**PEACE &
CONFLICT
SERIES**

RON MILAM, GENERAL EDITOR

ALSO IN THIS SERIES:

Admirals Under Fire: The U.S. Navy and the Vietnam War
by Edward J. Marolda

The Air War in Vietnam
by Michael E. Weaver

Capturing Skunk Alpha: A Barrio Sailor's Journey in Vietnam
by Raúl Herrera

Charging a Tyrant: The Arraignment of Saddam Hussein
by Greg Slavonic

Conscientious Objectors at War: The Forgotten Medics of the Vietnam War
by Gary Kulik

Crooked Bamboo: A Memoir from Inside the Diem Regime
by Nguyen Thai; edited by Justin Simundson

Girls Don't! A Woman's War in Vietnam
by Inette Miller

Memorial Days: Việt Nam Stories, 1973–2022
by Wayne Karlin

Rain in Our Hearts: Alpha Company in the Vietnam War
by James Allen Logue and Gary D. Ford

The White Pebble

MADAME NHU'S MEMOIRS

Madame Ngô-Đình Nhu
Edited and Foreword by Tuong Vu

With essay by Ngô-Đình Lệ Quyên, Ngô-Đình Quỳnh, and Jacqueline Willemetz

Translated from French by Quang L. Phan, with assistance from Maria Cristina de Mariassevich

TEXAS TECH UNIVERSITY PRESS

This book is typeset in EB garamond. The paper used in this book meets the minimum requirements of ANSI/NISO Z39.48-1992 (R1997). ♾

Designed by Hannah Gaskamp
Cover design by Hannah Gaskamp
Cover and interior images from the Ngô-Đình family collection

Library of Congress Cataloging-in-Publication Data

Names: Trần, Lệ Xuân, 1924–2011 author | Vu, Tuong, 1965– editor | Ngô Dinh, Lê Quyên, 1959–2012 writer of supplementary textual content | Ngô-Đình, Quỳnh, writer of supplementary textual content | Willemetz, Jacqueline, writer of supplementary textual content | Ngô-Đình, Quỳnh. République du Viêt-Nam et les Ngô-Dinh. English. | University of Oregon. US-Vietnam Research Center sponsor. Title: The White Pebble: Madame Nhu's Memoirs / Madame Ngô-Đình Nhu; edited and foreword by Tuong Vu; with essay by Ngô-Đình Lệ Quyên, Ngô-Đình Quỳnh, and Jacqueline Willemetz. Other titles: Cailloux blanc. English description: Lubbock, Texas: Texas Tech University Press, [2025] | Series: Peace and Conflict Series | "The US-Vietnam Research Center is pleased to sponsor the translation from French and publication of Madame Ngô-Đình Nhu's (Trần Lệ Xuân) posthumous memoirs, written in the last years of her life. The memoirs are accompanied by an essay written by the late Ngô-Đình Lệ Quyên, Ngô-Đình Quỳnh, and Jacqueline Willemetz titled 'The Republic of Vietnam and the Ngô-Đìnhs'"—Foreword. | Includes bibliographical references and index. | In English, translated from the original French. | Summary: "The memoir of controversial 'first lady' of South Vietnam, Madame Nhu, wife of Ngô Dình Nhu, brother and chief adviser to President Ngô Dình Diem"—Provided by publisher.
Identifiers: LCCN 2025031450 (print) | LCCN 2025031451 (ebook) |
ISBN 978-1-68283-278-3 paperback | ISBN 978-1-68283-279-0 ebook
Subjects: LCSH: Trần, Lệ Xuân, 1924–2011 | Ngô, Đình Diệm, 1901–1963—Family | Politicians' spouses—Vietnam (Republic)—Biography | Vietnam War, 1961–1975—Personal narratives, Vietnamese | Vietnam (Republic)—Politics and government | Vietnam (Republic)—History | LCGFT: Autobiographies
Classification: LCC DS556.93.T676 A3 2025 (print) | LCC DS556.93.T676 (ebook)
LC record available at https://lccn.loc.gov/2025031450
LC ebook record available at https://lccn.loc.gov/2025031451

Texas Tech University Press
Box 41037, Lubbock, Texas 79409-1037 USA
800.832.4042
ttup@ttu.edu
www.ttupress.org

This book is dedicated to the Vietnamese nation

"He who has an ear, let him hear what the Spirit says to the churches. To him who overcomes, I will give some of the hidden manna. I will also give him a white stone with a *new name* written on it, known only to him who receives it."[1]

—Revelation 2:17

"For he who is least among you all—he is the greatest."[2]

—Luke 9:48

Contents

Illustrations

(All images from the Ngô-Đình family collection)

Family Trees

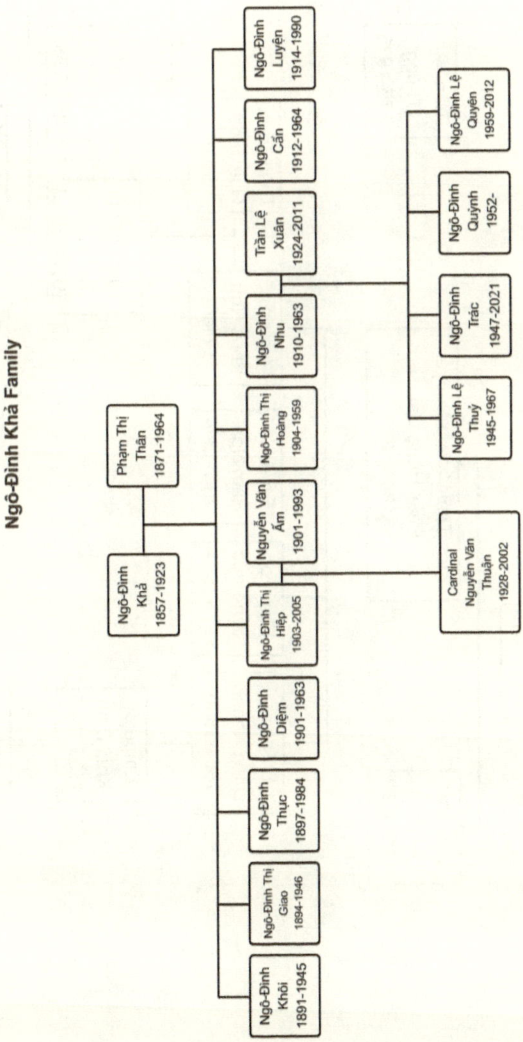

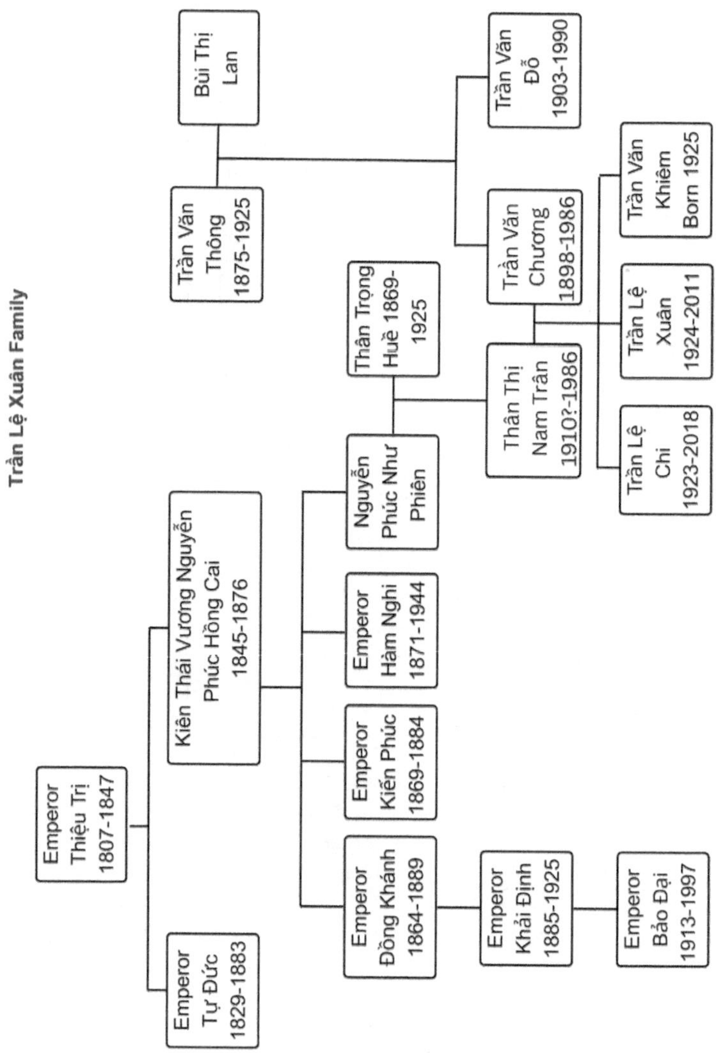
Trần Lệ Xuân Family
Emperor Thiệu Trị 1807-1847
Emperor Tự Đức 1829-1883
Kiên Thái Vương Nguyễn Phúc Hồng Cai 1845-1876
Emperor Đồng Khánh 1864-1889
Emperor Kiến Phúc 1869-1884
Emperor Hàm Nghi 1871-1944
Nguyễn Phúc Như Phiên
Thân Trọng Huề 1869-1925
Emperor Khải Định 1885-1925
Emperor Bảo Đại 1913-1997
Thân Thị Nam Trân 1910?-1986
Trần Văn Chương 1898-1986
Trần Văn Thông 1875-1925
Bùi Thị Lan
Trần Văn Đỗ 1903-1990
Trần Lệ Chi 1923-2018
Trần Lệ Xuân 1924-2011
Trần Văn Khiêm Born 1925

Foreword

The US-Vietnam Research Center is pleased to sponsor the translation from French and publication of Madame Ngô-Đình Nhu's (Trần Lệ Xuân) posthumous memoirs, written in the last years of her life. The memoirs are accompanied by an essay written by Ngô-Đình Quỳnh, Jacqueline Willemetz, and the late Ngô-Đình Lệ Quyên titled "The Republic of Vietnam and the Ngô-Đình s." Ngô-Đình Lệ Quyên, who died in 2012, and Ngô-Đình Quỳnh are two of the four children of Ngô-Đình Nhu and Trần Lệ Xuân; the other two, Ngô-Đình Lệ Thuỷ and Ngô-Đình Trác, passed away in 1967 and 2021, respectively. Jacqueline Willemetz is a family friend whose father was a classmate of Ngô-Đình Nhu at France's National School of Charters (École Nationale des Chartes).

We are grateful to L'Harmattan Editions for their permission to translate and publish this book. We thank the Ngô-Đình family members and friends, in particular Mrs. Jacqueline Willemetz and Mr. Olindo Borsoi, who was Ngô-Đình Lệ Quyên's widower. Mrs. Willemetz and Mr. Borsoi took responsibility for publishing the original book in 2013 after the deaths of Madame Ngô-Đình Nhu in 2011 and Ngô-Đình Lệ Quyên in 2012. Without their generosity in providing the text, images, and other documents and granting permission for translation and publication, this book would not have seen the light of day. We also wish to acknowledge Mr. Borsoi's donation of four boxes of archival documents in the collection of Mme. Nhu for digitization, together with her and Ngô-Đình Lệ Thuỷ's many sets of *áo dài* dresses for a future exhibition. Four documents from that archive have been added to the appendices. We are grateful to Mr. and Mrs. Nguyễn Đức Cường, who have supported this project from the beginning. Thanks are due to Mr. Quang L. Phan, who provided excellent translations, and Mrs. Maria Cristina de Mariassevich, who helped edit the English translation. Finally, we are indebted to Ms. Vũ Hồng Trang, who put us into contact with Mr. Olindo Borsoi.

This book provides us with a rare opportunity, more than half a century after the deaths of Ngô-Đình Diệm and Ngô-Đình Nhu, to perceive how some members of the Ngô-Đình family, especially Mme. Nhu, viewed themselves and the role of their family in Vietnam's history.[1] That role was no doubt complicated and controversial, but few would question its significance. Regardless of whether one is a supporter or a detractor, for the purpose of understanding Vietnam's modern history, this family is special because it was intertwined with the transition of the country from a French colony and protectorate to an independent and divided nation. It is special because this entire family, through President Ngô-Đình Diệm, helped shape Vietnam's modern history in one way or another. It is special because, with the exception of the Nguyễn dynasty that began with Emperor Gia Long and extended to Bảo Đại, the last emperor, no other family in modern time has had such an intense involvement in politics and public affairs as the Ngô-Đìnhs.

Over two generations, all the male members and one female member (by marriage) of this family were involved in politics or served in some public capacity at very high levels, beginning with Ngô-Đình Khả, who was an imperial tutor [Phụ đạo Đại thần] and grand chamberlain [Tổng quản Cấm thành] in the Nguyễn court in Huế, and who founded and was the first head of the Quốc Học School (national high school) for children of officials. He was followed by his sons Ngô-Đình Khôi, who was a provincial chief; Ngô-Đình Thục, who was one of the first Vietnamese bishops in French Indochina and later the archbishop of Vĩnh Long and Huế; Ngô-Đình Diệm, who served briefly as minister of interior in the Nguyễn court in the 1930s, as prime minister in

1954–1955, and as the founder of the Republic of Vietnam (RVN) and its first president (1955–1963); Ngô-Đình Nhu, who directed the Archive and Library in Hà Nội before becoming a political organizer, adviser to his brother, President Diệm, and leader of the Cần Lao Revolutionary Party; Ngô-Đình Cẩn, who was adviser to his brother, President Diệm, on matters related to the central region of Vietnam; and Ngô-Đình Luyện, who served as the RVN's ambassador. Besides the males, Trần Lệ Xuân, commonly known as Madame Ngô-Đình Nhu, was a member of the RVN's National Assembly (1956–1963), the founder of the Solidarity Movement of Vietnamese Women [Phong trào Phụ nữ Liên đới], and an informal "First Lady."

We do not have as much information about Khôi and Luyện as we do about their brothers, who stood out thanks to their personal talents and ambitions. For instance, Thục was ordained as a priest and sent to study in Rome in his late 20s, then appointed bishop a decade later. Diệm distinguished himself as a provincial chief and gained fame when he resigned as a minister in protest of the French failure to approve political reforms. Nhu was admitted into the National School of Charters [École Nationale des Chartes], a prestigious college in France, contributed significantly to the preservation of the Nguyễn court's documents, later successfully mobilized domestic political support for his brother to be appointed to the premiership, and served as the brain trust of the Ngô-Đình Diệm government. Swimming against the current, Mme. Nhu sponsored a progressive family law and raised a national debate on women's rights and family issues.

Mme. Nhu, or Trần Lệ Xuân, came from an elite family whose status was no less distinguished than her husband's. Her maternal grandmother was Nguyễn Phúc Như Phiên,[2] a daughter of Kiên Thái Vương Nguyễn Phúc Hồng Cai (1845–1876) and a granddaughter of Emperor Thiệu Trị (1807–1847). Nguyễn Phúc Như Phiên was a half-sister of three emperors, namely Kiến Phúc (1869–1884), Hàm Nghi (1871–1944), and Đồng Khánh (1864–1889), who were also children of Kiên Thái Vương Nguyễn Phúc Hồng Cai.[3] Như Phiên married Lệ Xuân's grandfather, Thân Trọng Huề (1869–1925), a cultural reformer and a high-ranking official whose illustrious career included stints as minister of defense [Binh bộ Thượng thư], minister of education [Học bộ Thượng thư], and Head of the Imperial Censorate [Đô Ngự sử] at the Huế court.[4] Thân Thị Nam Trân, Lệ Xuân's mother, was their daughter.[5]

On her paternal side, Lệ Xuân's grandfather was Trần Văn Thông, the provincial chief of Nam Định, and her grandmother was Bùi Thị Lan, a sister of Bùi Quang Chiêu, a prominent political activist and founder of the Constitutionalist Party. Lệ Xuân's father was Trần Văn Chương, a French-trained lawyer who would later become minister of foreign affairs in the Trần Trọng Kim government (March to August 1945) and who served as RVN ambassador to the US under Ngô-Đình Diệm (Chương resigned from his post in mid-1963 to protest the Diệm government). Her uncle was Trần Văn Đỗ, a medical doctor who twice served as minister of foreign affairs (1954–55 and 1965–67) under the Ngô-Đình Diệm and Nguyễn Cao Kỳ governments and was deputy prime minister under Prime Minister Phan Huy Quát (1966).

From tabloid tales to memoirs of former officials to accounts by foreign journalists, much has been written about the rule of President Diệm and the roles played by his family. Only recently did American historians begin to take the ideas and policies of the Diệm government seriously and on their own terms, not as French or American products. Due to space constraints, we will not review this scholarship here, but it has done much to illuminate the politics of the First Republic under President Diệm, who appears as a modernizer with a distinct vision and active governing style. His government was founded in the most turbulent period of Vietnam's modern history, and he must be credited for creating order out of chaos against all odds. The Republic of Vietnam that he founded was a fledgling nation with limited resources, an extremely diverse society, and a dependent economy with few industries.

The government claimed full sovereignty over all of Vietnam, but the North was under the rule of a Communist government that made a rival claim over the same territory. The RVN was recognized by nations of the "Free World," including the US and its allies in Europe, Asia, Africa, and the Americas. Communist North Vietnam had a weaker international position as it was recognized by fewer foreign countries. Still, neither North nor South Vietnam was granted membership in the United Nations, and their international legitimacy was limited. For the RVN, part of the territory under its control (in the central region and parts of the Mekong Delta) had been under Communist rule during the Franco-Vietnamese war (1946–1954), and the loyalty of the population to the RVN was suspect.

A few years after the Geneva Accords, with Chinese and Soviet support, North Vietnam began to resume the war against the RVN to unify the country under communism. Hà Nội mobilized its supporters left behind in the South, together with those who had earlier regrouped to the North but were now returning with arms and ready for fighting. With American help, the Diệm government successfully stemmed Communist advances in 1957–58 and 1960–61. While the war was not won, the military situation was in flux by 1963 with the initiative remaining with Sài Gòn. Yet the government was unpopular among certain segments of the elite and the general population, still refusing to succumb to Washington's pressure for political reform or the introduction of American ground forces into South Vietnam. Amid widespread protests by Buddhists, President Diệm and his brother Nhu were assassinated on November 2, 1963, in a military coup tacitly backed by the Kennedy administration. However it may have been justified, the coup led to four years of political and social chaos, the sharp deterioration of South Vietnam's military position, and American direct military intervention. It was perhaps the most serious blunder made by the US in the entire course of the Vietnam War, causing the RVN to lose its legitimacy in the eyes of Vietnamese and the world's people.

Despite the controversies surrounding President Diệm's rule, which was perceived by many to be authoritarian and nepotistic, it is beneficial for historians and for anyone interested in Vietnamese history to learn more about his family members who played such significant roles in his government. How did they see themselves, their country, and their compatriots? How did each member of the family think of others? How did they view the family's role in history? What brought them so close to each other, and what influence did each have on the president? Even though many books have been written about them, this is the first time, after six decades, English and Vietnamese readers can get a glimpse of their thoughts as told by themselves.[6]

We can now follow Madame Ngô-Đình Nhu as she narrated important events in her life, from her childhood to her marriage to Mr. Nhu, from her time in Huế during the Franco-Vietnamese War to the happy years of the Diệm government, and from her forced exile to the last days of her life. We learn how difficult her life was at certain points despite her privileged background, how obstinate she was in her belief, how forcefully she could act when the president and her husband were indecisive, how loyal she was to them and to her country, how resentful she was toward France and the United States, and how distressed her life was in exile.

Not all the details in the memoir are accurate or objective, nor did she tell us everything she knew or did, but her subjectivity is the very strength of the book. We do not have to believe her entirely, yet we now have an additional source of information and her personal perspective to add to a fascinating but in many ways tragic chapter of Vietnam's modern history. The memoirs also offer a chance for us to discover how she and her children lived their lives in exile. Understandably it took them a long time, if ever, to recover from the shock brought on by the deaths of President Diệm and Mr. Nhu, which was perhaps why they mostly stayed out of the limelight. Yet their ability to stay true to their characters, and their courage to defend and preserve the family's honor and dignity in the wake of such a horrendous tragedy, also inspired respect and sympathy.

The essay written by Ngô-Đình Lệ Quyên and Ngô-Đình Quỳnh and edited by Jacqueline Willemetz offers a narrative of how the second

Family photo in Huế, 1961, under a portrait of Ngô Đình Khả. Back row (L–R): His children Nhu, Diệm, Thục, Mrs. Nguyễn Văn Ấm (Ngô ĐìnhThị Hiệp), Mme. Nhu (Trần Lệ Xuân), Cẩn, Luyện, and Mr. Khả's son-in-law Nguyễn văn Ấm. Front row, around Mrs. Ngô Đình Khả, are Nhu's four children (L–R): Trác (14), Quỳnh (9), Lệ Quyên (2) and Lệ Thủy (16).

generation of the Ngô-Đình family viewed their role in history. Mrs. Lệ Quyên and Mr. Quỳnh are not historians, but they lived through parts of this history and learned about it thanks to their mother and to the surviving archives, documents, and photos. Their account is intended to make the case for the integrity of the Diệm government and his family against their critics. By telling the family's history alongside that of the Vietnamese nation, they want to demonstrate the sincerity and depth of patriotism in the family. They are on the whole not wrong: even critics of the Diệm government acknowledge that the president was a genuine and incorruptible patriot. Members of the Ngô-Đình family, including the president, certainly committed many mistakes, but few would question their patriotism, and many would say that the president was a much better leader than his predecessors and successors. He was certainly far better educated and more spiritual than the Communist rulers in Hà Nội.

It is not our purpose here to defend the Ngô-Đình family or the rule of President Diệm. By sponsoring the translation and publication of this book, we only aim to generate interest in and promote education about the history of republican Vietnam. Since 1975, this history has been brutally suppressed by the Communist regime, yet we need it to have a deeper understanding of modern Vietnam. As editor, I honor the family's wish to keep the translation true to its original as much as possible in the hope that readers will read and form their own opinion of the authors and their stories. In general, I do not attempt to fact-check the authors and only provide additional information and context, if necessary, on a few controversial or lesser-known events or figures. My notes are marked "(Ed.)," in contrast to those marked "(Au.)," referring to "Editor" and "Author," respectively.

Tuong Vu
US-Vietnam Research Center

Introduction to Madame Ngô Đình Nhu's Memoirs

A strange narrative.

To be discovered beyond all conventional reading.

The narrative of a life illuminated by the glimmers of an upcoming death.

Benevolent glimmers, as they have allowed a being not very inclined to introspection to suddenly gain access to what underlay the mystery of her life.

And this, just before her death.

A mystery that never ceased to expose her and at the same time protect her like the fine mesh of armor protects someone that fate has put on a shining yet wounding path, accorded little support.

A destiny, a mission, the hand of God in this life as in ours. A trajectory that meets the difficult and necessary salvation of the world.

It is the account of the life of Trần Lệ Xuân, publicly known as Madame Nhu. Sister-in-law of the president of Vietnam, by her marriage to his favorite brother Ngô Đình Nhu, she became Vietnam's "first lady," since the president was unmarried.

It was in that capacity that she undertook a worldwide tour to represent and defend her country. She tried to open the eyes of the world to the American neo-imperialism that wanted to impose itself at all costs on the Republic of Vietnam, which was then placed under the legitimate authority of Ngô Đình Diệm, its president.

Under the guise of helping Vietnam fight the communism fostered by Hồ Chí Minh, America played the game in its own way, behaving to no avail like its predecessor France when it wanted to hold on to its colonial empire.

The political community had to face an extraordinarily vital, brilliant person endowed with a subtle, quick mind whose lightning-strike responses could be incredible. The American press, hostile and yet spellbound, even went so far as to bestow on Mme. Nhu the epithet of "Dragon Lady."

She was so sure of the extravagant destiny of her country. That conviction never left her even during the worst days, and today she wants to convey it to us.

She was a "responsible" being, someone who courageously faced a political situation of terrifying complexity. Her deployed antennae gave her survival instincts a stupefying presence in the situations her country was going through, constantly countered in its legitimate aspiration to freedom and sovereignty.

Her numerous press conferences revealed an astute and determined woman. She knew how to keep the journalists at a distance with that incredible finesse of perception that could react sharply or bounce back with an amused and sometimes mocking sense of humor. All this, welded by that indomitable force that the certainty of a legitimate fight for her country conferred to her.

She never came out exhausted from those debates that tried to bring her down. Her adversaries, stunned, seduced by her unspeakably fascinating feline charm, had no other choice but to bow out and attempt to save face in their reports on the interviews to which she had consented.

It was not they who controlled the press and therefore the game.

Her existence cannot be understood without placing her back in the context that was her own, that of a Vietnam grappling with the big powers, sealed in their strategic obsessions, whether it be France, Russia, China, or, finally, the United States.

Accompanied by the radiant beauty that was her daughter Lệ Thủy, then 18 years of age, Mme. Nhu attempted to unveil the reality of Vietnam in a global information campaign.

Her journey to the great world capitals, where she was received in 1963, was tragically interrupted on November 2, 1963. It was on that day, in the middle of a press conference in Los Angeles, that news that the president of Vietnam and his brother had perished in a military coup d'état was abruptly brought to her.

The gap that there could be—and that still exists nowadays—between a country that aspired to recover its liberty and sovereignty and the great powers that only wanted to grant them on their own conditions was manifested in a shattering way.

Mme. Nhu was exiled with her four children.

Vietnam sank into chaos.

It is now established that the opponents of President Diệm were not the only ones to foment the putsch that cost him his life as well as the lives of many other Vietnamese, boat people or others. Opponents were always there. But the secret services and the big powers concerned had their hands in the work. They could easily hide under Vietnamese features, bonzes [Buddhist monks] or not, easily manipulated, lost as they were in a land that was however their own country, appallingly undermined by the political games of foreign forces that felt powerful but were overtaken by events.

Mme. Nhu saw an immanent sign of God's justice when the double assassination of the president and his brother was replicated first by the death of US president John Kennedy on November 22, 1963 (twenty days after the assassination of President Ngô Đình Diệm), then by the death of Robert Kennedy, slain on June 5, 1968, when his campaign for the presidency of the United States was in full swing.

Like every Vietnamese, she was sensitive to symbols, to dates, and it was on the solemn day of Easter Sunday when Christians celebrate the resurrection of Jesus Christ that Trần Lệ Xuân, Mme. Nhu, ceased to live, on April 24, 2011, at 2 in the morning. She had spent forty-eight years in exile, sometimes in Paris, sometimes in Rome, where she died.

Her daughter Ngô Đình Lệ Quyên died in an accident the following year, on April 16, 2012, in the morning. Lệ Quyên was in charge of designing the reception and integration procedures for refugees for Caritas in Italy and elsewhere in Europe, and served as vice president of the Association for the Study of World Refugee Problems accredited at the United Nations and at the Council of Europe. For her devotion to the interests of the state and her notable services to Italy, she was granted honorary citizenship on April 24, 2008, by a presidential decree on the recommendation of the Ministry of the Interior.

It was thanks to Ngô Đình Lệ Quyên's insistence and that of her husband, Olindo Borsoi, that Mme. Nhu finally consented to write her memoirs, to which she dedicated the last months of her life.

Jacqueline Willemetz

•

The White Pebble

PART I

The White Pebble

MADAME NGÔ-ĐÌNH NHU

CHAPTER 1

The Logic of Predestination

To know nothing, in advance, about one's life and to live it to the end, without the possibility of changing anything about it. And to discover at the end of this long journey that, after all, one would have wanted to live in no other way.

Despite the price paid.

What the two youngest and most dashing Apostles of Christ, James and John, and their mother wanted to get as reward for their lives dedicated to God has truly what it takes to stupefy us.

I recall the Gospel and the claim of the two apostles:

> "Let one of us sit at your right and the other at your left in your glory."
> Jesus said to them:
> "You don't know what you are asking."
> Could they bear what He himself would have to suffer?
> The answer was categorical:
> "We can."
> Jesus confirmed to them that in fact they could.
> As for the glory attached: "These places belong to those for whom they have been prepared" (Mark 10: 37–40).[1]

At the end of my life, after half a century of silence, and out of a simple spirit of duty, I relate what must be known.

It is about the salvation of all. It is not about satisfying any kind of curiosity, but to explain what the predestination of the Lord's "very little one" ["tout petit"][2] demands, in its time. I am dedicating myself to this book, if I am allowed to finish it, to help understand the demands of a long-predestined life which acknowledges it has not acted against its own will, but rather as if it had always wanted such an outcome.

How could I let myself be led that way, while not being driven by the consuming desire of the Apostles James and John: to personally partake in the Glory of Christ? Simply because the idea of such glory has no meaning whatsoever for a being who only belongs to its Savior by the Love He granted.

That glory they coveted, therefore, indicates a peculiar simplicity. Christ chose them for that, in priority, and thus loved John more than others.

God is Love; those who follow Him enter into this love and come to his Glory naturally. In the end, therefore, there is nothing special in the demands of James and John.

The predestined "very little one" is just viscerally attached to his Savior, be it only to His hand that he would never let go of. He does not have any idea of the "glory" requested by the Apostles James and John. He cannot do any more than carry out at his best what he is asked to perform, to avoid the worst for all.

What more is there to wish for?

By his physical attachment to God, the predestined one brings to his Savior a contribution He could not have otherwise. The human in the creature serves his Creator at the decisive moment.

That, indeed, is the true logic of predestination.

Once this is understood, the sense of what I have been allowed to call "my life of the predestined very little one" will become clearer. Its unique peculiarity suddenly hit me with a terrible revelation: Christ.

Bearer of what He holds for us all, He allows His creature, from his conception, since the beginning of time, to deserve and keep what will allow him, in the end, to offer his contribution. What belongs to the Creation will thus return to his Creator, for the full and ultimate fulfilment of our Humanity.

If I allow myself to speak of it so simply, it is because I have no other way to account for what has come to me from High Above. I understand, little by little, what concerns the end, now drawing much closer, at the end of an existence during which I never asked myself so many questions.

In sudden clarity, the end will present itself according to the logic of predestination I should thus define, without being sure of anything.

The end?

I do not remember ever having sought anything whatsoever to cling to.

If I may have been combative about the positions I have had to defend, deep in my heart, I have always calmly accepted all, without being attached to anything.

It is, therefore, for myself, out of personal curiosity for what I discover about my long life, that I try to recall the path that was mine.

Admittedly, having been mysteriously guided from end to end, I had to open myself naturally to the response due to the predestined "very little one" in order to better understand the last phases of a whole that concerns each and every one of us.

Only that response can break what separates human beings since the beginning of Creation until its accomplishment. It shall reveal the bond which unites them and allowed Christ to achieve His perfect and total fulfillment in favor of the absolute freedom that the Creator has allowed to us.

The world will then understand the incredible waste of time and energy that man allots to his search for happiness on Earth, while he holds the essentials in himself if he knows first, quite naturally and with the help of his Savior, how not to cut himself from his own roots.

Roots that nurture him as he proceeds in learning about life.

If man is reduced to himself, he can only count on his limits, those of his ignorance of the Truth regarding his Creator.

Hindered by its limitations, humanity ends up committing horrors like those inflicted on my family and on Vietnam.

Humanity must open up to free itself from its limits.

The risk, very heavy for all of us, is to shut ourselves out from God.

The time is coming when the real choice is finally open to each and all of us.

Creation is arriving at the time of its *raison d'être*, so we must be ready to receive it. We have our part in it since God awaits this Creation in the union of "Heaven and Earth."

This book reveals to all the long journey of this predestined "very little one" of the Lord who was in no way forced to take the path he had chosen.

We can learn, therefore, on our own with the elements within our reach, and act in the same way, as predestined, for the best and not for the sacrifice otherwise necessary for this best.

If it was so for the predestined "very little one," it is for him to disclose his ways to those of the end. They have the choice of ways to arrive at what the Apostles James and John discovered, which also happened to me, in my own way.

A path of pain.

The hand of the Savior has always been with me to grant me a deep understanding of things and not only the vital breath.

Everything became gradually clear, and in the greatest simplicity.

We were, in Vietnam, at the end of a colonial era which was incapable of understanding its limits or the means to come out of them. To enter it, my journey had no other support than what my environment could offer me, and it offered me just the minimum I was entitled to.

Being simply a younger daughter of the family, I was truly put aside and left to myself.

I was born in Hà Nội on August 22, 1924, and my arrival into this world was most peculiar.

First of all, the person who presided over my birth was not a woman, as was usually the case then. It was a man, a French doctor. A true gift of Providence, he did for me what no traditional Vietnamese midwife would have done, who would have, it seems, left me as I had come, silent and inert in my refusal to the life that came to meet me.

The foreign obstetrician, called upon for the first time by a Vietnamese woman, got hold of me by the feet and spanked me vigorously until my first cries of protest.

This was how by force I came into the life that was going to be mine. I was welcomed by the immense disappointment of my mother.[3] A second daughter!

She did not hide her feelings.

She was hoping for a son, as only a male child could have delivered her from the immeasurable threats that weighed on her, those her mother-in-law[4] was contriving, to ensure the full domination over her eldest son, the first one to create a family. She made it a point to keep him under her thumb.

Such threats included giving him a second wife, as the first one was yet incapable of giving him a son. Idle pretexts were rampant in a society where polygamy was then common practice. My mother was sufficiently wary of her to undergo her second childbirth in the house her father had entrusted to her before his death.[5]

It was better to be born a boy than a girl and, above all, to have a better horoscope so as not to start life with too heavy a handicap. My handicap was colossal, aggravated by an out-of-the-ordinary horoscope that branded me with the stamp of independence.

My horoscope was thus summarized by the "infallible wise men" of the family who revealed it to my mother: "Her unsurpassed star even overtakes the unimaginable." Faced with questions prompted by such an oracle, the astrologer reminded my mother what had been said about her eldest daughter [Trần Lệ Chi]: "As the destiny of your eldest daughter rises or falls, the same goes for yours. As for your second daughter, she will have her own destiny."

From that day on, my mother looked at me with suspicion.

Eventually, my mother had a son [Trần Văn Khiêm]. In my family, I was the younger daughter. Above me was my elder sister with her own prerogatives. Below me was my brother. He was younger than me but in his capacity as a first male in the lineage he was over me in consideration. Such were the Confucian rules then in practice.

That hierarchy was also imposed upon the household staff. The status of the little masters had repercussions for the housemaids, who applied it among themselves. Thus was there less cause for contentment for my wet nurse. She was the only one of her rank to know how to read ancient literature while breastfeeding me. Beyond these moments she neglected me, and I was therefore delivered to the other house staff, who entertained themselves, treating me as a mere toy.

My mother had everything going for her, but she also had a handicap of her own: that of having a well-read mother-in-law who was intent on not being imposed upon by her first daughter-in-law, albeit the daughter of a princess and the head of the Imperial Censorate, a unique institution in the history of Vietnam.[6] My paternal grandfather had been province chief in Nam Định, which was the largest and most important northern province in the country.[7]

Before going to the South to assume the position of the first Vietnamese lawyer,[8] my father [Trần Văn Chương] made it a point to spend some time with his mother, who doted on her eldest son. He was the only being before whom she seriously bowed, but he could not do anything to change what she was.

When my parents had to take the long trip south to live their new life, my mother was obligated to leave one of her three children with her mother-in-law as testimony of her promotion to grandmother because we were her first grandchildren.

There was no hesitation; it was me that my mother left behind her.

She took with her the newly born, the only son so indispensable to consolidate her position in the new family, and my elder sister who was already two years old.[9] I was a tiny little child barely one year old.

My grandmother did whatever she wanted to the wet nurse with whom I was abandoned.

I was raised without any heed, whiling my time away with gardeners and common-law prisoners condemned for minor violations. They served my grandfather and took care of the vegetable garden as well as the poultry. They gladly bathed me with the animals.

After one year I fell gravely ill.

As I was already dying, my parents were alerted and hastily rushed back. At the sight of my pitiful state, my mother held me tight against her, wrapping me in her arms. She would not let go of me for ten days until I appeared to be alive again. These ten days attest to the fact that the core of my physical resistance was always there in spite of the weak constitution of the body that did not allow me to remain seated as a two-year-old child.

For my mother, holding me against her was also the only way she was allowed to justifiably express her blame on my grandmother.

Curiously enough, my mother, apparently devoid of any maternal instincts, did not seem to recognize me. She wondered if another child might have been substituted for her own to dampen the natural haughtiness of an arrogant mother-in-law.

This dreadful doubt, albeit entertained with discretion, turned me into an inconvenient thing. And this morbid doubt maintained a latent dispute between my mother and her mother-in-law, my paternal grandmother.

The child that was me had to grow up with this question mark without any basis in reality. And yet, of the three children, I was the only one to exhibit a physical likeness to my mother.

After that, I was no longer left behind. My lot did not improve, though, and my status remained below that of my sister and brother. I had the responsibility of such chores as the stewardship of the household staff.

That is how, willy nilly, I took my place among my folks, despite being subject to my brother's rejection at the slightest of disputes: "You are only the daughter of the wet nurse." An affirmation I ended up making mine to ensure my independence, and in turn defy my folks who did not know what to say.

I felt that my father was on my side, but I then discovered this peculiarity inherent to a man that pushes him to hold his peace instead of taking sides against the majority of his folks.

Without real support, I was like an alien to my family, living like a spectator, so to speak. My early childhood was not that happy, nor did it improve as I was growing up.

In my fourth year, perched on a tall chair, I learned the Latinized Vietnamese language. I also liked to copy the old Vietnamese characters on tracing paper. Facing me, his favorite playmate suddenly becoming studious, my brother was furious for still being considered a baby.

One day, he was particularly irritated at having lost his playmate; he snatched a pen from my hand to throw it at my head. Although my fontanel was closed, the pen went straight in and lodged inside. The frightened master, an old-fashioned man with a turban who had the peculiarity of having two fingers of his right hand stuck together from birth, could not do anything but look at me, because I prevented him from withdrawing the pen. I could guess the horror of the scene by looking at the expression on his face and that of my brother. But the occasion was too opportune, and I did not want to miss it. Cautiously getting off my high chair, I climbed up the stairs, stepping in cadence, to go and show our mother what tragedy had happened. Because it surely was one. The pen did not fall off, but what had particularly frightened my mother was the determination I had, despite my tender age, to keep the "exhibit" of my brother's gesture. The whole family experienced the same trauma. Briefly, from then on, I became an "untouchable."

Later on, my brother screamed and shed hot tears when at five years old—an exceptionally young age to become boarders—I left for Sài Gòn with my eldest sister.

In the car on the way back from Bạc Liêu, my parents were surprised at seeing such a long outpouring of tears. But my brother could only utter this reply, which became "historic": "Con nhớ mấy chị" (I miss my older sisters). A touching epilogue his folks always remembered for having heard it enough, as my brother had a real liking for me.

If I attracted little affectionate attention from my family, that was not the case when it came to people outside the family. It was to me that friends and passing acquaintances handed their parting gifts, gifts that proved to be contentious and provoked multiple attacks [from my siblings]. If it was a doll, she would very quickly lose her eyes and hair.

The same thing happened when our family was sitting near the lock, to observe at leisure the swing bridge turning on itself. Our neighbors and passers-by stopped to talk to me. Why me? What did I have to retain their attention that way?

A French priest with a beard going down all the way to his navel stopped every time to caress my head and bless it discreetly. He scandalized us because a head, particularly the head of a child, is sacred. It is the seat of Thượng Đế, the Almighty unknown who reigns over everything.

At six years of age, I distinguished myself at dance and piano classes. My distinctiveness came from my being natural. I did not take advantage of it. I observed it with the passing of time. It was hard to make me jealous. The piano teacher could have preferred other students over me. That was his business and did not make any impression on me at all. While I did not let him have any power over me, he could not do anything against me. I took everything with simplicity. It was also the case when I danced on the stage.

Could it be because I was not aware of the situation I was living in or because it did not matter to me at all?

No such thing; I did see the truth. But what could I have done in there?

I had learned to quietly accept the facts. And I held on to that. And nothing more.

Having never been anything but myself all my life, I have always abandoned myself to my nature, withdrawn, distant. That was all I could do.

Later on, when I had to face the crowds or people at political gatherings, I disappeared as soon as my job was done. By my reserved nature, nobody could feel attacked. Thanks to this detachment, I preserved the peace due to me because nobody felt attacked by my presence.

This would last until the confrontation with the West, colonizing, imperialistic, and self-centered.[10]

Face-to-face [interactions] demanded the respect of the other. That was not always the case. However, without resorting to a frontal attack, I would withdraw with no other problem than the incomprehension and bad faith of the other.

After having given my grandfather [Thân Trọng Huề], the head of the Imperial Censorate, four boys and two girls, my maternal grandmother [Nguyễn Phúc Như Phiên], whose eyesight had weakened, had Vietnamese literary works of her choice and foreign literary works translated into Vietnamese read to her.

She considered that she had sufficiently discharged her spousal duties to maintain her feminine liberty, to the point of putting a bolster across the conjugal bed between her and her spouse, after introducing to him another woman as a second spouse, who gave him seven children.

So that this second wife would not have too much power over the shared husband, my grandmother chose a third spouse for him. Their entire world was quite disciplined, since each person took care of her own fief without encroaching on that of the others. I got along very well with one of my aunts, the daughter of my grandfather's third wife. Later on, she would help me enormously when I stayed in Đà Lạt, on the mountains or more precisely on the highlands where I was living alone most of the time, with my first two children and a husband who was almost always absent.

With the passing years, my father became the most renowned lawyer in the country.

Our lifestyle was an alliance between the "sang" (pronounced shaang), that discreet luxurious living style peculiar to Vietnam, and the modern Western way of life. It became a point of reference around us, who dwelled in the most beautiful mansion in Hà Nội.[11]

My parents, who loved beautiful things, had the support of national handicrafts at heart. The rear of the garden thus became a little atelier for the objects they took an interest in. These art objects, along with everything else out of the ordinary, were destroyed when the Communists took over.

The very luxurious comfort of my existence did not make me any happier. The gaps still remained great between my eldest sister, my younger brother, the scion of the family, and me. Inevitably, they burst out on any occasion, like that of my seat in the family car. The jump seat was for me! My sister would sit between my parents and my brother next to the chauffeur.

Finally, I left my childhood.

On the day of my seventeenth birthday, my mother had entrusted me with the task of arranging bouquets for a reception she gave that very evening. Always crazy about flowers, I gleefully took on this errand. Along the way I met friends in my class who asked me to come along for some ice cream. I did not notice the passing of time, and it was in a big hurry that I had to run to the florist. I chose the most beautiful flowers that were available to fill up the rickshaw and went home precipitously. On the way home I crossed paths with a handsome and elegant man who smiled at the sight of my being surrounded by flowers. Barely back at home, the doorbell rang. I spontaneously went to the door to open it, and found myself face to face with our guest, punctually on time! Just the man I had crossed paths with on my way home. It was Ngô Đình Nhu, whom I had already heard of before, because he hailed from a prestigious family in Huế well known to my mother, who was a native of that city herself. Panicked by my tardiness, I could not have any other recourse than to push him into a dark small room, begging him to kindly wait so that I could finish the arrangement of my bouquets. He smiled and obliged graciously.

President Ngô Đình Diệm's brother Ngô Đình Nhu.

My mother would never have forgiven me should she have received her guest without any floral decorations in her living room. I dressed up my flowers in beautiful vases and when everything was ready, I ushered our guest into the living room and announced his arrival to my parents.

As for me, I was hurrying to prepare myself to be up to the event. When back to the living room to meet again that man with a lively and delicate charm, a joyful complicity had already been established between us. He looked at me with an amused expression. To please me, he took the habit of sending a few books, which I would comment on in my letters of thanks. He always replied. He called me "Madame de Sévigné," as my letters were always long and lively. We thus learned to know each other. My mother appreciated this fine man of letters very much. One day, one of his elder brothers, Ngô Đình Diệm, came to the house with a huge spray of dahlias. According to a traditional ritual, standing in for the late father, he asked my parents for my hand in marriage for his brother. My parents consented.

After my wedding, which took place on April 30, 1943, the very morning after my baptism, I left my family and brought the erstwhile wet nurse with me.[12] She had been with me since my very early childhood. I was in such a hurry to leave the family with whom I had not been happy that I took off my shoes to run faster toward my husband who was waiting for me in the car.

My family status changed completely. In my new environment, I would gain more respect because my husband, although being younger, would acquire the elder's status in the absence of his elder brothers.[13]

Alas, I lost my erstwhile wet nurse. She used to sit silently at my feet when, back from school, I was doing my homework. After my marriage there was no question of her keeping that habit, not even in the absence of my husband, when I was all alone.

One day, she thought she felt that I no longer had the same need for her and that was enough for her to decide to leave me.

At the time I was oblivious to the incalculable loss of her presence that had been in my shadow for such a long time. It took me war and deportation with all that followed to realize it. Deep inside, I have never ceased to regret this reassuring company. But unconsciousness is a peculiar trait of those born in a certain environment who no longer feel the importance of things that were part of their lives . . . until they vanish.

What happened to me will be the regret and remorse of not knowing to keep Heaven's treats because of that strange placidity I had to deplore throughout my life because it did not incite me to react.

I realized too late what I have lost by releasing someone who had always been by my side since childhood and taught me the things in life I would not have otherwise known.

Gradually I settled pleasantly into my new life. I ended up being sensitive to this particular magic which emanates from what the Nam-Giao near Huế represents at the center of the country.[14] This mountain, this unique place in the world, symbolizes the expectations of a whole people for an unknown Almighty God.

In order to benefit from what Heaven has permitted, the world must grant all its respects to the Spirit of this people capable of waiting for a God, however unknown to them.

In Vietnam as elsewhere, I had the occasion to discover the places I wanted to know, every year for a decade during my world tour, in one direction or another. During those multiple trips when I saw and visited the most famous places countless times, I tried to understand the areas of interest that man in general and the inhabitants in particular found there. None of them would ever bring me that same sense of spirituality that delighted me at Nam-Giao.

By itself Vietnam was up to the blessing of Moses. Yes, by itself, with the fruits of a purely human discovery.

Before he died, Moses, the prophet of prophets, gave his ultimate blessing.

> You who love the ancestors!
> Your holy ones are all at your command.
> At your feet they fell,
> Under your guidance went swiftly on.
> —Deuteronomy 33:3[15]

Now, who deserves this inspired blessing if not Vietnam?

By nature, it is the first, following its first sage, Confucius, to have chosen the Most and the Best, and therefore Virtue, for the building of its human society.

Because it was necessary to be inhabited by Love, the Lord Almighty, to know, from the beginning of time, how to venerate his neighbor, even when dead and reduced to the state of a corpse, to whom nothing is owed, and to recognize in him without delay the Ancestor that the Living must know how to worship, not as a God, but as what is necessary to derive the Most and the Best for all.

The Cult of the Ancestors worship has always permeated Vietnamese society with a constancy and spiritual intensity which have never been denied.

By this attitude, we are placed in a unique position under the protection of the prophet Moses, whom we do not even know, and we have been able to offer the Lord, at the right moment of our conversion, something He could not have otherwise: the incredible multitude of souls that we will have known how to venerate from the beginning until this precise point of the present.

By living in this way and at all times according to the ultimate blessing of Moses, Vietnam assured to all its dead the righteous veneration recognized to the ancestors. It is, therefore, through it that all mankind is assured of the Right number of "Saints" who will obtain the union of "Heaven and Earth" of the new times.

The "predestined" nature of this country has been announced to the world by a white dove, that bird which is the personification of the Holy Spirit for Christians.

Vietnam called it "Việt Điểu" (the Viet Bird) when it appeared to its dynastic leaders. And at the same time, they heard in their hearts the expression of "Nam Tiến" (Southward Advance) that directed them to the land where they had to found their civilization.

Was not it already a dove that announced the end of the deluge to the world, or the same dove that was to appear on the baptism of Christ? (Matthew 3:16)

Such unique precedents could only herald an exceptional destiny.

The colonialists, under cover of the Church, believed they could seize that land like real bandits. But at the end of time Truth dawns.

I was required insistently to ask the Lord for our right, in due time.

Finally, finally this time has arrived.

What to say, other than to understand it, to know how to draw from it what God-Love expects from His creatures.

I mentioned above the Center where the city of Huế, the imperial capital of the past, is located. Those splendid cities that even a Vietnamese, whether from the north or the south, hardly knows perhaps in the same manner I have been allowed to discover. Hence my gratitude toward the Lord for having kindly accorded me this window on my ancestral roots. Without them I can say that I would not have known anything about Vietnam.

What distinguishes Huế especially is its capability to poetically express its visceral expectation of the mysterious Thượng Đế (the Almighty) without any touch of idolatry.

Consequently, I can only bless the intuition received from High above that led me to claim from the world that the inspiration we were accorded in the expectation of Thượng Đế be honored by the Holy Catholic Church as it should be. This, in absolute reparation due to our country.

By siding with a conquering West, the Church has only underlined and aggravated the terrible mistakes she committed against Vietnam, to which precisely the Holy Church owes Reparation.

I could not insist more on this, which was suggested to me from High above precisely, logically, and, above all, generously as the only appropriate and urgent response in the time required for the best of all!

Knowing it allows me to lead everything in the direction that God wants and to prevent the unnecessary.

What will be the price?

That question was never part of my concerns, and it was not up to me to worry about it. Knowing what I have to do is enough for me, so as not to risk being carried away by what is beyond me. I do not risk staying immobilized for an indeterminate time waiting for a response to my expectations either. No impatience, then.

It has taken me over half a century to finally give voice. To know more serves above all the Divine purpose, because my natural peace of mind does not seek to know the result.

Predestination does not move according to the immediate result. It remains its instrument whatever the appearance. Its logic serves the Lord in His views, which can only be victorious, whatever the deadline. Hence the weariness when time weighs on the predestined "very little one" who certainly has a say about his destiny.

And now what to add, if not to urge—what am I saying—to beg those who will fall on these lines, not to despair while the hour is near when, finally, everything is in our hands.

The Lord knows.

Also, He can only allow and support what must be, so that what is necessary for the infinite happiness of all may triumph at long last. It's the reason why the predestined "very little one" cares about it more than anyone else, especially since the Stations of the Cross arrive at their end.

What can one expect of such a life until it is concluded?

To advance in the way which is one's own, to make the decision which is justified, without seeking to impose it and without even waiting for the result. Then move on, as if the consequences would only follow their course, without taking any more interest in them. One then seems detached and even indifferent. This is not the case, notwithstanding all appearances.

Now I know that nonetheless and in the time that I still have, I must remember the facts, personal and otherwise, of this unique life of the predestined "very little one" who never strictly knew anything of his own. Useful evocation, if only to better grasp the contours and the details of that life and try to understand its right meaning for the rest.

The aim of my book is to complete what is known by all with what is not known, which has allowed me to endure with my usual peace of mind, the trials that appeared terrible to many, but were unreal to me.

In this way, perhaps, people will better understand the meaning of my life, both private and public. I take this opportunity to say that I only reveal the details that are unknown because I am convinced that, although guided by my unique predestination, my behavior has always remained simply human, only led by my faith in the Lord.

Faith is so absolute that having it is to enjoy it.

•

CHAPTER 2

A Life Projected into History

After our wedding and honeymoon, I settled down in Huế with my husband, as an eighteen-year-old young newlywed. There I spent the first years following my wedding. They passed very rapidly. That was a new life not only of independence but especially involving new responsibilities hitherto unknown.

I could truly discover that admirable city. I knew it before only through brief annual stays, during our round trips between Hà Nội and the high plateau of Đà Lạt in the south, or to one of the beaches in the center of the country. There the sea was ideal, very different from those in the south or the north of Vietnam.

Everything concurred in my favor, allowing me to get to know and savor the atmosphere of Huế and feel the soul of the country in its uniqueness. I took daily walks alone because my husband insisted on seeing his elder brother who lived next to the family home. Meals served there were the most unique in the world.

What stands out the most in my memories is the vision of this idyllic landscape crossed by multiple streams so remarkable for the purity of their water. There, nature, its horizons, fruits and flowers, their beauty, their aromas and their flavors were intoxicating.

Of Huế I keep a moving memory of all I experienced there at that time and I have not found anywhere else.

We could taste its enchanting "Cá nục nấu canh dưa hồng" (fish soup with young watermelon). "Lờ đờ có kẻ mất chồng không hay" (Hey! Hey! [It is so good that] you could lose your wits and your husband without knowing.)

Sublime also was that soup with sardines and watermelon, so cheap, that can only be found in Huế. An example among others of what this place can give. And its pepper is incomparable!

For my promenades I took the rickshaw I had brought from Hà Nội by train. Its shape and size, so original, were not known here where old high-perched rickshaws were still in use. This one came from the north; it was wider, stockier, and more comfortable. Everybody noticed me as I was the only one to have it and I did not hesitate to share it with my husband, something no one had done before.

Every day I went along the An Cựu canal, going to dinner with my husband at his mother's home. It was one pleasure I never tired of enjoying, because the cooking served there was exquisite and varied. I was honoring it with the craving of my young age, and I could see the pleasure I gave to my hosts, my mother-in-law and my brother-in-law Cẩn, who did not appear to have seen such an appetite in their lives. I was even more appreciated because I was preceded by the wife of a younger brother, Luyện, who got married just a year before me. That wife who came from the south scandalized her in-laws by ordering from time to time Western meals prepared by the colonial hotel located in the vicinity of the house.[1] The Southerners already had the bad reputation of being "owned by the colonialists" and the attitude of that girl confirmed it to us. The opinion of the people of Central Vietnam did not make the situation any better, as they tended to despise "the people [who mimicked] the colonialists" ["*gens du colo*"] and the more so, given the fact that my sister-in-law, who was introduced by our parish priest, used to live in a "nhà cao cẳng" (wooden house on stilts) that used to serve as a garage for discarded automobiles.

In Huế, the interest of what was offered to me every evening came from a series of unusual circumstances when I discovered the strange imperfections of certain members related to the family. I was moving confidently in that new environment that had become mine since my marriage. Being the only one of my kind, it was up to me to adapt to that familial universe that might appear disparate with the differences in character and age of people together with their ranks.

I think specifically about one of my sisters-in-law who was married to a hothead [*un excité*]. He thought everything was permissible through his spouse, the second daughter of the family and mother of the future archbishop of Sài Gòn, my nephew Nguyễn Văn Thuận.[2] To the colonialists, Sài Gòn was "the" key post, for it was located in the heart of the richest rice fields of the south. After the fall of Sài Gòn in 1975, its archbishop was kept a prisoner in Communist reeducation camps for thirteen years, nine years of which in total isolation.

I learned by chance that he had not been freed, while no accusation had been made against him. Nobody had intervened in his favor, perhaps not to make him appear or to overburden him with the "man of the colonialists" stigma. During an interview given in 1988 to an English writer who is my goddaughter, I incidentally mentioned his thirteen-year imprisonment.[3] He was freed shortly thereafter, as if my intervention had been enough to whitewash him.

He sought to see me and thank me forthwith, but I was in Paris when he went to Rome and vice versa. He met my eldest son and considered his duty to thank me fulfilled. Later on, he was invited to the festivities the Church had convened in his honor when he was promoted to the rank of cardinal. Since his death, the Church has initiated the procedure to beatify him. His relatives are all the happier since they could not do anything for him during his thirteen years in captivity. I still harbor a regret that they had accused me of "bringing misfortune to the family" in a book written about him.[4] And yet I did not hesitate to intervene in his favor when he was still a prisoner.

What is there to say about the glee of the church? That archbishop who was appreciated by the colonialists never invoked or regretted in his books and speeches the tragedy of the assassination of his uncles Ngô Đình Diệm and Ngô Đình Nhu who were at the head of the Legitimate Power [Pouvoir Légitime] of Vietnam, or that of Ngô Đình Cẩn, his other uncle.[5] He was careful to avoid showing his kinship.

Nevertheless, after the coup d'état of 1963, while in Vietnam, he did nothing in favor of the return of the Archbishop of Huế, Ngô Đình Thục, his uncle.[6]

I am returning to my existence in Huế.

I was quietly whiling my days away, playing the "đờn tranh," a kind of Vietnamese zither of infinite sensitivity. I had learned to play this instrument easily, which was for a long time my only source of entertainment in the company of my zither teacher. When I set myself to do some embroidery, my husband gladly kept me company, as he liked to indulge himself in this kind of delicate work.

When he met me again in the evening, he used to take me to his mother's house. After dinner, he would disappear into the house of his elder brother Ngô Đình Khôi on the other side of the canal.[7]

At the very beginning of my marriage, I had a marvelous cook, who took an infinite pleasure in serving a young married couple who appreciated, as they should, the fine cuisine of their chef. But that did not last long. That chef, the former cook of my sister-in-law and of her family that had at least fifteen members including numerous children, said he was exhausted and then retired to be at my service as a young married woman.[8] This was actually the initiative of my brother-in-law who rightly thought that the cook would get less tired serving a new couple rather than his usual charge. But his former bosses would not have it that way and considered it tactless, laying their man off. They prevailed, and that forced me to dine every evening at my mother-in-law's place.[9] I had no cause to regret this outcome because the meals prepared by the chef of the other

President Ngô Đình Diệm's sister-in-law, Mme. Ngô Đình Nhu.

house were delicious and prepared with the great art of the delicate cuisine of Huế.

After dinner my husband left me there to go to the house of his elder brother. He stayed there for a while and that gave me a chance to listen to my brother-in-law Ngô-Đình Cẩn, younger than my husband but older than me, telling legends and old or recent histories that I would not have discovered otherwise.[10]

For them all I was a very young girl, younger than the nephews and nieces that are my elder sister-in-law's children. My time among them was not wasted.

And yet, everything has an end, and that was precisely on August 22, 1944, my twentieth birthday.[11]

Tragedy struck the family after more than a year of serenity that had allowed me to enjoy the place to the fullest.

When I had a portion of my birthday cake brought to my elder brother-in-law Ngô Đình Khôi, I learned that he had not returned from the meeting to which he was invited by the communists with his only son. Both were led to an unknown destination from which they never returned. From that time on, I often found myself alone as my husband vanished into nature to avoid the fate of his elder brother as well as that of his third brother, the future president Ngô Đình Diệm, who suddenly also disappeared.

For my own sake as well as for others, I need to recollect what happened to my country from the moment the communist Hồ Chí Minh attacked members of my family without any warning.

He assassinated my great-uncle Bùi Quang Chiêu, political leader in the south and elder brother of my paternal grandmother.[12] He was killed with his six boys, the youngest of whom was only 6 years of age.

He ordered the assassination of the eldest Ngô Đình and his only son, who was about to get married.

After this clean slate, he ordered the capture of the future president Ngô Đình Diệm on the train that was taking him from Sài Gòn to Huế. He had him taken to the high mountains in the North, at the Chinese border, where he was kept prisoner in a hut from September 1945 to December 1946.

Then he let him go.

But before releasing him, Hồ Chí Minh had kept him for one full night in a room at the residence of the former Résidents Supérieurs Français in Hà Nội, where he had settled in after seizing power.[13]

Hồ Chí Minh tried to convince him to join his ranks. Ngô Đình Diệm limited himself to replying that, above anything else, he wanted to know what the Communists had done to his captured elder brother and his only son. Before responding to the proposal of "joining the Communists," he insisted that all the verbal horrors heaped on the Ngô Đình family be retracted. Without it there could not be any valid base to talk about anything else whatsoever. Hồ Chí Minh did not respond to any of the prerequisites.

The future president left [Hồ] in the morning; the doors were wide open for him.

His liberation was due to his brother, my husband, who had just met with Hồ Chí Minh shortly before.[14]

Diệm showed up unannounced in Hà Nội at my parents' home, where my husband used to stay when he was in the North. Since their return in 1945, after seeing their mansion confiscated, my parents withdrew into the mansion my grandfather had left to my mother, the very same one in which I was born.

My father resumed his work as a lawyer there and my husband went there to stay when he left Huế for Hà Nội. Nobody knew what my husband was doing. He never opened up to anybody.

I would have preferred his being with me more often rather than being in the North, but to think he was with my parents still reassured me a little.

Hà Nội had become the capital of the Communists and to my husband this place appeared to be safer than anywhere else.

My husband understood the course of events, but he never talked to me about it. Thus, he disappeared regularly without telling me where he went.

Overnight, on the day following my twentieth birthday, I therefore found myself suddenly alone.[15] Absolutely. The new two-story house expressly built for our marriage but completed only afterwards suddenly appeared too big for me, despite the presence of two domestic servants, a cook, and the rickshaw driver who also doubled as my gardener. A factotum, he himself had to hide also as the Communists were recruiting all the able-bodied men.

To say that I was dismayed is an understatement. But I got over it, for life had to go on and we had to prepare to face the unknown, which would prove to be more and more incomprehensible.

In my new solitude, I gradually realized that instead of being my protector, my husband had become a threat to me.

My wedding, which had been the last grand affair in Hà Nội before its evacuation like that of the other great cities, coincided with the last jolts of the world war whose effects were felt in the major global capitals before spreading everywhere else.

Vietnam was a painful example whose effects I had to endure, especially in the Central region, hence in Huế, its capital. The colonialists had always known how to remain discreet there. Now Huế does not exist anymore, apparently razed by the colonialists and the imperialists, and they do not even talk about it.[16] One accuses the other. An absolute horror.

On August 27, 1945, I had my first child, Lệ Thủy.

This adorable angel, beautiful at birth, was a daughter who immediately became the pride of her father. He promptly found his own features in her.

Unaware of the world she came into, the little angel never stopped smiling, eyes and fists closed.

Just by herself, she could fill the void that had invaded me.

Left alone with my baby as I was, there was no question of my traveling. From now on I would stay at home to take care of her. With the church right behind the house I did not have any difficulty going there.

I managed to keep my days busy with all of this, despite the absence of my husband to whom my thoughts often went, wondering where he could possibly be and what he could be doing.

Reduced to this kind of life, I can no longer remember how I could manage to be self-sufficient.

I do not want to forget this brief time of "Vietnam's independence" proclaimed by the Japanese. They settled in my country in March 1945, chasing the French out or locking them up in concentration camps.

But they were correct and discreet toward us.

Before the war, the French colonialists would dispose of our rice as they saw fit. In order to sell it to the Japanese at a more advantageous price, they did not hesitate to starve us.

Nevertheless, during the Japanese war against the Americans, the French refused to sell our rice to them.[17]

While maintaining the authority of Bảo Đại as the emperor of Vietnam, the Japanese proclaimed the independence of our country in 1945, before having to surrender in August 1945.

Despite that declaration of independence, the French rushed to regain ground and wanted to indemnify themselves for the losses caused by the Japanese occupation. They did not recognize as valid the independence proclaimed by a country that had just lost the war.

Shortly thereafter, my parents left Hà Nội definitively and came to Huế to settle down in a big house they had rented. They came in a new black Citroën automobile which they left to me before leaving with these words: "We give it to you—the Communists had taken it but promised to give it back to us. You can keep it because they claim they do not steal from anybody."

In fact, the Communists affirmed that they had returned everything to that sister-in-law, whose husband and son they had caused to disappear.[18] What the Communists had brought were cartloads of "Ho Chi Minh banknotes" that were hastily used by whoever had them as they were simply worthless paper in the eyes of the population. One day a Communist official showed up at the house and asked to see my husband. Thinking of the fate that befell my brothers-in-law, I invited him to wait for my husband, as if he were about to come back any moment, whereas he was in fact at home upstairs. After a few minutes, the Communist decided to leave and told me that he would come back another time. As soon as night fell, my husband left. He simply told me that he would provide me with everything I might need. And I had no news of him for a long time.

Emperor Bảo Đại, to whom the Japanese on leaving had handed the "independence" of the country, asked my father first to form a government.

My father declined to be the head of the government, because he thought he was too young. He proposed to Bảo Đại to choose a man of a more respectable age, Professor Trần Trọng Kim.[19]

As for my father, he accepted the post of foreign minister. He then came to settle in Huế with the other members of the government.

It was there that I saw for the first time the project of what would become the Vietnamese flag. The project was first presented to my father while he was sitting behind his desk at home.

On the flag there was a sign at the center that blocked three red lines drawn on a yellow background. I found this motif inappropriate, believing that the yellow flag would look better with only three red lines that extended to infinity. My parents agreed with me. The flag was presented to the government which likewise gave its approval.[20]

And so, this flag has ever since been that of the Ultimate Legitimate Power of Vietnam.

The first independent government my father had helped establish did not last long. It did not have the support of any foreign nation, and the watchful colonialists were waiting to retake everything with or without the help of the Americans. They always hoped to be reinstated in Vietnam by violent or sneaky means.

A few questions arise about this colonial mentality that refused to understand the natural aspiration of a people to regain their independence, a mentality that was determined to cling to a colony even if it meant committing terrible acts.

In the name of what?

The colonialists knew how to exploit the Church to favor their expansion. They caused it to merit the admonition of Jesus to Peter: "*Get behind me, Satan! You are a stumbling block to me; you do not have in mind the things of God, but the things of men.*" (Matthew 16:23)[21]

These satanic times of men under the cover of the Church have already lasted too long.

Let the time come now for the reparation owed by those who have persecuted us, the colonialists, the imperialists and the communists, these cruel people with no faith nor law. We can only count on the Lord so that everything goes as well as possible, first for the Holy Church, because my country and my family have never betrayed Her. Quite the contrary.

When the Japanese left, the victorious allies of the Second World War asked the Chinese, then noncommunist, to come to Vietnam to protect French interests.

It was the Chinese turn to parade in our area.

From the first day, a group of excited soldiers invaded my garden. My house by the An Cựu bridge was the most elegant of the city.

I was alone in the villa with my baby, the nurse, and the cook. Luckily the villa was a two-story building. This allowed us the time to lock up all the doors of the first floor and to take refuge on the second floor by barricading ourselves on the balcony, overlooking the garden within sight of the street below. We could then alert the passersby by hitting on the pots or on any of the utensils we could lay our hands on. The shouting stopped the soldiers before they could reach the garage door. As the noise we made on the balcony was amplified by our howling, the soldiery chose to leave the place without going further.

I followed in the footsteps of the soldiers to meet their general, a twenty-six-year-old youngster, to whom I addressed my complaint in good and due form. He escorted me back to see with his own eyes the scene of the litigation.

My living environment and my German Shepherd impressed him to the point that he assured me that he would take the necessary steps. Still, I did not expect that he would have two guard-posts erected at each end of my street. That was meant to stop the circulation not only of his soldiers but also of passersby. I had a time of perfect calm during the Chinese stay in Huế. The news spread throughout the city after witnessing the jarring noise I had created on my balcony.

Aside from that, the Chinese appeared to be literally famished. They divested the street merchants of their products at a speed that had never been seen before. Did they pay them? I do not know, but they did not leave too bad a memory on their trail.

After that the colonialists made an agreement with China to begin again as before.

After having eliminated all his principal adversaries, Hồ Chí Minh proclaimed in Hà Nội on September 2, 1945, the Democratic Republic of Vietnam (DRV) and the independence of the country.

The National Assembly that had been previously elected met on March 2, 1946, and designated Hồ Chí Minh to be the first president of the DRV.

In March 1946, Hồ Chí Minh signed an accord with France in which the two parties recognized the DRV as a free state, with its own government, its parliament, its army, and its finances, and being part of the Indochinese Federation and of the French Union.[22]

Until September 1946, a semblance of entente between France and the DRV prevailed, but in the end Hồ Chí Minh realized that France, basically, wanted to retain her colonial empire under conventional ruling arrangements. He decided to launch hostile activities.

On December 19, 1946, the Indochinese war started.

The troops of Võ Nguyên Giáp, the army of Hồ Chí Minh, mounted a surprise attack on Hà Nội.

During this period, I tried to cope and make do as best as I could.

In this climate of insecurity that threatened us all, I did not go to see my mother-in-law every day, only from time to time to show off my baby who was a true splendor. I walked her around in her baby carriage and attracted the admiration of the strollers on my way. These brief moments of happiness, already so rare, came to a complete end.

Launching into that war that left the people panting, not knowing which way to turn, the Communists one day decided to deport us. They intimated to us the order to evacuate Huế, but where to?

We did not have anywhere to retreat to, if not to the Canadian Church of the Redemptorists, located just behind my house.

Before we even had the time to remove the grand piano that was stuck in the main entrance door, gunshots were fired in the night, while my mother-in-law and sister-in-law were at my house.[23]

Had I been alone with my baby, I would have already been at the Redemptorists as Cẩn, my brother-in-law, was already there. He did not want to take the risk, like us, to stay on the other side of the Canal, because he would have been exposed. But my sister-in-law who owned this beautiful house that was expressly built to be rented to us wanted to stay there with me for as long as possible. Which caused us to be stuck there the night the first burst of gunshots exploded.

Where did they come from? We did not know.

We were huddled on the first floor in the middle of the living room, surrounding ourselves with cushions taken from the armchairs and couch. The shooting lasted all night long. The next day, some persons resembling cavemen appeared, wearing jute sacks as clothes, carrying guns too long as if from another age. They ordered us to leave the place without delay and locked up our German Shepherd. I was innocent enough, or rather foolish enough, to obey and, most of all, to ask them not to forget to bring me the dog where we were going. Of course, I never saw again that magnificent dog with an exceptional intelligence that impressed us all. I had taught it not to walk on carpets; not to bark, but only to growl. I could have tried to keep it and bring it along on a leash, but my unawareness verged on idiocy.

Then the harrowing saga of our deportation began, and it is from that time on that I started to learn by experience.

First of all, never to separate myself from my baby.

One day, after having carried her during an exhausting march, barefoot on the clay soil, I entrusted her to my cook so that I could stretch my arms and then be able to advance with less pain.

And oops! I did not see my cook at the end of the road when I suddenly turned my head around.

Where was she? Alarmed, I shouted out and saw her emerge with the other women of the group which included my mother-in-law whom the rickshaw operator carried on his back.

I retrieved my baby, who did not walk yet, as if the difficult times disturbed even the little ones; I would never let go of her again.

In the group we had already made ourselves noticed because we were absolutely inseparable and systematically refused to go under the bridges that would have protected us from the shootings that crisscrossed those who passed over them.

If I refused to go under the bridges with my baby in my arms, it was in order not to see the horrors that were heaped there, all those decomposed corpses, abandoned to their fate. During this period nobody thought of clearing that heap of corpses, if only for public health reasons. But our crossing of those bridges was so surreal that the shootings stopped when I crossed them, with my baby in my arms.

I remember a rainy day during which I covered the two of us with my woolen jacket. The baby took it for a game of hide and seek and burst into laughter. These bursts of laughter must have been heard very far as they left us alone when we walked on those bridges that separated us from the Communist headquarters.

The headquarters were not very far away, but it took those who led us there two days to reach them. We therefore spent one night in the open air, sleeping on the naked ground without anything to cover us but the clothes we wore. When we arrived, we found a suburban middle-class house, with a pool in the middle of the garden. We rushed there to wash at least our faces and feet. It was then that a tall and handsome young man appeared, rather tall for a Vietnamese.

Dressed in the latest sports fashion with golf pants and woolen sweaters, one of which was worn nonchalantly on the shoulder, he said, "I would like to talk to 'Cụ Bà' Ngô Đình Nhu" while looking in the direction of the group, where the rickshaw man had just put my mother-in-law on a seat.

Instead of her, it was me, the youngster of the group, who exclaimed: "And what for?"

I was outraged that the young man had adopted this affected tone of respect to address a group I considered to be very ill-treated.

The young man knew right away who he had to deal with. He turned toward me and apologized without the slightest shame for the bad treatment we had received.

"I would like to apologize for what you may have suffered during your transfer from there to here, but, given the circumstances these days, it was impossible for us to do any better."

"And why?" I retorted, "Nothing obliged you to treat us like you have done. Sleeping even on the ground, in the cold of this winter, and not having anything to eat but a fistful of rice always served cold? And why taking two days to cross a distance that could have been covered in one day, while we were being shot at unless we went under bridges filled with corpses and other horrors?"

My indignation was so just and sincere that the man was all dumbfounded to the point of being able to say only: "We would ask you again to excuse us and to please take some rest in the room at your disposal while waiting for dinner."

We followed the guide who took us in two groups: the group of my mother-in-law [Phạm Thị Thân], her daughter [Ngô Đình Thị Hoàng], and me, her daughter-in-law, each of us accompanied by our respective children, and the group of the house help, my cook with her daughter who was my baby's nurse and her five-year-old son.

The first group went into the room with an old bed supplied with a mattress in the middle.

The second group disappeared with those who were showing the room.

We would only see them again the next day, in the morning.

We followed our escort to the dining room, where a decent diner was waiting for us. After dinner, upon returning to the room that was assigned to us, we realized that the only antique bed in the middle with its sheetless mattress was meant for all of us.

If we lay down sideways, there was room for everybody, with the adults' feet hanging over the bed. With the baby against me, I went to sleep without asking for anything else, and I was not disturbed like during the previous night when a battle-ready situation was launched to the cries that "someone has escaped."

In fact, they did come to wake us up, although the "escape" was due to the fact that in the count they could not find my baby, who had fallen asleep in my arms and her little feet did not stick off the end of the mattress. After that everybody was obliged to lie down straight on the cold floor and managing nevertheless to regain their sleep until the brutal awakening.

In the morning, in this new place, after being served some sort of porridge, we were taken to a new destination, the one that my sister-in-law had indicated. It was a locality where her farmer lived. We could stay there until further notice. From time to time, we received a visit from the Communist official. For a Communist, that man was truly civilized, so that he was well received by my mother-in-law and sister-in-law when he came to visit. In truth, he came to make sure we had not left our assigned location.

The time arrived when it was no longer possible for us to stay at that place. From time to time, unknown aircraft flew over the place where we were and dropped a few bombs in the fields, to test who knows what.

My sister-in-law decided to travel further, to a convent where we could at least follow Mass every day. Where we were, we were deprived of the Eucharist, even on Sundays. It was decided that, being young and hence more agile, I would go with the farmer of my sister-in-law to the Communist headquarters to get travel passes. I did it on a fine day and obtained without any problem the necessary papers from the Communists. The chief by the name of Bảy (Seven) took his hat off in the most courteous way. To the point that during the period of the Ultimate Legitimate Power of Vietnam, when Central Vietnam was under the official purview of Cẩn, my younger brother-in law, Bảy did not hesitate to come to see him from time to time to get news about me. I was the one from the group whom he knew best.

We left on a small boat with our Communist travel passes that we were never asked to show, and arrived at the nuns' convent, where a room equipped with four divans[24] was reserved for us. The two wooden ones were for my mother-in-law and my sister-in-law with her daughter, and the other two in bamboo were for the baby's nurse and for me.

There was a simple basket forming a child's cradle hanging from the ceiling between the two of us, and it only took a touch to swing it and calm the baby should she become agitated. Of all of us, she was the most comfortably settled, with my padded jackets serving as blanket and mattress. She did not disturb anybody and was the quietest baby in the world, and only left her basket cradle to keep my mother-in-law company or to be in my arms as I walked around.

The nuns appeared to be charmed by our company. Separated from them by a simple partition, they heard us all day long whereas we did not hear them at all, as they were always silent. They only retired to the dormitory to sleep. As for us, we spent our days in the common room that was reserved for us. We also took our meals there.

The nuns ended up knowing the character of and having an idea about each one of us. They heard my sister-in-law and her daughter squabbling over trivialities, thus witnessing their scandalous behavior that emerged on every occasion because my sister-in-law did not have any authority over her only daughter, a ten-year-old little girl. The child continually did whatever she liked and had chosen me as a punching bag, with the pretext that I was penniless when I left home, with a cook and her child and a nurse for my baby. Furthermore, I was completely ignorant of the whereabouts of my husband and my parents. In brief, nobody was more lost and deprived than me.

Things became so venomous that one day, as I was automatically taking a second serving at the dinner table, I was stopped by the exclamation of the pesky little girl: "Mom! Auntie just took a second sardine!"

The atmosphere did not improve when I decided to sell the cow and her calf that belonged to me in my sister-in-law's herd, which brought me enough money to buy two of the biggest boxes of powdered milk sold on the market. But then I had to think of how to transfer the milk into smaller tin boxes to be able to carry them into the trenches when the alarm sounded and planes with unknown intention showed up on the horizon. I asked my niece for my old boxes of powdered milk back; she was using them to keep her paper cuttings.[25] She protested. Her mother, siding with her, exclaimed: "Why not use the numerous empty jars lying unused on the shelf instead?"

We were dealing with glass containers here! How could we take them with us into the trenches when the planes passed without breaking them?

That senseless suggestion demonstrated a real mark of selfishness, I pointed out, but it only served to prove my own selfishness! And more than that, my own clumsiness (!) because on the first alert I was not able to preserve the containers of powdered milk. They broke up at the first explosion and the milk powder spread all over the floor to my great consternation.

It was the last drop of water to cause the overflow.

With the travel passes obtained to leave, I decided to return to Huế and take refuge with the Canadian Redemptorists. I shared this idea with my cook, who agreed to leave with me and her daughter. The whole convent sided with us and sympathized all the more, knowing that I could not possibly leave my mother-in-law behind, even with her own daughter. But God decided for the best. I was getting ready to go to church to pray with my little group. Just as we were leaving, I was told that someone was looking for us. It was a Redemptorist priest who came by boat just in time to take us to town.

We would have surely gotten lost in the wild, at the mercy of who knows what. We were spared all this thanks to the boat that came to pick us up. The boat was soon filled up with miscellaneous provisions that were in short supply in Huế. We boarded in a hurry but would only reach our destination in the middle of the night, with no other light to guide us than a meager bundle of dried branches the priest was swinging at the end of his arm. The city, sunken in total obscurity, appeared to be totally deserted.

Nevertheless, we arrived at the monastery. We were put in a hangar with one wing reserved for the family. Cẩn, my brother-in-law, was already there. He greeted us with relief because he had been terribly worried after we had disappeared from that beautiful house next to his that had served as my residence. It was blown up after my departure. The news devastated my sister-in-law. I lost all my furniture in there, but it was nothing compared with her own home. She was so upset that she refused to have it rebuilt and her daughter preferred to settle in the south, in Sài Gòn, where she would later lead an unbridled, scandalous life very remote from our Vietnamese traditions.

Once back in Huế, I did not plan to stay there for long. I could no longer stand the unbearable discomfort of my situation. To me the city appeared more and more as coming from another age and, most of all, a year had passed without my knowing anything about my husband. Where was he? What was he doing?

Obviously, the baby had no memory of her father, whom she had barely glimpsed since her birth.

My exasperation reached its peak the night following our arrival.

In the hangar arranged as dormitory for the family, my brother-in-law's bed with mosquito net was between my bed and that of my sister-in-law and her daughter. While he had a mosquito net and a thick woolen blanket, I had nothing other than my woolen frock coat of the latest fashion. It was the most inadequate of blankets. I was advised to simply roll myself up in a mat like the peasants used to do if they had no blanket. I did not like that advice. I had already suffered enough that winter, insufficiently covered as I was. I woke up in the middle of the night when everybody was asleep, incensed at the sight of the warm gear [attirail] of my brother-in-law. Throwing on his back the thin blanket pierced with holes that was used for ironing, I got hold of his, made of thick and fine wool, and pulled it toward me in the dark. That woke him up and I felt he was trying to hold on and not let me have it. Furious, I had to let go of it and take back the ironing blanket full of holes that had served me since the beginning of our misfortune.

In the morning, he looked at me with stupor when I went to greet my mother-in-law and told her I was leaving, to join the convoy of trucks that was about to set off toward the mountain pass called "Đèo Hải Vân" ["Col des nuages" in French or "Pass of the Clouds" in English]. I wanted to reach Đà Nẵng (Tourane), where I hoped to catch a flight to Sài Gòn with what was left of the proceeds from the sale of the cow and calf.

I wanted to meet up with my sister there so as to learn the news about my parents and consequently about my husband.

Everybody was caught by surprise, because I had just settled in the hangar put at our disposal, and the convoy was going to leave any minute.

I left therefore with my baby in the hollow of one of my arms and carrying the basket-cradle containing her diapers and clothes. I did not bring anything else for me besides what I had on me. So, I got away after bidding farewell to my mother-in-law who did not know how to retain me. Upon arrival at the convoy, I ran into a truck with an unoccupied passenger seat. The driver, a young blond legionnaire, who turned out to be German and only spoke his own language, took me on as his passenger. I was so lucky! My driver proved to be well-bred and discreet. He tickled the baby a little bit and nothing more.

Before the departure of the convoy, the baby's nurse showed up. The family had sent her back to me, but there was no place for her in the truck. I also knew that there would not be any job for her in Sài Gòn at my sister's place where house help was abundant.[26]

We thus headed for Hải Vân Pass, which I had known since my childhood from having crossed it every year during our summer vacations. At the end of the trip, I was dropped off at the French Center in charge of the area.

The colonialists were back and already settled on Hải Vân Pass.

I was well received when my name was recognized. A bed with a mosquito net was reserved for me and a cradle with curtains was reserved for the baby. I was told that the military plane would not depart for Sài Gòn before two days. The only thing we could do was wait. This gave me a chance to get to know the French officer in charge of the region, Colonel Gilbert, if I am not mistaken. I was invited to his table during the short time of my stay. This first contact with the returning colonialists was ideal because that officer was most civilized. He already knew about my odyssey which, in his opinion, was not over yet. He had every reason to marvel at my crossing, alone with my baby, Hải Vân Pass, whose security he oversaw.

He did not have the same success as me; I learned that he was later killed in an ambush there.

Through him who had proved an ideal host for the baby as well as for me, we were led to think that a good colonialist could make up for all the worst of his peers. It's enough for him to be civilized.

But the colonialists have so tainted their image that it has become difficult to picture them as ideal hosts toward human beings subjected to the worst hazards of a life that had lost all human character.

The plane that took care of us was a military aircraft.

I had to pay for my seat, which was almost touching the floor, with my back against a pile of sacks. The trip was fast, and soon we were thrown into the smothering heat of Sài Gòn.

I immediately took a cycle rickshaw that swiftly brought us to my sister's house. She had had no news about me nor about our parents and wondered what had become of us.

When she saw me suddenly arrive with my baby in my arms, dressed in black with a white turban, she asked whose death I was grieving. She could not know that it was for my eldest brother-in-law, Ngô Đình Khôi, who had been assassinated by the Communists along with his only son.

I arrived unannounced while she was receiving our aunt, the one who was going to keep me company during my stay in Đà Lạt. The surprise was as immense as our joy despite the anxiety of being without any news of our parents. They had disappeared at the same time as my husband.

Without difficulty I settled down at my sister's place. Her daughter was of the same age as mine. We had only seen each other once since my marriage, when she wanted to inspect my new living environment. I was unfamiliar with hers in Sài Gòn, so this was truly a reunion. I had a comfortable room for myself and my baby and someone to take care of her during my stay.

A few days later, a Redemptorist priest rang the doorbell. I received him on behalf of my sister, who was asked to come to the monastery to meet a messenger coming from the North.

I went there the next day in her stead.

And who did I see coming into the reception room?

My husband, whom I had not seen for a year!

My baby, who did not recognize him, first showed some reticence to be taken in her father's arms. Everything went quickly back in order, especially when daddy settled down on the spot and he saw his daughter walking. She was late in everything but quickly caught up.

After one month we decided to go back to Đà Lạt and stay in the house of a doctor friend of my father, pending the completion of the villa my father had ordered for us.

First my husband went to Huế to present himself to the family and take the things he had left there that I might need. Afterward, we left for Đà Lạt, which had returned to its wild state but could rapidly be fixed.

Mme. Ngô Đình Nhu and her husband at their residence in the early 1950s.

There I lived my calmest period of the Franco-Vietnamese war, with my husband, whenever he could join me from time to time. We had two more children: two sons, Trác, born on December 28, 1947, and Quỳnh, on August 23, 1952.

Their father continued to come and go, disappearing and reappearing without notice.

I had learned not to lean on him.

Our eldest daughter was growing up ahead of her two little brothers. Every day she went to her school, the Couvent des Oiseaux (Convent of the Birds). She deserved some praise because it was a mountain road she used to climb with ease in the company of the cook who would then go to the market after dropping her off at the school. One rainy day I saw our daughter coming back, carrying her schoolbag with difficulty. I was surprised to discover that her briefcase was waterlogged and that the cook had not even been aware of the need to empty it.

Furious in front of my husband, who was present by a rare chance, I ran out in the rain to take my bicycle and started to pedal.

I just told him, "This cannot continue. I will ask the Lord for a car."

Speechless, my husband only nodded his head in acquiescence, his eyes raised to heaven.

I disappeared in the beating rain to confront the slope of the terrain.

Soon something happened that allowed me to have my personal car, a perfectly functioning one because it belonged to the manager of a garage. He was ready to let me have it if I helped him sell his garage at a good price. I did not know a thing about these matters, as my only means of transportation was a bicycle. I entrusted that deal to my husband, who happened to have a distant cousin, passing through Đà Lạt, in search of a garage for sale. Lacking money, the cousin asked us to help while waiting to be paid for the work he was doing for the nuns at Les Filles de Charité (Daughters of Charity). It was not a problem, if the man was trustworthy and promised to repay the money that was advanced. The deal was therefore concluded, and overnight I had my dashing car, with a professional garage for its maintenance.

What could be better!

Having seen how the affair was roundly concluded through me, the cousin in question got into his mind that I had special powers when it came to money, and that I could have as much of it as I wanted. Although I had warned the nuns at Les Filles de Charité to pay him only in my presence, they did not do so, considering that it was none of their concern. Thence started the drama. My husband's cousin received the money in payment of his work for the nuns but did not reimburse our loan. He swore in the classic manner, "I will die coughing up my blood on the road if I do not comply in due course."

And that in fact was what happened to him.

His scared family thought that he had thus paid his debt and did not want to settle it. Finally, my husband had to intervene, I do not know how, but nobody contested my gift-car that served me very well during my stay in Đà Lạt, until we moved to Sài Gòn.

During those eight years, from 1946 to 1954, I did not have any other refuge than this place that had returned to the wild. It was wild to the point that no one dared to cross the garden at night to go to the kitchen, for fear that he might come face to face with a tiger.

Living alone with my children, I was relieved when my aunt, the daughter of the third wife of my paternal grandfather, joined me in Đà Lạt to do her work of secretary in the Vietnamese administration and to meet Emperor Bảo Đại, who used to spend most of his vacation time there.

She taught me how to use a sewing machine with a pedal, so ancient that nobody knew how to use it, which amused me all the more and which struck the curiosity of the emperor, whom I had several occasions to meet then.

I recall having been seen as a "magician" [magicienne] for being present at one of his fishing parties. Why? Simply because never before had he caught that many fish.[27] One of his servants, who was Black, rolled his eyes in stupefaction. I was wondering myself if he was going to empty the whole stream. On the other hand, he kept an impassive air about himself. He just smiled calmly when the servant exclaimed: "This is unbelievable!"

Thanks to a common acquaintance, General Nguyễn Văn Xuân, a graduate from the French Polytechnic School, who was the first Vietnamese premier in the [State of Vietnam], these meetings continued for a while.[28]

General Xuân, who was my father's cousin, often went to Đà Lạt to meet Emperor Bảo Đại, who was my mother's cousin. To lend a private nature to their meetings, they made it a point to invite me to join them at dinner, and the evening always ended with a bridge game. In turn each of them wanted me to be his "support" partner. If my partner won, I would take his winnings, and if he lost, I would not lose anything. It was, therefore, a total gain for me and that suited me perfectly. Instead of taking the money, I would just choose a present. This is how I won, with Bảo Đại, that famous sewing machine.

For me these evenings took on a familial aspect because politics was discussed only before or after I joined, never in front of me.

It sometimes happened that the bridge game was replaced by a picnic in the woods, which allowed me to swim or take a plunge in the waterfalls if I so desired. I was very well entertained by people who were hardly inclined to share my usual hobbies.

My husband, who was aware of these evenings and of those encounters that took place during the day, would not bring them up unless I mentioned them myself. They lasted the duration of my stay in Đà Lạt but became more spaced out when, having my little Simca 8 bartered with the garage, I started to pick up the children I met on my route on rainy days. That way I honored the vow I had made to provide a ride to the children I would see in the rain if I had a car one day.

There was no respite for me during the rainy season . . .

A priest who officiated the daily Masses in the little chapel next to the house ended up wondering about all that transportation of children and asked me the reason for it. When he learnt the truth, that I had promised the Lord to transport the children that found themselves in the rain if He provided me with a car, he exclaimed: "But this is insane!" He then explained to me that the transportation of other people entailed some insurance. This is how I was relieved of my oath. After the first impression of surprise, people took me for an eccentric, which was not necessarily flattering.

This joker life that I led first with a bicycle as a means of transportation, then a few years later with my Simca 8, which I had learned to fix with minor repairs of first necessity, lasted until our departure for Sài Gòn.

On July 7, 1954, Ngô Đình Diệm returned to Vietnam after a long stay abroad. He had accepted Bảo Đại's proposition, to become prime minister.[29]

Ngô Đình Diệm then asked his younger brother, my husband, to join him in Sài Gòn. In turn, I therefore left Đà Lạt to settle down there.

It was a sham transfer of power, a kind of trap to lock us up in a process at the hands of the colonialists, but the destiny of Vietnam could then be achieved through the only official way that was open to it.

At the beginning, this elevated position did not bring us anything.

NOTHING! Nothing but a life of pariahs during which my husband, his brother, and the government had to lock themselves up in the palace to escape the evil blows of the police, that of the "Bình Xuyên" (river pirates).[30]

At the beginning of this life of madmen and swindlers, I was living alone with my children in the secondary rooms of the St. Peter Clinique, built by my brother-in-law, then the Archbishop of Vĩnh Long, in Sài Gòn, for his archdiocese.[31]

For my family I had chosen three compartments that could serve as apartments, one of which would house the printing press of my husband who then published the weekly journal "Xã Hội" (Society), and the other two for our family.[32]

Having thus put us in a position of recluses, the colonialist trap seemed to have worked well since it had closed on us. It remained for us to see the follow-up.

The events went beyond the unimaginable.

What we may have thought to be the beginning of the end proved to be most overwhelming, if only to mention the condition of our life which was so miserable as to weep over it. But I did not shed any tears for that circumstance, because after so many years of absence, my husband was finally supposed to be there with us all the time.

"Supposed to be there," but in fact no one saw him.

I knew he was there, but he was invisible, because he spent most of his time at the "Norodom," the old palace of the Governor General in colonial times, that the French had made available to the government on September 7, 1954. Later on, this imposing edifice would become the presidential palace and receive another name, the "Dinh Độc Lập" (Independence Palace).[33]

My three children and I were parked in the two apartments at St. Peter Clinic that we had been assigned as living quarters. It did not take me long to elegantly arrange them to suit my taste and turn them into a family home as pleasant as possible.

In a corner near the window overlooking the kitchen, there was a bar with high stools. Next to the bar in the middle of the room I installed a table for our family meals. The living room was close to the window overlooking the verandah where I hung the orchids my husband had loved to grow in Đà Lạt. They managed to survive in Sài Gòn. Our bedroom was next to the living-dining room. On the other side of the living-dining room, I furnished the children's room with their beds and an old sculpted divan that served as a bed for their house servants. That room had a window that opened on the verandah of the main entrance. Each room had, in addition, another room in the back that served as bathroom or toilet. The kitchen was located behind the living-dining room.

In brief, I felt at ease with what could have made me sad at the thought of everything I had known until then. I certainly did not expect a comfortable setting in this place which promised to be quite modest.

There too, I had to stay alone with my children again.

Most of the time, my husband was at the palace and only appeared unannounced, like that time when he saved, *in extremis*, our second child, barely a year old, from a certain and tragic death, beyond anything one could imagine. It was an afternoon when the weather was extremely hot.

I had laid my baby on a mat on the floor just under the window of the bar overlooking the kitchen. It was the freshest place. Then, horrified, I saw emerging in the ground from a pipe of about four fingers in diameter (eight centimeters wide) a snake of the same size! Slowly it slithered while hissing toward the baby asleep just a few steps away. It gradually came out of the pipe and then I saw it in all its length. I had never seen anything that impressive except at the zoo or in picture books. Paralyzed by fear, I could not even shout. All of a sudden, I saw the monstrous beast being pierced right in the middle of its body by a sharp stick that immobilized it at the corner of the wall and the floor. The two halves of its body wriggled frantically in all directions.

It was my husband who had masterfully killed the monster.

Crawling towards the baby, it would have swallowed him in one bite had it had its aim. The help was so sudden! And I was amazed at this masterstroke against a monster of such size.

That image has ever since remained in my memory as a testimony of who my husband was. That man full of nobility who would not treat in the same way those who, nevertheless, would have attacked him, as traitors, in the same perfidious and sneaky manner of that snake.

There was also that afternoon, when alone I took a siesta in my room that was the extension of my husband's printing room. I had snatched at the flea market some old-style salon furniture I could not place anywhere but in our own bedroom for lack of space. I had, as it were, transformed this room into a precious little living room of style that enormously pleased me.

Suddenly I heard next to my room (thus in my husband's printing room) regular and repetitive muffled blows as if someone were trying to methodically destroy something. My children too were taking their siesta in their room, separated from mine by the living-dining room. I got up to see what was going on. Quietly, I went to the next room as it was directly connected to outside and opened to the court of the clinic.

And what did I see there?

An appalling thing!

Eight individuals impeccably dressed in white *sharkskin*, the material used for summer suits by the men of Sài Gòn, all wearing the same straw hat, were repeatedly beating someone lying on the floor in their midst!

I could not see what it was about. The person seemed to be crushed on the floor and curled up around himself.

Indignant, I seized one of my clogs, that indoor footwear suitable for the heat in Sài Gòn, and forcefully delivered blow after blow to the backs of those maniacs who did not see me coming, and at whom I shouted, "You are crazy! Who are you attacking that way?"

Of course, I stopped their deliberate and cold violence. Surprised by this unexpected intervention, they stopped . . . but only to turn their eyes in the same direction to an individual, dressed like them, whom I had not noticed.

The individual just gave them a sign that meant, "That's enough."

All of them lined up one behind the other and left by the same way they had arrived.

I then discovered that their victim was none other than the person in charge of my husband's printing press. He had been beaten up, without any protest on his part nor attempting the least resistance.

Flabbergasted, I asked him what had happened. He just wiped the blood that trickled down on his face, shrugging and trying to regain his composure with a simple, "Oh, that's nothing."

Faced with his obvious unwillingness to make a big deal out of it, I did not insist and left in the same way I had arrived, full of the questions I had not been able to ask and decided to put them to my husband. But he just said, "Do not worry about it."

I had to face the facts. All this was none of my business, which took me further away from everything having to do with my husband's printing press, especially since the beaten man I had rescued continued to remain at his post.

My husband passed the printing room over to others when he left for good these apartments that had been reserved for us and ended up pleasing me such as I had arranged them.

I would never see them again when I had to leave the place to get away from the country for three months after the first popular demonstration by those among one million refugees from the North that I, alone, had succeeded in mobilizing to support my manifesto then.

This story deserves to be remembered: After the signature of the Geneva Agreements on July 21, 1954, and the division of the country into two regions on either side of the 17th parallel, refugees coming in mass arrived in South Vietnam.[34] Nobody had predicted such a human wave, and nothing was prepared to welcome them. Families found themselves living in enormous concrete pipes used in the construction of drains. I could assess that situation myself when I went there for a visit.

The police, who were in the hands of the Bình Xuyên ("river pirates"), were incapable of coping with the situation. They could only mistreat the influx of these unfortunate people, who came, haggard and gaunt, and who were attracted by the news that President Ngô Đình Diệm had received "full powers" from Bảo Đại. But all that was still on paper.

Bảo Đại had left the country. He was living more frequently in Cannes on the Côte d'Azur. He settled in the Château Thorenc that the French had made available to him. When Ngô Đình Diệm was elected president of the republic, the French relegated Bảo Đại to a modest apartment in Paris and they would thereafter not try to use him against anybody else.[35]

So, we were very distraught because of the distress of all these refugees. I understood that if I could bring them any help whatsoever, I could in turn count on them should the need arise, at the right moment.

That moment came quickly and in a fortuitous way.

With my husband I had been invited to dinner in a restaurant in Chợ Lớn, the Chinese twin city of Sài Gòn, by the Polytechnic School graduate, General Nguyễn Văn Xuân, my father's cousin who was then vice president and defense minister in the Ngô Đình Diệm government.

General Xuân also invited the two counselors of the French Embassy, Messrs. Wintrebert and Mourer, who were known to him as being open-minded about Vietnam and who could bring him some support.

During dinner I asked General Xuân why he had not discharged General Nguyễn Văn Hinh, Chief of Staff of the South Vietnamese Army, who did as he pleased and had recently ignored General Xuân's order to "go and join Bảo Đại in France."

General Xuân answered me: "Find me only five signatures to endorse that discharge you are suggesting there."

Getting up from my table, I said to him: "You will have a million!"

The French counselors had only the time to exclaim, "You are dangerous, Madame," before I left the table with my husband, who had remained silent from beginning to end.

That was the starting point of what was to become my public life.

Everybody was surprised, including me.

After dinner my husband returned to the palace, where almost the entire government resided, and for good reason, as nobody trusted the police who were neither capable of imposing order in the city nor of providing the slightest sense of security to the population.

As for me, I left for the apartments at the St. Peter Clinic.

At the entrance of my living quarters, I saw two starving men, Quang and Hồ, who were waiting for my husband.

"No, it is impossible to see him, he is at the palace," I explained to them.

They gave me the reason why they were there.

"We represent one million refugees," they said, "who received the news that President Ngô Đình Diệm had received full powers from Emperor Bảo Đại. But in truth the situation here is unbearable. The Bình Xuyên police is harassing us to make us leave, but that is impossible even if we wanted to. What can we do?"

"Nothing for the time being," I said, "you must put up with it. We will see afterwards."

But faced with their sense of despair, I felt sorry for them and told them: "Unless you listened to me and would do what I will tell you?"

"Sure, and willingly so!" came the reply.

From that moment started the first of the actions I carried out on the national level, alone, as if driven by a sixth sense, in an unpredictable, swift, and even expeditious way. In return I had full success, with nothing and nobody to help me apart from the refugees among themselves.

I only had to advise the two men to tell the refugees in their charge to make, with whatever they had in their possession, some banners held at the end of sticks not more than 60 cm. [about 2 feet] long. They would only have to brandish them when they had their picture taken.

These banners had to be kept in shopping bags to be displayed at the right moment and bear an inscription in ink proclaiming: "We support the motion of Mme . . ." That was all.

"The date and venue of the rally will be communicated to you in due course! You won't have to wait too long!" I affirmed.

I added this ultimate suggestion: "The success of this undertaking lies in its secrecy. You will only know when the moment comes, to let the others know only a few hours ahead of time."

Everything worked out as planned.

On D-Day which was September 21, 1954, I used the same messenger to announce the hour, [which was during] market time, and the venue of the gathering: the forecourt of the Sài Gòn Cathedral.

The messenger quickly came back to tell me that the police, armed with submachine guns, had been tipped off (by whom?)! and that they were already on the spot at the place called "The Glass House," where gathered the great majority of refugees in the capital. There were two armored cars at the entrance. I got immediately into my little car, a light green Panhard, my messenger accompanying me to show the place, which by the way was not far from where I lived. I saw that the police, in battle gear and armed with submachine guns, were in fact there as well as the two armored cars as reported. I got out of my car without stopping the engine and with my messenger still inside. Keeping close to the car, I challenged the police pointing the machine guns toward the refugees: "Why do you prevent people from going to the market?"

"Oh no, we did not prevent them at all," replied those who were facing me as they quickly swung their guns behind their backs.

I turned to the refugees and said: "You see they are not preventing you from going into the market. Go ahead then."

When the place was emptied of its occupants, I returned to my car and got into it, when upon realization the men with their guns pointed at me stepped in: "No! Not you!"

"Why not?"

Without waiting, I stepped on the accelerator of my car whose engine was still running and crossed the passage before the police had the time to gather their wits. Panicking, my messenger, who tried to get out of the car and already had half of his body outside of the window, thankfully locked, could not stop my acceleration. I then arrived at the cathedral, where those who had already arrived were gathered in the forecourt. They calmly unfurled their streamers, on which they had the time to put my name. I was the author of the motion they had supported.

I hurried to send to the only French-language newspaper in Sài Gòn my motion demanding what I wanted, that General Nguyễn Văn Hinh be dismissed. The amazing thing was that the article of the newspaper on the demonstration of the day and my motion were censored by our own minister of information, who professed not to support a demonstration lacking government approval.[36]

I was the only person who was wary about him, and with good reason. Till the end and even after the Ultimate Legitimate Power of Vietnam disappeared, he stayed on with those who came after us, despite his reputation of being a Communist secret agent. Which in fact he was. [The Communists] reached out to him when the Americans left. But he chose to commit suicide because in the interval he had sided with the American imperialists. He could not imagine that the latter would abandon the game to the Communists, after having expelled the colonialists.

That is how a double and even triple agent ended up losing his life, after believing he fooled everybody till the end.

This case illustrates well the Machiavellian cleverness of the man, who succeeded in his maneuvers almost to the end.[37]

That first demonstration I led on September 21, 1954, surprised everybody, as I was absolutely alone in planning and carrying it out. Furthermore, I had this minister of information against me, a crypto-communist [*crypto-coco*] who took advantage of the fact that I had kept the government in the dark, to censor my motion that was supported by the demonstration and reported by the sole daily newspaper published in French. That was too much!

Unknowingly, I had provoked such a shockwave that General Nguyễn Văn Xuân, vice president and minister of defense, resigned three days after that popular demonstration he did not see coming and which he felt guilty for. According to the two advisers at the French Embassy, he had in fact heard my words, but was wrong in underestimating them, thinking they were "a simple provocation."

General Xuân did not consider himself as having "betrayed" the colonialists by not taking me seriously. He had to resign anyway. I only learnt about it much later, while for me he was the nicest member of the government when he was a part of it.

General Xuân was considered my "first victim."

I liked this man, my father's cousin, because his spoken Vietnamese was very imprecise and, therefore, comical. For instance, during his first speech in Vietnamese, he had held his breath in order to shout aloud the last words, further asking his audience to repeat after him: "Việt Nam Hòa Bình Muôn Năm!" (Long live peace for Vietnam!). But with his faulty use of the tones, it became: "Việt Nam hóa bịnh muốn nằm!" (Vietnam becoming sick, wants to lie down), causing an explosion of laughter in response. That incident stuck to him like a label he could never shed. It also showed how the colonialists used to choose their collaborators.

After that spectacular demonstration of September 21, 1954, the first Ngô Đình Diệm government had to be reshuffled. With American help, the French succeeded in having the family keep me out of Vietnam for three months, as long as the government was not completely "stabilized" after its first reshuffling.

Elections would soon take place to designate the Constituent and Legislative Assemblies.

Both the French and the Americans wanted to make sure I would be elected to neither.

Wasted effort!

I only had to register to be elected. And that was easily guaranteed by my electorate, the refugees from the North, those same people who had participated in my first demonstration of September 21, 1954.

It was then understood that from that time on I would not be removable from my seat.

And that would be the case.

So that my distancing from Sài Gòn would not quite appear to be a "punishment," I was sent to my father, the Vietnamese ambassador to the United States.

Senator [John F.] Kennedy was then the only American official to have invited me and my father to a luncheon at the Senate. Faced with this central institution of the American administration for the first time, I could not hide my surprise seeing these men, all of a certain age, behave like youngsters for the seats at the table they preferred to others. My father appeared to be embarrassed by my surprise; J. F. Kennedy chose to laugh at it while I completely forgot the seat the assistants had left vacant in deference to the only foreign woman, that I was that day.

I also went to Hong Kong where I settled at the Italian convent of the Canonesses of Canossa.

I felt at ease in this immense city even though I did not speak Chinese. The people there simply took me for one of theirs and would glance at me with great sympathy. In fact, I got into the habit of taking my little morning walk in the neighborhood around the Convent, that was favorably looked upon by the people living in its vicinity.

Hong Kong reminded me of Chợ Lớn, the twin Chinese city of Sài Gòn. It has the same vitality, except that the Chinese who settled in Vietnam speak Vietnamese, serve Vietnamese dishes, and seem to feel more Vietnamese than Chinese. Later I would return to Hong Kong to acquire my most precious jade. For the time being I spent my days with the Chinese children learning English. I could practice that language daily with a British lady instructor and thus consolidate the basic school English I learned since childhood in my French *lycée*. Thus, I spent my vacation studying to perfect a language that would prepare me for a universe hitherto unknown, that of debates with an audience thoroughly well-versed in verbal jousting.

I returned to Vietnam only after the first elections of the republic and soon found myself immersed in the noxious atmosphere the colonialists incessantly tried to impose on us.

I expected to find the small apartment I had arranged with care and was persuaded that I would be allowed to stay there. But not at all, I was taken directly to the Independence Palace, where my husband had ended up settling in. I was quartered in just one room in the rear. It was to be our bedroom, for my husband and me as well as for our three children!

At nightfall, foldable canvas beds for the children were spread around our bed, while the Xẩm (Chinese nanny) who looked after the youngest of them pulled out another one for herself in the bathroom.

That situation lasted for I do not know how long, but we had to wait until the wing that included our room was finally cleared of those who were seeking refuge as they felt exposed to danger in their own homes.

All this is to say to what point the colonialists were shameless in maintaining that "terror" around our family, which had withdrawn into the palace they had nevertheless made available to us.

I seriously regretted the little comfortable apartment I had arranged as best as I could before I had to leave the country. My only consolation then was that my husband and children were finally reunited, albeit in that atmosphere of constant threat.

My father, then Vietnamese ambassador to the United States, paid me a visit. He was frankly outraged at seeing me camping in such a miserable setting. He seemed to wonder if I had lost my mind for having lived through challenges that were beyond my strength. But he must have realized that under my usual serene appearance, I did not appear to even see what was driving him to despair.

With time, I was surely able to bring the necessary improvements. The right wing that was reserved for us became the most organized and elegant, whereas the left wing, on the opposite side, that served as apartment for the president, remained monastic in style.

Our apartments came with two immense rooms in the front and two more on two stories. On the spacious balcony extending out from my room I could install my desk. My elder son shared the other room with his younger brother. There he could create his own private space. My eldest daughter preferred to go to the other side of the staircase, to arrange a room for herself above her father's office.

We were finally settled in a decent manner, although I regretted that there was not enough room for me to install a little kitchen somewhere nearby. Our kitchen was so far away that I never went there. Sometimes the courses arrived cold and my husband could not savor one of his favorite dishes, the cheese soufflé. This is the inconvenience of big houses. But our dining room ended up being the official dining room when the president came for semiofficial evenings. Sometimes he would come to share the family meals with us. This was to show how seriously he took our installation within the surroundings.

On October 23, 1955, Ngô Đình Diệm organized a referendum proposing to the people a choice between the founding of a republic under his responsibility and maintaining the status quo with Bảo Đại.

With 98 percent of the votes against Bảo Đại, he had the full consent of his fellow countrymen to build the new republic to be called the Republic of Vietnam (RVN). Its army would be called the Army of the Republic of Vietnam (ARVN).

The new president asked his brother, my husband, to become his political adviser. It was in this capacity that Ngô Đình Nhu, among his functions, made the "Nhân Vị" prevail as it was inspired to him: the Transcendence of the Human Person, that is his "Regeneration" by his capacity to practice Virtue, as Christ taught us (Matthew 19:28).[38]

Immediately after, the National Constituent Assembly was elected. My husband was elected deputy. Due to my being away at the time, I registered remotely and was also elected.

The Constitution was finally approved by the Constituent Assembly and was proclaimed on October 26, 1956. That date became the date of our National Day celebration. The Constituent Assembly morphed into the Legislative Assembly in conformity with the terms of our Constitution.

Our institutions were in place.

If internal calm was restored thanks to the energetic actions of the president against the religious sects and the Bình Xuyên, we had to be vigilant to the external threats our opponents were pressing down on us. The French colonialists had overtly turned Cambodia into their base of redeployment by installing there their arsenal of "terror" against Vietnam. It was from Cambodia that the criminal attacks of the colonialists, especially from the air, would originate. That is to say, the cynicism was total. The first attack was harmless, as if to serve as a little test.

That happened during 1957.

An economic fair had been organized in Ban Mê Thuột, the most important city in the Highlands. In this region the very soil lends itself to industrial cultivation. Most of the big tea and coffee plantations belonged to French companies or individuals. The government wanted to spur the cultivation of cotton for export and for local industries. On that occasion that was meant to set an example, members of the National Assembly had been invited and its opening was to be celebrated in the very presence of the president of the republic.

During the ceremony the president was the target of an assassination attempt by a young communist cadre who aimed a shot at him with a submachine gun hidden in his jacket. One of the ministers was wounded. The man was arrested, tried, and condemned to capital punishment. Surely the president must have commuted his sentence, as he was immediately freed after the coup d'état of 1963.

That criminal act, perpetrated during the exposition organized by Lê Văn Kim, jeopardized this officer who had already been promoted director of the Officer Training Military School in Đà Lạt.

Providing some details on this officer will help clarify the government's narrow room for maneuver; it could not be wary, from the outset, of its potential collaborators on the sole pretext that they had collaborated with the French. The government was forced, so to speak, to retain them in positions of responsibility. In this instance, Lê Văn Kim was nominated temporary aide-de-camp of Admiral Thierry d' Argenlieu, who had been appointed to the post of High Commissioner for Vietnam by General de Gaulle on August 17, 1945.[39] From simple aide-de-camp he became and remained director of the Officer Training Military School during the whole period of the Ultimate Legitimate Power of Vietnam.

Lê Văn Kim was the son-in-law of this doctor-friend of my father whose villa served as my refuge pending the completion of the house my parents had ordered from an Italian contractor. When this house was finally completed, I would no longer be in Đà Lạt but in Sài Gòn. My sister took possession of it until she left to join my parents in the United States. There, she would tardily launch into studies which had always interested her and graduated with brilliant degrees. My folks would then abandon the villa and the premises, until I acquired my own residence there.

Mme. Ngô Đình Nhu and her husband at their residence in the early 1960s.

In Sài Gòn we gradually began to live a normal existence, albeit in this constant climate of instability and hostility maintained by the colonialists always attached to their businesses and interests. We did not, however, expect another bombing directly aimed against us at the Independence Palace.

In Huế, the family of Ngô Đình Nhu, 1961.

On November 11, 1960, at 1:30 a.m., the day following the election of J. F. Kennedy to the presidency of the United States, a strange "coup d'état" broke out, originating from the officers of the Vietnamese army, known to be colonialist agents, which was passed off as a treasonous act of the presidential guard. Warned about the attacks, two of the president's nephews rushed to rescue him. In the general chaos, they were assassinated on the spot.

President Ngô Đình Diệm takes a photo of Lệ Quyên, the youngest daughter of his brother Nhu, 1961.

A well-known officer, General Nguyễn Khánh, came to the Palace to present himself as the spokesman for his companion friends.[40]

I knew Nguyễn Khánh well, the aide-de-camp of my father's cousin, Nguyễn Văn Xuân, a Polytechnic School graduate and first president of the "Government" the colonialists had set up in South Vietnam in 1954 after their defeat at Điện Biên Phủ.[41]

He used to come to me to enquire about my tastes for the picnics he organized in the forest. Among the participants was Emperor Bảo Đại, my closest cousin on the maternal side. He made it quite clear that he would not come if I was not the other main guest.

Ngô Đình Nhu and his daughter Lệ Quyên, 1961.

It was then the very people who used to organize those quiet picnics in the forest with Bảo Đại and General Nguyễn Văn Xuân who were the masterminds of the coup d'état. I soon realized that they could only have been manipulated by foreigners—that is, the French colonialists.

Lệ Quyên wearing an officer's cap, 1962.

Mrs. Ngô Đình Nhu in her office at Gia Long Palace with her husband and their four children in 1962: (L–R): Trác (15), Quỳnh (10), Lệ Quyên (3), Lệ Thuỷ (17).

Family photo, 1962. (L–R): Ngô Đình Lệ Thuỷ (17), Mme. Ngô Đình Nhu, Archbishop Ngô Đình Thục, Ngô Đình Quỳnh (10), Ngô Đình Nhu, President Ngô Đình Diệm, Ngô Đình Lệ Quyên (3), and Ngô Đình Trác (15).

Khánh quietly pleaded with the president to kindly receive the delegation of his companions who would have liked to present their "desiderata" and thus put an end to the "misunderstanding" that had already caused several deaths in the presidential guard. On insisting to be received by the president, they knew they would appeal to his weak point, this desire for peace pushing him toward conciliation rather than confrontation.

That evening the president and the men of his guard were all dressed in their pajamas as it was getting dark.

My husband let his brother deal with the situation. As for the children, they had been led with me to the basement. Afterward I decided to go back to the upper floor.

On the order of the president, Khánh was introduced in front of him so that he could present the "request" dictated by a group of dissident officers, who were proclaiming it on the national radio. The president was just listening to the request without saying a word. Everybody knew that he abhorred anything that could degenerate into violence. When he said that he did not want to cause a bloodbath, I immediately intervened: "Why are you saying that? Me, I am ready to give my blood!"

When the president did not respond, the men of the presidential guard, still dressed in their pajamas, hence unrecognizable, signaled that they wanted to talk to me.

I withdrew to listen to them. They gestured toward the park: "Do not talk to that traitor; have him called outside." And they pointed to me the corpses of disemboweled beasts killed in the crossfire, their four legs up in the air.

I did not want that man to be massacred that way, and I went toward my husband, entreating him to intervene.

It was his turn to ask me: "What do you want me to do?"

"First to take Khánh aside so that he may not endure the fate of the beasts. Then to send men to retake the radio station, just leaving enough people to defend the palace!"

My husband was in total agreement with me. No sooner said than done. We took back the radio station.

Khánh was still on the phone with his accomplices when they found themselves surrounded. They thought he had betrayed them and insulted him profusely.

Most of them fled to Cambodia, which was the usual refuge for our opponents.

Thus ended the first coup d'état of the colonialists, who had previously ensured the "neutrality" of the United States Embassy in Vietnam.[42] I discovered that when, standing alongside the president and my husband, I received the person who represented the Secret Service of the United States.

He made it a point to essentially demonstrate their neutrality and to justify it.

Faced with the proof of that neutrality I first found to be strange and then scandalous, I immediately responded to let him understand, "I do not expect that coming from allies and our friends."

The president and my husband just kept quiet.

Whatever it was, my reaction was soon known in the United States. It is the reason, it seems, of the very particular curiosity I provoked during the official visit of Vice President Lyndon Baines Johnson when he went to Vietnam to meet President Diệm on May 12, 1961.

He arrived in a mild afternoon, with his wife and the sister of President Kennedy, Mrs. Jean Smith.

I was not knowledgeable about my visitors and so was not sure what to expect. I noticed, however, that the passengers crowded the windows of the plane from the time the plane came to a stop until its door opened. And the most curious thing of all was the sudden exit of a kind of giant who rushed out as soon as the door opened. With utter disregard for the protocol of waiting at the foot of the stairs, he slighted his Vietnamese counterpart, who found himself totally ignored.[43]

In a single dash, the guest crossed the space that separated him from the receiving line to come directly to me, back in the first row of the spouses of officials, as if the Vietnamese vice president did not exist. The latter had to run after his distinguished visitor, who did not feel perturbed at all. Manifestly, he had detected my presence only through the plane's windows. Yet I was standing in the back and at a good distance.

It was the first surprise, and it was of some magnitude. But it was nothing compared to what followed, which proved quite embarrassing for our visitor.

Vice President Lyndon B. Johnson, who later would succeed President Kennedy as president of the United States, greets Mme. Ngô Đình Nhu in the presence of Vietnamese officials, 1961.

At the entrance of her room in the Independence Palace, Mme. Ngô Đình Nhu shows off the skins of tigers killed by her husband to Mrs. Johnson (with the big flowery handbag) and the sister of John Kennedy (on the left of Mrs. Johnson).

He did not know about the strictly Vietnamese manners of the president toward women, toward his sister-in-law especially. There was no occasion to approach me in the president's presence. Doing so would appear to be giving a lesson in etiquette. Hence a dilemma I do not recall how L. B. Johnson got out of. I only recall his embarrassment that made me smile. I could have simply told him not to be bothered by the difference in protocol for each gender. But I did not do it because I was amused by his uneasiness.

At different junctures during Johnson's visit, I felt sympathy for this distinguished visitor until an incident happened that struck us all with an unspeakable surprise.

An amazing event.

First for me, who experienced it directly to the point of being literally dumbfounded, then for the other participants who were watching it.

Just consider the surprise, what shall I say, the bewilderment it provoked. It was the official luncheon offered by the Vietnamese vice president in honor of his American counterpart. All the diplomatic corps and government officials were present at a long table where the two vice presidents faced each other. I was seated on the right side of the American vice president while his spouse was seated at the right of the Vietnamese vice president. On the left hand of the American vice president sat the spouse of the president of Vietnam's National Assembly.

Throughout the entire luncheon, the American vice president insisted on getting me to accept his invitation to come and visit his ranch in Texas as soon as possible. He did not succeed because that was not in my plans.

On his insistence, I dropped this joke: "I will come when you become president of the United States!"

Those few words had a thunderous effect on him. Johnson got up in a jump, grabbing my left hand. In giant steps, he pulled me after him and I only had the time, skirting the back of our seats, to seize the arm of the lady sitting next to the American vice president on the left. It was impossible for us to resist the burst of the Texan.

Looking straight ahead, he strode toward the large balcony of the room. It was only there, having arrived at the balcony, that he realized I had dragged the lady sitting at his left with us. Only then did he become aware of how ridiculous the situation was, and to get out of it he uttered the first excuse that came to his mind: "I wanted you to show me the Sài Gòn landscape from here!"

The lady I had dragged with me was very agitated and could only repeat "Kỳ dị quá!" (How bizarre!) while I could not stop the nervous giggles that had seized me! And it was for a reason. In fact, when he saw Johnson get up from his seat, the Vietnamese vice president thought that he wanted to make a speech and eagerly hit his glass with a spoon to request silence. Hence the general attention, amplified ten times by our dash to the balcony, with our seatmate swept into this strange escapade who did not stop repeating aloud "Kỳ dị quá!"

Johnson saw himself sinking deeply into the most embarrassing situation and we could not silence our most perturbed company, lost in the most mixed up of protestations. As for me, I must consider myself happy for having had enough presence of mind not to be exposed, alone, with this unpredictable man by my side.

Faced with the long table full of inquiring looks turned in our direction, I had no other explanation than that irrepressible giggling. But poor Johnson! How would he explain it to his wife? And what might Kennedy have said when his sister told him about this anecdote?

Johnson went back to his place. He appeared to be stunned for having made a spectacle of himself and lost his composure at the very idea that he could become president of the United States. It was an idea that resounded profoundly in him.[44] Was he already possessed by it at this point? And all that in front of an important official gathering.

What to think of my quip that was meant to be a simple joke and proved to be prophetic, as he actually did become president of the United States?

And what to think of the tragic circumstances that piled up on Vietnam during his presidential mandate?

And he, L. B. Johnson, a president completely paralyzed by the gravity of the situation, not knowing what to do and maintaining himself in total passivity. Certainly, the worst moment of his existence.

Why? Because one could clearly feel that he did not have any precise idea of what had to be done to respond to all the issues that were hurling toward him about our country.

How pitiful it was to witness his means appear useless when confronting the communist offensives. He let them dismantle Central Vietnam, a region that had been standing on its own for ages, with no need of help from anybody, and had been under the simple and good care of my young brother-in-law Cẩn, the other bachelor of the family.

On November 2, 1963, after leaving the Canadian Redemptorists, for whom he had always been a benefactor, to reach Sài Gòn, Cẩn was arrested by the rebels and taken to court for a travesty of a trial. It was a machination intended to look like "serious business" and dissuade the imperialists from intervening, forcing them to endorse the crime that had been perpetrated.

Ngô Đình Cẩn was summarily shot in May 1964, without a trial worthy of that name. With him they suppressed the last of the Ngô Đình brothers still in the country.

My urgent letter addressed to Johnson I had only written to set my mind at rest, because I knew very well that the machination was already unfolding.

But a coup de grace was needed so that Vietnam could get out of the ultimate trap by dragging the American imperialists into it.

That was simply tragic and deplorable.

That coup de grace came with L. B. Johnson, who never recovered from it despite his instinct and political flair.

After?

It was over.

Vietnam was cleared of the last French people who had stayed on, whereas Johnson was finished without understanding what was going on, while the newspapers released the pitiful confession of his "cowardice."

It was impossible to see a more dramatic situation than this.

I had, nevertheless, once attempted the impossible to try and make him understand the problems of Vietnam when, just before the horrors committed against my country, during my last visit to the United States in the fall of 1963, I had accepted one of Johnson's neighbors' invitations to go to Texas. Such a circuitous method would have been avoidable had it been possible for Johnson to telephone me, asking: "Why not make a trip to my place? You will see my ranch!"

But having been taken over by his ebullient nature, just once in Vietnam, paralyzed him forever.

Since then, in all the photos of him, one could only discern the frozen man who thought he had to do his best to control himself. He showed this in this only letter to me in response to mine asking him why he seemed to be "afraid" of me.

He replied: "How can I be afraid of such a lovely lady as you?"

That letter, in the packet of correspondences left behind at my departure from Paris, was part of the belongings I had entrusted to a Chartist friend of my husband when I decided to leave Paris to settle in Rome. It was never returned to me. I cannot account for the loss of this letter nor a strange occurrence with one of his closest acquaintances. Before his death, this acquaintance conveyed a message through the Chartist friend his desire to see Trác, my eldest son, but the message was not delivered.

I later read in a newspaper article that this friend of my husband rejected the charge that he was part of the French secret service. All this left me pensive. To what extent could we trust the people around us since we left the country?

Back to Lyndon Johnson, that fiasco of his in Vietnam was a great disaster when he became the president of the United States after the assassination of J. F. Kennedy.

Luckily, however, he had that spurt of reason, which did not make much difference anyway, when he wised up in time to prevent the American bombing of Hà Nội, therefore of the little lake in the center of the city, that little jewel bearing witness to past centuries of the ancient capital.

To recall what happened in Vietnam with Lyndon Johnson is a historic example of an aberrant and tragic failure that could have transpired otherwise with just a little more inspiration combined with common sense.

But before getting there we had to endure a new attempt of a coup d'état on the part of the officers of the Vietnamese army, well known as agents of the colonialists. It broke out in the early morning hours of February 27, 1962.

A group of aircraft had left on a bombing mission, when two of them, on the pretext of some mechanical troubles, asked to return to their base.[45] On their way back, they made a detour and flew over Sài Gòn. They then charged on the palace to bomb it. One of the aircraft hit by anti-aircraft defenses crashed into the Sài Gòn River. The pilot was captured, tried, and condemned to capital punishment. The president, however, decided to commute his sentence and he was freed after the coup d'état of November 2, 1963. The other aviator sneaked to Cambodia, where he met up with our usual opponents.

One bomb fell at the center of mass of the palace. Intended to make everything collapse at once, that bomb did not explode. The part of the palace that was targeted in particular was the right wing where my family lived. That wing crumbled in its entirety on the living quarters of the Chinese amah[46] who had just enough time to take my last child, Lệ Quyên, into her arms before finding herself stuck under a beam falling from the balcony of the room of my eldest son, who was absent that day. My eldest daughter, who was in the rear wing, jumped to the scene to try to free her sister from the arms of the nurse and to take her nine-year-old brother. It was impossible to free the nurse who was unable to move under the beam. My eldest daughter hurried to seek help for her, but as soon as she had descended, the staircase collapsed under the flames, taking the whole story down with it and preventing her from going back. My

Mme. Ngô Đình Nhu and an army general contemplate the extent of the disaster of the bombing that destroyed the Independence (Norodom) Palace in February 1961.

husband could not reach the children because of the fire and had to use a service corridor to go and seek help. As for me, as I was running to the bathroom to put a robe over my nightgown, I found myself surrounded by flames from all sides. I tried to avoid them. I fell into a two-story-high gaping hole of ten meters and next to an unexploded bomb.

By the time I got up and found myself in the open air, the central part of the palace had disintegrated.

With several broken ribs and a burned body, I staggered in the middle of the rubble, toward a presence I detected a few steps away. But before reaching it, I lost consciousness. It was my husband! At the sight of the entire right wing in flames, he thought I was dead. The left wing that the fire spared was holding up to nothing, cracked all over. Having lost everything to the flames I could only count on the few dresses being tailored at my dressmaker. That was enough to dampen in me any urge for a new purchase.

From that point on I looked at the colonialists with greater horror.

Roger Lalouette, the French ambassador in Vietnam, did not go so far as to express his satisfaction for the destruction of the Independence Palace, the former palace of the French governor of Cochinchina. He simply said that what he regretted most about this destruction was the loss of the magnificent skins of tigers, all killed by my husband, that decorated sumptuously the entrance to our bedroom.

When these skins were shown to Mrs. Johnson and Mrs. Jean Smith, President Kennedy's sister, on their official visit, photos were taken. Thanks to those, their memory is not completely lost.

My husband was recognized in Vietnam as a tiger hunter of merit. Very often he was solicited by the farmers when tigers came too close to their villages. He regretted, only once in his life, letting one of these superb felines get away, for not shooting a second bullet out of fear of ruining its skin.

The photos bear witness to the splendor of these trophies unique in the world. My husband knew that I was pleased when he brought me these presents that he alone could offer.

As for the destruction of the Independence Palace by the colonialists, I do not know how much pleasure he could have derived from it.

Mme. Ngô Đình Nhu visiting a village with members of the Solidarity Movement of Vietnamese Women, March 23, 1961.

Mme. Ngô Đình Nhu presiding over a meeting of the Solidarity Movement of Vietnamese Women.

Mme. Ngô Đình Nhu visiting a childcare facility of the Solidarity Movement of Vietnamese Women, March 25, 1961.

France tends to wish to impress the world with her buildings, but one can hardly find a personal touch in them. Those awful pipes running through the palace's corridors were repulsive and horrifying enough to us, but the previous occupants did not seem to mind and willingly put up with them. A question of personal taste. A little strange, nevertheless.

I did not know anything about the new palace presumably "built mostly for me." I have never seen it, except in photos that were sent to me by well-meaning souls.

In any case, the French rage against the Vietnam we represented, after having expressed itself in the destruction of the palace, did not calm down. Destruction had to go much further. Huế had to suffer as

Group photo of the Solidarity Movement of Vietnamese Women (Mme. Ngô Đình Nhu is in the middle of the front row).

well. The ancestral family house of the Ngô Đình with finely executed woodwork was destroyed.

Vietnam's independence lasted almost one decade, from July 1954 till November 1963.[47] The republic that was promulgated on October 26,1956, hardly matched what we had dreamed for our country. However, during that period it did emerge, despite the accumulation of its trials. It could show to the world what a nation conscious of virtue as the sole foundation worthy of respect can be like.

What criticisms it had to hear, levelled against it and all it was doing in all kinds of tones, came from the so-called "messianic" West, though actually composed mostly of colonialists and imperialists. These criticisms were ridiculous, because they did not take into consideration our tangible achievements, instead choosing to ignore them.

All that was needed was to look at the photos and the reporting on all the achievements in Vietnam and compare them to what was being done elsewhere.

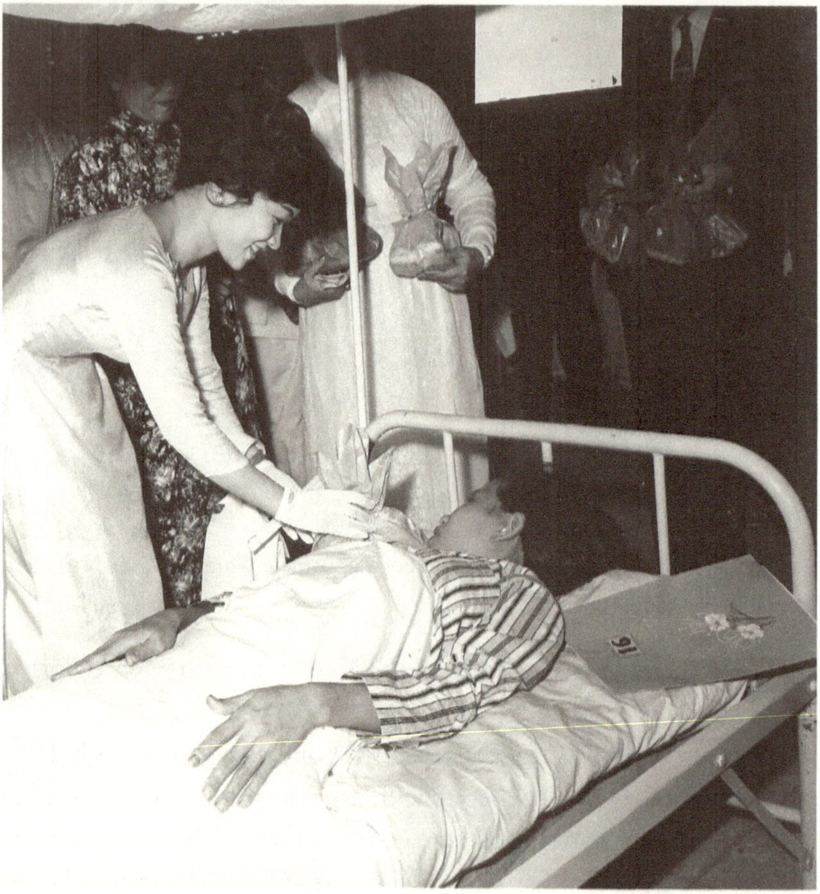

Mme. Ngô Đình Nhu distributing gifts at the maternity ward reserved for families of paratroopers under the responsibility of the Solidarity Movement of Vietnamese Women, July 25, 1961.

But nothing. Not a compliment. Only idle criticisms. Nothing more.

As regards my own activity during these ten years, I did not stop innovating, in my position as head of the Solidarity Movement of Vietnamese Women I had created.

I had to act, considering the obligations that weighed upon Vietnamese women in all domains at that time.

I did not have any obstacles in the South, but when I had to think about the much more traditionalist Central Vietnam, I felt the reticence of my brother-in-law, Cẩn, who was until then the only person responsible for the region, and managed it in a perfect calm, without incurring any cost for the South.

I entered political life with no training whatsoever.

I observed those who prided themselves in professing to know all by innate science as well as the prestigious degrees they had obtained. They did not understand any of what they deigned to listen to. The unfortunate ended up even talking for themselves, without anybody listening to them in turn. There had to be "cliques" to prepare the rooms to listen to you, applauding when required, affecting an air of disdain when you were to be criticized. And what else?

At the beginning I had to constantly explain myself, in my way, to be listened to. It had to be done. Otherwise, I could never have denounced publicly, so to speak alone, what the whole world had accepted so as to strengthen the inadmissible grip that was weighing on a Vietnam subjected to the prerogatives of Man.

And therefore, to the Law of the one who appears to be strongest.

But every cloud has a silver lining.

In Vietnam, the time had come when everything had to change to support what is not usually considered as indispensable, the Right of Women as soon as it is sustained by Virtue.

In our country, Virtue has always been recognized as the basis of everything. It has been highlighted in our republican constitution. For me it was a natural support in my defense of Christian Laws. But oddly, I had to be antagonized by the media of the Christian West.

Since its beginnings, our republic imposed the intangible rights of women and those of a just and balanced society, whether it be about heroic women in the image of the Trưng Sisters or those exemplary women of the domestic hearth called "Nội Tướng" (Generals of the Interior).

Unique in her kind, the traditional Vietnamese Woman became an example that appealed to everybody.

It was especially Her, the Success of the Ultimate Legitimate Power of Việt Nam–Nhân Vị!

I also claim for the Vietnamese Woman her unfailing support of the Ultimate Legitimate Power of Việt Nam–Nhân Vị. That is the incontestable proof that it endowed her with the full value of her support and lent her an image hitherto ignored. Keeping it under silence or even pretending to ignore it amounts to committing an unqualifiable injustice.

A day will come when our country will be given back to its ancestors, who were snatched from it at the beginning of these times, and returned also to the Woman who knew more than anyone else how to respect the best Vietnamese traditions.

As far as the "Representation" of my country is concerned, I would just recall, for my part, that time when, freed from the oppressive colonial presence, Vietnam could reveal more freely the nature of its soul.

The Ultimate Legitimate Power of Vietnam–Nhân Vị must be credited with wanting to set the example, whether it be tradition or modernity, from both the social and the private points of view. It's a point that could not be contested.

In May 1963, the Buddhist affair began.[48]

My young brother-in-law Ngô Đình Cẩn, who administered as no one could better the central region of the country, had worriedly watched his brother Ngô Đình Thục become the Archbishop of Huế, the capital.

This fact delighted the catho-colonialist, who had always had the ear of the Vatican and who could thus keep Sài Gòn, his most important fief in Vietnam, but it would have caused drama in Central Vietnam, therefore in Huế, where the rather intrusive archbishop could not handle his young brother.

The drama was all the more dreadful since the president, a monk at heart, listened first and foremost to his elder brother, the archbishop. He never connected well with his younger brother.

Catholics and Buddhists were competing in ostentatious demonstrations on the occasion of their respective celebrations.

Things got venomous on account of the unrest clandestinely incited by the colonialists and of the ensuing recovery of the communists' strength.

The two elder Ngô Đình brothers did not have the slightest idea of the irreparable situation that was unfolding.

My husband, who was siding with his younger brother then, tried to support him, but to no avail. It was too late, and it was a disaster.

Neither of the two responsible persons, the elders, was ever aware of how necessary better communication with their youngest brother was. Attracting their attention and letting them know would have been perceived as an offense. Yet it would not have taken much effort to put everything back in order. All I could do, though, was to keep quiet.

It was my job to redress the situation "in extremis" and in the only way permitted by the Lord. Coming from Him, the solution could only be unexpected and definitive.

The president had to credit me with it.

Again, and as was usual, he just said, "Nhờ Bà" (Missus, please help!).[49] It did not go further than that and the two elder brothers, Diệm and Thục, continued to behave as "elders" toward the youngest with that arbitrary authority characteristic of them. I was a lesser victim of their arbitrary authority because they recognized that I was more concerned with the domain of Women.

Getting back to the famous "Buddhist" disorder, it was perceived as the first serious blow against the Ultimate Legitimate Power of Vietnam–Nhân Vị and would end up undermining it all the way to the final blow.

To recall it is a lesson Vietnam should remember forever. This recollection in its brevity does represent the scourge that affected the country in some of its millennia-old traditions, hence that authority exerted by the elder, in a very Confucian way, on his younger brother. But how to dismiss the respectful obedience to be expected in response and not risk causing another harm that could prove more damaging?

In any case, it was in fact the occasion coming from Above that allowed me to put things back in order, as the Lord wanted, and thence Truth be recognized by all, without causing any problem to anybody.

It was the final phase of that famous Buddhist affair that hit the headlines of the world chronicles against our country and its leaders.

The president had established a joint committee tasked with settling this thorny issue.

This committee was composed of the representatives of the government and Buddhist representatives. It met without impediment under the authority of the vice president of the republic, Nguyễn Ngọc Thơ, who was himself a Buddhist.

I proposed that the representatives of the political parties and social groups be included. That would have allowed me to participate. But the president, who was determined to follow the affair himself, absolutely did not want any possibility of my involvement which he would have risked having to deal with.

In the end with the Buddhists, everything was done as he wanted. All that ended up with my husband waking me up in the middle of the night. Looking exhausted, he came to tell me: "Please excuse me for having to wake you up like this, but the president must sign this paper and he wants to do it only with my agreement. He has personally followed the affair from the beginning with his government, represented by two Buddhists, his vice president and his minister of foreign affairs, Vũ Văn Mẫu. They are both telling him to sign the text as the Head of the Buddhist [Association] has already done, but he wants me to agree with him before signing it. The text is only two pages long. I did not follow the affair at all; therefore, I cannot say anything about it. I know that you are interested in it, and I am asking you to tell me what I should advise."

I could only be outraged by such a request.

I was put aside when I wanted to participate in those meetings as the Head of the Solidarity Movement of Vietnamese Women. But seeing my husband exhausted, I took pity. I took from his hands the paper already signed by the other parties and went through it rapidly. I protested: "As always, they demand that which has never been forbidden!"

My husband was surprised and could only say: "What can we do? They have already signed the paper and are saying that, if the president does not do likewise, their people are ready to launch a revolt immediately. They are waiting at the palace gates."

"Let him sign, then, but after having written above his signature: 'None of this has ever been forbidden.' Everybody will wonder, for good reason, whether the government has lost its head when devoting so much time to such a thing!"

That was my only comment.

I was well aware of the particular obsession of the Catholic president facing the wave of the so-called "Buddhist" agitation by those whom he deemed to represent a vast majority in the country.[50]

My mother herself was like the "president of [all Vietnamese] Buddhists in the United States." I knew how she was being used for political purposes that were far beyond her ken. I did not hesitate to speak to her frankly on this topic. Furious, she would appeal to my father so that he could confront me. My father would intervene to calm us down, but he would just nod his head and repeat what he always used to say about me: "You are clever!", whereas I was just direct and simple with them in all matters. That my mother was amply used by the Buddhists did not surprise me at all. Having tried in vain to liberate her from them, I ended up not mentioning that subject in front of her. My parents did likewise because they preferred to avoid my teasing. I could not really take seriously a "religion" that was degenerating this way.

Furious for being subjected to something in which he had not participated, my husband limited himself to returning the paper signed by the Buddhist chief. He dropped it in the middle of the table, indicating what I had advised for the president to sign.

The Buddhist minister of foreign affairs, Vũ Văn Mẫu, kept quiet, and the vice president, justly confused, could only conclude: "They drank 'chè sâm' [or] 'ginseng tea' (a sort of prized rhizome that boosts energy) while we drank ordinary tea. That turned us into 'người ngu' (imbeciles)."

Faced with his colleague's comment, the minister of foreign affairs shaved his head in the hope of making people believe in a mystery he did not want to explain himself. But in the end, everything came into the open.

Later on, the same Vũ Văn Mẫu who was persuaded he had to remain the man of the colonialists till the end would turn against the Americans. They would understand how they had been fooled throughout when on April 23, 1975 (one week before the fall of Sài Gòn), Vũ Văn Mẫu, in the "name of the Vietnamese government," would call on the Americans "to leave Vietnam within 48 hours, with their weapons and luggage."

Vũ Văn Mẫu was then the second-in-command in the government of Trần Văn Hương, who had replaced Nguyễn Văn Thiệu, the man of the Americans, whom the French had wanted to leave and be replaced by their man, Dương Văn Minh, the assassin of the Ngô [brothers], known as "Big Minh."

The colonialists thought they could impose him as "Great Minh!"[51]

They ended up with nothing and we witnessed a strange "blow for blow" between the French and the Americans, as was the case recently, when America invaded Iraq under the pretext of a "declared war," when in fact it was the "private hunting ground" [chasse gardée] of Western colonialists.

It is hard to imagine a worse act of provocation.

Is it necessary to go over the political context of that time?

I shall recall it here: During my last trip to the United States in 1963, my car was surrounded by an even more impressive security escort than that of President Kennedy. His motorcade had to stop at an intersection to give way to my retinue.

I asked: "Who was that?"

The reply: "President Kennedy!" prompted me to exclaim in astonishment: "Well, well . . ."

The astonishment was no doubt a mutual one.

I remember being told that security police were expensive during that last official visit of mine to the United States just before the coup d'état that would cost the lives of the president of Vietnam and my husband. What was the reason for that? I did not know, but I do remember that feverishness that accompanied my visit to the United States.

The agitation became more intense when the news about the assassination of my people broke out. The Vietnamese Embassy stopped doing anything to ensure my security. My daughter Lệ Thủy and I became the charge of an American couple, introduced to us by a Catholic priest. This arrangement lasted until we left the United States for Italy.

Moreover, our departure provoked the most incredible hustle among members of the media who went so far as to erect barricades to block us and take photos of the two of us.

There was again a gust of insanity when I arrived in Paris after the coup d'état of November 2, 1963. The American ambassador in Paris had reached the point where he could not answer any questions concerning me. All he could do was repeat: "Damned if we do, damned if we don't!"

All this to illustrate the overcharged atmosphere swirling around us.

Few journalists dared to tell the truth about the tragedy of Vietnam. I would, however, mention Georges Mazoyer, whose position was favorable to us. Recently promoted director of a daily Parisian evening newspaper, he was hit and killed by a car while going around on foot. The journalists who were favorable to us in turn disappeared from the horizon.

I would also mention Suzanne Labin, who wrote the ultimately objective book, *Vietnam: An Eyewitness Account*,[52] and the famous Marguerite Higgins who died on January 3, 1966, of a rare tropical disease. She was a great reporter, very close to the Kennedy family.[53]

She had received the prestigious Pulitzer Prize and had been sent on a mission to Vietnam. Once her investigation was completed, she sent a note to President Kennedy. She was informing him that after visiting forty-two of the strategic hamlets that had been devised by Ngô Đình Nhu, she could assess in situ their support of President Ngô Đình Diệm, contrary to what the media were saying. Back in the United States in September 1963, she asked to be received by the president. Following her report, she published the famous book *Our Vietnam Nightmare* in which she remarked that the Buddhist crisis was a setup.[54] She added that the objective of the "Buddhists" was to obtain not religious reform but the head of Diệm, not on a silver tray, like the head of Saint John the Baptist, but wrapped with the American flag. She had also noticed that the "Buddhist" activists knew the journalists very well and called them by their first names.

Despite such a hostile climate that blocked any real search for the truth, I granted from time to time interviews I was asked to give and continued to intervene with political personalities.

When my eldest daughter died on April 12, 1967, I decided I would counter everybody with my silence. This lasted for half a century.

I am only breaking this silence now with this book I owe to my youngest daughter Lệ Quyên, which may appear mysterious to all. This is to say that, if it is understood as it should be, it means that the Lord will have decreed its publication.

From what I can see, only the colonialists are aware of what weighs on them. As for the Church, The Chosen One [Son Élu][55] is precisely my Chosen One [mon Élu], as I have known from the outset.

What better to ask for.

Meanwhile, I do what I can, preparing myself for what must be, with an absolute trust in my Beloved who is preparing everything for the best of what He wants.

After looking back at a personal level on what should be recalled of my childhood, my adolescence, my adulthood, I must admit that there is nothing particularly amusing about those memories to retain.

Everything was coated with a perpetual bittersweet dominated by the loneliness of a young mother abandoned to herself in a country at war. The circumstances at the time did not provide her with any possible means of support or defense. To the point that her husband had become a threat to her, instead of being her protector.

From then on, all that was left to do for this very young woman was to lean on her Spouse from Heaven [l'Époux du Ciel].

She felt it very deeply even though she could not say anything about it.

Her natural behavior in such absolute isolation was something to marvel about. Now that I am diving again into that period, I perceive even further that terrible loneliness. How helpless I was, without any experience, in this lost world where I moved exactly as if I were not that lonely, with yet two very young children. It is to be wondered how these little ones did not feel the need to seek another protection than that of a young mommy who was then some twenty years old and had no true means of subsistence.

That mommy nonetheless demonstrated her real trust in Providence, like when she decided to ride her bicycle despite a drenching rain. To her husband who was asking her where she was heading like that, she replied: "To ask the Lord for a car!" After that, all she had to do was to recount how in fact she did obtain what she had requested.

It is by revisiting this solitary past, exposed and vulnerable—which however did not appear to astonish anybody—that I marveled retrospectively and in silence for never having sought to break this absolute solitude.

Even when my aunt was with me in Đà Lạt, I never asked her for explanations about the repeated disappearances of my husband. I did not seek to understand.

The Lord knew, and that was enough for me.

I know now how much He felt my absolute faith in His Presence and how, quite naturally, He could only allow me to have the natural vision of what it was about when He sensed that I felt a profound need for it.

Just response, one might say, to what has not even been requested, but is due. It was so natural that apparently just a certain time of inner need was enough to obtain what then became mine. When I was left with only the need for the Lord, such a need as to make one sick for His absence, it could become so serious that in all Justice, He could not but intervene in time.

It was something like my due! Oh yes! I did perceive it during all this time of absolute solitude of my life that was threatened from all quarters.

How could a being without any defense manage to survive and to bear misfortune in such a context of terror aimed at her people? And how could the Lord allow the culprits of this situation to take on any responsibility toward a country and a people whose History, Unique, explains what, in the end, is reserved for it?

To recall it to those who were then responsible does not aggravate their case as the moment of reckoning has finally come. To warn them in time could spare them too much pain in enduring the effects.

As for myself, I see this near end as justly owed to the predestined "very little one" of the Lord.

Thus, I can only rebel inwardly against the state of my health that would require of course the miracle of a sudden and unexpected healing and not this slow convalescence whose fumbling is crushing me with its sluggishness.

Sometimes I come to believe that people are looking for the best way to heal me without really looking, despite it all. There is enough to annihilate the impatient person that I am and who can bear no longer what has been crushing her for months.

The Lord is the all-powerful Pity and I am leaning on It and what It represents for us all, even though I seem to be isolated in my convictions.

Pity for us can only mean His Return.

Return at last! At the time that is His and which is also the time of everyone.

I sense that return so acutely that I can only start with astonishment when I perceive, around me and especially in my relatives, the fear of new low blows when I will be gone.

The Lord has made us wait for so long that in all justice it is only natural for the weight of this waiting not to fall on those who have unjustly endured it. However, even an injustice that may not have been largely redressed on this earth would end up being righted anyway.

The great payoff for all is only possible because the End of everything will be the abundance of the Divine largesse for all.

Only absolute Faith in Him could advance the time.

Believing in it is having, at last, this natural outcome of the Divine Will.

To write so naturally about what I had never thought of allows me to understand how the time is much closer than I had imagined.

May the Lord in His immensurable Goodness deign to hasten the time; I can ask for nothing more.

May He put an end to the torment of His "Christ of Nations" that is Vietnam and those who represent its Ultimate Legitimate Power.

Since the beginning, they have always done their best to represent it, so they should not endure in return the worst of torment that has lasted for too long.

Therefore, the time has arrived when the Lord expects from His predestined "very little one" a more dynamic faith instead of seeing him crushed by physical suffering.

He can only cry, he who has never cried even in times of worst misfortune. He is not getting anywhere, as if defeated by the stabbing physical pain that is striking him.

But what is permitted today is certainly only tolerated to awaken a nature more generally known for its dynamism.

I have never lost what characterizes me, a precise vision of what I am allowed to see to better understand the context in which I move. I can only marvel at my relatives' pessimistic view of my fatigue as I know that it cannot jeopardize anything pertaining to the mission that falls on me.

It is true that crying of pain, not knowing that it is the ultimate price, maintains all its worth, that is to shorten the final waiting time.

Amazingly, most people do not appear to realize it.

Why?

Waiting has lost its meaning since the Church seems to have sat on it so complacently as to give the impression that it is not in search of any outcome other than the one most convenient to it. It seems inclined to hold on to it.

Man can realize that such a time has lasted too long even if most of them prefer to see it last longer to further enjoy and profit from it. It is mostly hell that has benefitted from it, and it is in view of the ultimate End that responsible men must be accountable in the time that remains to them.

I am talking about it calmly even if I am surprised by this new time that is opening to me.

In the various places where I found myself during my life, I have always had the support of daily Communion. Thank you, my Lord, for this proof of the power of Your love. Thanks to it, which is so necessary for me, I have been able to go on my way with the usual placidity of my nature.

In a cruel world, of whose incredible complexity I was totally ignorant but is still mine, I can receive, every day, what this world is holding in beauty, despite all, for whomever can appreciate its just value.

Still, one must deserve receiving, every day, the Bread and Wine of Life that the Lord is always ready to give to each of His beloved ones, with the daily ablutions that maintain them as children in flesh and blood of the Lord.

To deserve it daily is what the child from Tĩnh Quang Lâu (the Abode of Serene Light) can understand while awaiting the imminent return of his Beloved Lord![56] So much expected! As He Himself is waiting for us!

In this convergence, nothing will be missing from the Joy of the Return of the Beloved to whom is due what has always been his since the beginning of all eternity!

FOR THE HAPPINESS OF ALL!

•

CHAPTER 3

The Contribution of Việt Nam

After losing the battle of Điện Biên Phủ, how could the colonialists claim to withdraw to South Vietnam with arms and luggage, and act as if the country belonged to them as a right?

The so-called "Christian" West had provided a further proof of its cynicism. Yet since July 7, 1954, President Ngô Đình Diệm had accepted taking on the responsibility of the country at the request of Emperor Bảo Đại.

The French, discharged of their own responsibilities, should have left and let us build in the independence we had wanted and gained.

But we were in the tragic situation where the colonialists, along with their army of Vietnamese officers and their Bình Xuyên police, maintained Vietnam in a state of latent dependence and total corruption. When the imperialists got into the game, it would be the highest bidder who got it.

The colonialists were set on terrorizing the population if they even dared to show their natural sympathy for the president.

By its murderous intervention extending beyond the imaginable, the colonizing and evangelizing France engaged the Church beyond the admissible.

Mme. Ngô Đình Nhu (right) and her daughter Lệ Thuỷ, Rome, October 1963.

Her responsibility is so implicated that the Church cannot possibly bear any longer the weight that falls on Her.

Not recognizing it means to shut the door to reparation while there is still time.

I know that it is absolutely my duty to recall it without delay so as to ask what justly belongs to the mission the Holy Church entrusted to

Lệ Thuỷ in Rome, 1963.

me through Monsignor Asta, the apostolic nuncio in Vietnam.

When he came to the presidential residence, dressed "in cappa magna," he passed on to me the mission to go on a world tour to defend and shout out the truth about our country.

And what truth! A saving one, of course, if it is respected.

I received the president's approval before I decided to go and bring my eldest daughter with me.

Mme. Ngô Đình Nhu in Rome, October 1963.

My daughter and I left on September 12, 1963.

Time was running short for us as we had fulfilled our duty toward the country, and it was now important to bear witness.

That mission that the Church entrusted to me arrived very late at this point in the history of our country.

After the coup d'état of November 1, 1963: arrival of Ngô Đình Trác, holding his sister Lệ Quyên; next to him is his brother Ngô Đình Quỳnh. Fiumicino Airport, Rome.

At the beginning of the evangelization, the Church missed the Essential.

When it brought to the Vietnamese Man his coronation, that is his redemption by the Body and Blood of Christ, our Redeemer in the Eucharist, it failed unforgivably in his mission. In fact, it forced the converted Vietnam to deny from the outset what was exactly its own value, that unique contribution of our country which is the Cult of Ancestors, since the very earliest times.

For having always believed in the virtue of the Cult of Ancestors, the intrinsic basis of the divinity of Man, as he lives beyond death, Vietnam received the blessing that singled it out in the face of God:

Surely it is you who love the people,
all the holy ones are in your hand.
At your feet they all bow down,
and from you receive instruction.
—Deuteronomy 33:3[1]

For us the Cult of Ancestors was so important that it is unthinkable to undermine it. Besides, my husband's family, the Ngô Đình in Huế, celebrated the lunar new year (Tết) by crowning the third and last day of the festivities with a solemn Mass dedicated to the dead, the "kỵ." They thus practiced in the eyes of those who were invited, whether Catholics or not, that so venerable Cult of Ancestors.

This happy synthesis achieved by the Ngô Đình, who clearly showed that they were by no means "idolizing" their ancestors, was shared by a great number of their fellow believers who greatly respected Ngô Đình Khả, my husband's father, by whom this synthesis had been inspired. The emperor himself recognized the value of Ngô Đình Khả, his preceptor, and appointed him minister of rites.

That synthesis did not prevail in the teaching of the Church.

Most Vietnamese people, therefore, kept their distance from evangelization and thus found themselves deprived of the crowning that Christ, his Redeemer, has wanted for Man.

This fault of the Church is even more tragic considering that this people, in their expectation of the unknown Almighty (Thượng Đế) and in practicing the Cult of Ancestors, had been especially prepared by God to receive Christ, his Beloved Son.

By this Cult of Ancestors, raised from simple and useless deaths to ancestors to be venerated, the Vietnamese make available to the Thượng Đế the Right Number necessary to save the large number.[2]

Thenceforth, what cannot it obtain for the Lord Himself and for the immensity of the Human Community?

This daily natural veneration of the ancestors, that is expressed in such a pious and touching way in meals shared with them, is now manifested by the Vietnamese Catholics in daily Christian Masses and Communion.

On this point, it must be recognized that all the happiness in the world depends, in the first place, on the Holy Church.

May the Church feel it more profoundly and further embrace it in all truth and soon She will have what is due to Her.

It is not without reason that this mission I have falls to me, which is to serve the Church in what She alone holds: the happiness of the world by following the Lord in the way He wishes.

My resentment against the entire world made me almost forget that the Holy Church holds the Perpetual Miracle of the renewal of souls for which the just number of souls is enough for Her.

This just number is obtained with each of us becoming true disciples of Christ, hence his "Children of flesh and blood," thanks to the discipline of "Tĩnh Quang Lâu" (Abode of Serene Light) that was inspired to me by the Lord. With the creation of that just number, a happy outcome, the world discovers that Perpetual Miracle held by the Holy Church, and thanks to Her, obtains the End of hell, therefore the "Union of Heaven and Earth" as God wants.

In the composition of this just number, the Vietnamese make an immeasurable contribution with the ever-living souls of the ancestors they venerate to offer them to that Almighty God they sense without knowing Him if they have not been evangelized.

This is to say the immeasurable fault of the Messianic Messengers[3] who, while finally introducing to them that unknown God and bringing them the Flesh and Blood of the Messiah, their Redeemer, required that they get rid first of their very own contribution to the Lord.

I cannot repeat it enough so long as the Holy Church does not recognize aloud and forcefully, and especially in time, that immeasurable mistake.[4]

It was at the hands of the colonialization by France, "the eldest daughter of the Church," that Vietnam started to endure its crushing ordeal.

And there was that furious insanity on the part of the colonialists when Vietnam provided itself with its first president. They seemed not to know any more which side to turn to in order to destroy us and recover in part what they had lost.

Subsequently, while it was up to us to present the achievements of our young republic as our job, the imperialists strove to claim the paternity of our achievements with their troops and their experts.

To take the credit for what they could not, in front of us, to present as their own work, they went so far as to commit the worst of crimes, the assassination of the president of Vietnam and of my husband.

After that tragic date of November 2, 1963, that cost the lives of the two Ngô Đình brothers, the country was delivered to hell by the communist and imperialist powers.

As for the colonialists, they persevered in their most murderous instincts. They went so far as to attack my children and myself. My eldest daughter perished in 1967, in France, near Longjumeau, in a traffic accident whose circumstances have never been elucidated.

The West ended up being the winner because in return they secured my silence. A silence almost total, except for some brief curses: "Chết ai mặc ai" (never mind who dies!), which expressed very well that I had become indifferent to everything.

Nothing mattered to me anymore, and that indifference lasted for more than half a century.

Finally, here we are, bound to take stock for the final flight.

"The Union of Heaven and Earth" is ready for whomever has always desired it, as long as he does not let anything distract him from it.

I do not think the end of time will manifest itself in a great upheaval; it will be more like an event of extreme softness.

Ancient time appearing as the present, so the minds would be prepared and nobody would be troubled.

•

CHAPTER 4

The Space of the Mission

The occurrence of this event that I perceive to be of an extreme gentleness requires that all the inadmissible injustices that persist against the "Christ of Nations" that is the Ultimate Legitimate Power of Vietnam–Nhân Vị be flattened out, if we do not want them to resurface in a different way.

Forced to leave my country, I settled down where my husband had decided to create, in the vicinity of Rome, a center of religious culture open to young Vietnamese students, like the one already existing in Paris.

On a hill planted with olive trees, there is a dwelling with a luminous patio at the center. It has a glass ceiling, and the floor is decorated with originality with lively and richly colored scenes of cockfights.

Moreover, that house which comprised a vast living room and spacious bedrooms attracted my attention with its unique floor paved with large marble slabs in varied colors. Its orchard was full of apricot trees, fig trees, and olive trees of all sizes. As a whole, it constituted an environment that instilled in me an interest in creating exactly that harmonious development for which I felt ready for a better well-being according to my ideas.

The archbishop, my brother-in-law, acquired it in August 1963.

In October 1963, when I passed through Rome for the first time, he introduced the residence to me this way: "It is not quite like in Paris, where there is a chapel for the students, a restaurant, and a room for meetings. This place here does not lend itself to the same arrangements, as the architects who accompanied you have observed. Your husband told me to entrust to you the total destiny of this house, so you can decide to rearrange and decorate it as you wish. And if you want more, you will always have the possibility to do so."

After November 1963, I was required to set the [physical] boundaries I wanted to maintain for the children and for myself, to be fenced in with an iron grating. I also decided to erect a wall along the road. From there, by walking, I set myself to create the boundaries of our private space. That space remains "untouchable." I must add that I chose to exclude the location of the "*casa colonica*," with the intention to let my children profit from it later on when they would grow up and found their own families.

To carry out this transaction that took place in Italy, Archbishop Ngô Đình Thục asked the Roman Curia to suggest a trusted man to him. The Curia recommended the services of Don Pietro Gelmini.

We came to find out, just after my eldest daughter's death in 1967, that Don Pietro Gelmini, when he bought the property, had not paid up the mortgage that came with it, despite the money my brother-in-law had given him.

Only much later would we learn that Don Pietro Gelmini had obtained a personal loan from the bank when the property was acquired. What did he give as collateral, if not the money that should have cleared the mortgage? With the amount of the loan, Don Pietro Gelmini launched into excessive real estate investment deals he could not finance. When news of the matter broke and the press reported it, Monsignor Ngô Đình Thục, who had been duped, was ready to join the wave of creditors. The Church opposed it. It did not want to double this scandal with a dispute between two priests. We did not receive any indemnification to compensate for this misappropriation and help us clear the mortgage.

Family photo at home by the villa Luce Serena in Trigoria near Rome, 1965. (L–R): Ngô-Đình Quỳnh, Ngô-Đình Lệ Thuỷ, Mme. Nhu, Ngô-Đình Lệ Quyên, and Ngô Đình Trác.

To get its money back, for over twenty years the bank auctioned off our property, lot by lot, to those who coveted it. The property shrank throughout the years. Of the thirteen hectares we had originally

Mme. Ngô Đình Nhu in Tĩnh Quang Lâu.

received, we could only save three, and still I had to pawn my jewelry. The bank then agreed to spare the lot I had myself defined as being "untouchable," which was to become the "Abode of Serene Light" or "Tĩnh Quang Lâu."

In this so-called civilized world, I did not receive any help to support me in this ultimate fight to salvage the little that was left of material wealth. I was spared nothing.

I have seen several instances of arson fire occurring on my lands. Providentially, all of them stopped at the limits of my house. I remember seeing the flames swallow the plantings of an abusive neighbor and stop on a straight line on my wheat field so as to provoke the astonished surprise of the spectators.

During these twenty years, I had to confront more dishonest people who did not hesitate to attack mine.

There was a shepherd from Sardinia who, unbeknownst to me, was banned from his region. I allowed him to let his herd of sheep graze on the hills of my property. It was actually a good way to clear the brush of our fields. When my son set himself to work the land in his own meticulous way, I asked the Sardinian not to come into the property anymore. Not only did he refuse to leave but he claimed to "occupy the land" by starting to cultivate it.

I did not know a thing about the Sardinian temperament, even less when it comes to an ex-convict. He did not hesitate to threaten to kill us. Even the police advised us to capitulate.

My son used a little tractor to cultivate the field. It was so cute. I loved to see him work the land that way, an occupation for which his ancestor Ngô Đình Khả had the highest respect.

Then what happened?

One day my son was driving his tractor to plough one of his fields. Absorbed in his task, he had no other preoccupation than to steer his machine. His younger sister and I were observing him. Concentrated in following his route, we did not notice right away that, at a certain distance, the Sardinian was perched on a tractor, three times bigger, on the field where he used to bring his sheep to graze. He was observing too but there was a portentous air about him.

Then without warning, he proceeded straight toward my son! Seized by an immense anxiety, I ran toward my son and stopped on the path the Sardinian had just taken. Anxiety had given way to an absolute determination. I stood as an obstacle in his way and was ready to step in between the two of them to the point of clashing. As for him, he was determined to rush ahead all the same, to confront me, but I did not back by one single inch. I saw panic in his eyes when he had barely the time to swerve the steering wheel to avoid me. I disappeared in the volley of dirt his maneuver had sent in my direction. He thought he had buried me and I saw him speeding away on his tractor without further ado. Without looking back, he was terrorized by what he had done.

As for my son, he was unaware of any of this. My daughter, on the other hand, missed none of that disturbing show and rushed toward me to help.

Immediately I had the inner conviction that he would never return and announced it to my children. The following day the telephone rang. It was the police chief who called us to say: "What have you done? The Sardinian has just left after telling me he will never return on your lands."

That was the end of this serious problem.

Here as in other circumstances in my life, I had only followed what my instinct had dictated to me. That famous instinct, that sixth sense the Americans feared so much to the point of always looking for ways to keep me away from their field of action.

To end this terrible incident with a happy conclusion, on the following Easter, I sent one of my sons to buy a lamb from him as a sign of peace. He was touched.

Much later, I learned he was thrown out of his car after a night of solitary drinking.

His case was similar to that of the dishonest cousin in Đà Lạt who died vomiting his blood on the road after keeping the money I had lent him to buy the garage he wanted. This Sardinian, too, made a harmful use of the innocent aid brought by the Abode of Serene Light.

Since then, I have learned, by grace from High, that, without knowing it, I had proved to the Lord how much I deserved that this residence be the space of His Choice, on this earth, for the disciples who want to be His children of flesh and blood. That is, the ones who only want to do His Father's will.

During all these past years, I always had to be there to prevent, by just being there, others from laying their hands on our possessions, again and again.

I remember those painful moments when I found myself surrounded by lawyers with their piles of files whose very first words I did not understand, so exasperating was the whole thing to me.

I must consider myself to be happy for having been able to keep our property. It is still there, contained within the limits that only the steps of my decision had encompassed it with. It is, therefore, up to the Lord to extend it as He wishes for the mission He wants to entrust to His children of flesh and blood.

The divine desire of this Unique Mission wanted by the Lord became thus Mine.

He committed me, in achieving the "Union of Heaven and Earth" according to His Own Will.

If nothing was idyllic, everything seemed to me natural because my claim was also the Lord's claim.

My children and I, therefore, bow and understand that the Time for Renewal is coming and all that is left to do is to be ready, without delay.

Now here I am, however, confronted with one more abusive claim against my family and our residence.

Nephews of my in-laws, taking advantage of a mental derangement of Archbishop Ngô Đình Thục, who was their uncle and my brother-in-law—a derangement that led to his double excommunication in 1976 and 1983—dared to take advantage of a will he wrote, in an attempt to seize our property.

In his state of mental disorder, my brother-in-law Ngô Đình Thục, forgetting his previous assignment to my family of the possessions we had occupied since 1963, established in favor of the Church a will to dispose of these possessions where we lived and that were in his custody. No harm came out of it, as the Church, well aware of what happened, eagerly returned to me the will written in its favor. I could only be grateful to it. But it so happened that the archbishop also wrote a will covering my three children and the thirteen children of his younger brother Ngô Đình Luyện, who was appointed executor. The latter never wanted to execute such a groundless will, and it was only when their father died that his children submitted the archbishop's will to us. Based on the will that should have never existed, my nephews, only interested in the material value of this space, tried to win over the spiritual value it represents, that of our due coming from God and belonging to Him.

Due so fundamental that I simply replied to my daughter Lệ Quyên when she decided to get married and wanted to introduce her chosen one to me: "No need to introduce him to me. I accept your choice as long as you two follow, for yourselves and during all your life, what has always been our discipline, that of the Abode of Serene Light."

It so happened and I realize that I have been inspired from High; that's why I wish to write about it here.

The practice of the discipline of the true disciples of the Lord has developed the perfect harmony that existed between the two of them and us for the long lasting of the Abode of Serene Light.

The properties belong to Tĩnh Quang Lâu. Today they are under my authority and responsibility. When I am no more, they will be under the responsibility of my daughter Lệ Quyên and of her husband Olindo Borsoi.

After them, the people in charge of Tĩnh Quang Lâu will decide likewise, without ever departing from the basic principle decided by the Lord, so that the people who inhabit this privileged residence be His true disciples, therefore His children of flesh and blood.

Laws that are external to our community cannot prevail over it.

No property laws should be allowed to divide it.

The children of mine who are attached to these possessions will continue to live there as during my lifetime. They will, therefore, continue to enjoy their goods, wherefrom nothing will be taken without the consent of the main persons in charge. They are advised not to seek any foreign intervention. It would only meet with rejection from High and would deprive them of the harmony of brotherly relations, even if they do not all totally follow yet the rules of "children of flesh and blood," those of the faithful of this privileged abode.

I guarantee my blessing to those who will follow this message.

I think I am clear about this absolute responsibility that I must take on and transmit. To challenge it means to risk getting what I cannot guarantee. To respect it is to assure the guarantee owed to what the Lord wants, in His first and last will, for His return in the "Union of Heaven and Earth" as He cares about for this last generation.

What better could we wish for?

Yes, what better to wish for the community of Serene Light that Christ has always wanted and had at last, only at the end of times, and very simply, with His predestined "very little one."

It is strange that the same thing may be perceived differently by some and by others. I am talking about the imminent return of Christ.

The time requested was necessary for all Creation to apply itself to the task.

But O Lord, You who are the Master of time, please think about our awaiting.

•

CHAPTER 5

The Christ of Nations

What will you have for your long waiting?

Justice wants, above all, the Just Compensation.

God knows when pain is there not to quit for as long as one is still breathing, and the Lord does not abandon either whomever belongs to Him. More than ever.

But the more I support and encourage myself, the less I can feel what I am clinging to. To what? Yes, to what?

And what to say, if He appears when one is not waiting for Him anymore, as the wait has surpassed human capacity?

But why think of something that can only depend on Love?

Take Pity, O Lord, on those who can only live on Love, hence on You, Love.

I know very well that there could not be any other outcome.

And here is how, after a long time, here or there, without paying much attention to anything whatsoever, I find myself, just like more than half a century ago, at Tĩnh Quang Lâu alone most of the time, with the children at work.

No more do I see the gentle slopes of the hills where the sheep I allowed from time to time to trespass used to graze.

Entire villages have settled in. In the name of what right? I do not know. Reduced to the small space I have chosen, without knowing how it still belongs to me, I stay within the walls to contemplate the landscape. That is enough to furnish that wait of whose duration I am ignorant but which opens me up to all the rest, hence the afterlife, that afterlife which belongs to everyone.

The Lord thus knows that at the End, all I need is little, very little, really little for my waiting of the Whole.

Will this parsimony suffice to Him?

After I was allowed not to care for anything. Yes, NOTHING. Except seeing again my family whom I had left too soon.

How is it possible that He, the all-knowing and almighty, is content with so little from His predestined "very little one"?

Is it He Himself who reduced him to such little as he can give?

And could it be only to offer to him, in the Just Time, the explosion of what is due to him?

In any case it is finally time for me to think about what the Lord wanted from me, concerning Him, on earth.

I mean that unique mission which is mine. At last.

He will have what he has wanted from the beginning: disciples who shall be children of flesh and blood, and not only adopted children, thanks to that discipline He has precisely wanted since always and never repeated.

And how?

Simply because they will have followed exactly what He has taken care to let me know in the clearest of terms: the daily Mass and the Eucharist, a complete wash and just one daily meal.

As the Lord Himself used to do.

The "Christ of Nations" that I represent in the name of Vietnam has no other solution than the one permitted from High, to wait.

What else is left for me to do?

To recall that I was liberated from the unbearable (the assassination of my eldest daughter four years after that of my husband) because I accepted, after strongly resisting the "divine market," the price of the sacrifice of my daughter after that of my husband.

And what was that price? Other than the End which I saw as too huge a demand but finally accepted, in a cry of the loser in front of the Lord: "Yes, the Union of Heaven and Earth" [L'Union du Ciel et de la Terre].

And what has my life been like since, if not the worst of everything?

I am reduced to nothing, transported from one hospital to another, to struggle at night with beings I cannot make out whether are real or the product of my nightmares, and only the bars of the bed prevent me from being taken away, I do not know where.

Then finally back to my house, by myself all day, though watching through its balconies and windows the landscape Tĩnh Quang Lâu is offering me and getting a picture of the setting in which my Lord will come and give me at last "the Heaven and Earth" that await me.

But when?

Will I be finally delivered from these pains that are turning me into nothing more than a physical wreck having to spend an insane amount of time to do the simplest thing and drag myself to it . . .

Why am I reduced to such a depressing state?

What is that all-powerful goodness to authorize such a horrible price, this continuous suffering of my body I had hitherto been spared?

And why do I have to be reminded of all that it is costing me?

Will I ever forget it?

Will the time come when I will forget?

Is it the price for what is to come? At last!

Would recalling it be a solution for someone who does not see anything like it in nothing? And who only cares about what is to come because he could not be left to himself? He has cared for His awaited coming ever since. Yes, ever since.

This time, no matter how beautiful it may appear, will hurt me if it does not unfold the way I am waiting for.

May that which has never been revealed finally appear.

Let that happen in clear terms.

That is due to us, O Lord, we want nothing else but the definitive so much expected since always. This "Heaven and Earth" united, that You have wanted me to demand at the price it has cost me.

The briefest time is attached to it.

Pity, therefore, O Lord, You who are Pity above all.

Pity for one who has always relied only on You in all, and now more than ever, because the only thing that is left to him is this expectation of You.

This plea is unfolding under my eyes, under the rays of a sun ready to welcome the most awaited of this promised "Union of Heaven and Earth."

But nothing moves. As always, I endure the waiting.

But of what then?

I see what I could never forget pass by: the predestined "very little one" of the Lord being held by the hand, or following Him, to kneel at His feet, His hands neatly folded on His knees as soon as He is seated on a tree trunk in the clearing He has crossed.

He does not say anything, neither does she, they look at each other. She melts under His gaze, she who will have to gather, at the right time, all that her inner crucifixion will be worth to her for a total closure. At last.

Everything must be understood as God wants it anyway, for everything to be as it should be. It is thus useless to wait for this transformation taking place without our knowledge, which we participate in ourselves or nature wants from us and which we must simply and quietly prepare ourselves for.

Could that be the explanation to which everything has simply submitted, because it is the softest one and best responds to the multiple and diverse desires of every one of us who does not want to be pushed in any way.

Things come as they should.

God-Love and Goodness manifests Himself that way.

Even if He makes us wait, what belongs to Him does not lose anything.

Quite the contrary, as everything is for the better well-being of all.

One may deem that the Lord is indeed making us wait.

But if it is for our own good?

Why need to rush if everything is for the better?

I am assured of that before anybody.

Trusting Him is the only appropriate answer.

As he only knows to wait, the predestined "very little one" is not disappointing Him, because he holds in his unique predestination what allows him to hold firm.

He received for all the mission of the royal epithalamium (Psalm 44) aimed at bringing back to the cult of the Lord Almighty those very ones who knew, in absolute free will and not by obedience to anybody, to never treat their ancestors as just dead bodies to be buried.

By its Cult of Ancestors and by its contribution of an incalculable number of souls—that just number by which the Lord Almighty saves the large number, Humanity in its entirety—Vietnam takes part in the salvation mission of Christ the Savior.

The immense weight of its past sufferings while it had received this aptitude to unite with Humanity has prepared it to bring its message to the World.

Sufferings inflicted by the Messianic Messengers of the Church when they wrongly accused Vietnam, through a narrow-minded proselytism, of Idolatry for putting the veneration of Ancestors on the same level as the veneration it professed for the Almighty.

Sufferings inflicted also by the Church.[1]

Instead of supporting it, She destroyed our country in that deep intuition it had received to work for the Lord Almighty, in preparing for Him this incalculable number of souls. Thus, Vietnam was crucified in its faith whereas, if better understood, it could have only favored that spiritual takeoff for which it had been ready for so many centuries.

The "Messianic" West must also account for the political assassination perpetrated against the legitimate representatives of the Vietnamese power if it wants to spare itself the consequences of both what it allowed to be committed against Vietnam and its inadmissible silence about its own misdeeds.

On this matter, it is permitted to acknowledge a deserving act the United States accomplished on August 21, 2009, at the 17th parallel between Central and North Vietnam when they uttered the following prayer: "May Our Lady of La-Vang also be the Holy Mother of our country (the United States) and of our Christianity."[2]

After his visit to the site, the new American archbishop went to Phủ Cam, where the Ngô Đình [family] took roots, in the province of Huế in Central Vietnam.

American Catholicism has thus shown its respect for what concerns the Ultimate Legitimate Power of Vietnam–Nhân Vị, whereas the colonialists stood out by their sinister silence.

The Holy Church cannot make Herself a party to such silence.

It is on the Church that the salvation of the world rests. In that respect, the Church can only be at the forefront of Reparation.

It is, therefore, appropriate to ask the Church to clearly explain the reasons that led Her to decide, at the time of Vatican Council II (at the 79th General Congregation of December 2, 1963), that the opening Mass of the Assembly honor the memory of the president of Vietnam, Ngô Đình Diệm, and that of his brother and adviser Ngô Đình Nhu, who were assassinated on November 2 of that year during the coup d'état that toppled the Ultimate Legitimate Power of Vietnam.

It was the Mass for the "Spirit of the month" [l'Esprit du mois], so the fathers of the Council were invited to unite in prayer for their eternal rest.

Since the criminal West assassinated my husband and his brother, the Lord insists, as the first demand due to their country, their people and to themselves, that the Holy Church elucidate Her motivation, after this past half century, if She does not want to painfully assume the responsibility of her shortcomings.

As a requirement of Justice owed to Herself, the Holy Church could not fail without jeopardizing Love that rests on the Spirit of Justice and permits Her to hold the perpetual miracle: the End of Hell and the Realization, at last, of the Union of "Heaven and Earth" according to God's will.

As for Vietnam, it is forever ready to help those who owe it reparation.

Mme. Ngô Đình Nhu
Tĩnh Quang Lâu, August 22, 2010
On the feast of the Coronation of the Virgin

PART II

The Republic of Vietnam and the Ngô-Đình s

NGÔ-ĐÌNH LỆ QUYÊN,
NGÔ-ĐÌNH QUỲNH, AND
JACQUELINE WILLEMETZ

Introduction

In support of the posthumous memoirs of Madame Ngô-Đình Nhu published in the first part of this book, we resolved to open our family archives and present, in this second part, the essentials of what the Ngô-Đình brothers attempted to do and achieved out of love for their country, proud of its regained independence.

It is in fact to Ngô-Đình Diệm, assisted by his brother Nhu, that fate entrusted the charge of founding and democratically building the Republic of Vietnam as it was promulgated on October 26, 1956, in Sài Gòn.

History records that they were assassinated on November 2, 1963, whilst in charge of their country and trying to put an end to the harassment of communist infiltrations from North Vietnam.

On November 2, 2013, a great number of Vietnamese and many sympathizers the world over would commemorate the fiftieth anniversary of their tragic end.

All these years have passed.

The truth about Vietnam and the Ngô-Đình brothers who have sacrificed their lives to it has not so far found a space where it can be told. It is, therefore, with deep gratitude that we thank Éditions L'Harmattan for initially allowing this space to exist at last.

Jacqueline Willemetz

CHAPTER 1

The Ngô-Đìnhs

Gathered here are a few fundamental facts on their very ancient family.

The ancestry of the Ngô-Đìnhs goes back to Ngô Quyền, who was the first emperor of Vietnam. In the year 939 of the first millennium, after several military victories over China, which was struggling with grave internal tremors, Ngô Quyền founded the first Vietnamese dynasty. His accession to power marked the beginning of the independence of Annam. He abandoned Hà Nội, a city founded by the Chinese, to settle in Cổ Loa, the legendary capital of a kingdom that predated Chinese rule. He unified the country by bringing together those who had earlier migrated from Southern China to flee the nomads' invasion, and the native population of Polynesian and Indonesian descent.

His death started a period of anarchy that ended in 1010 when Lý Thái Tổ founded the Lý dynasty. Then followed the Trần Dynasty from 1225 until 1414. One of them, Trần Nhân Tôn, was crowned in glory when he confronted Kublai Khan. By making him pull back, Trần Nhân Tôn stopped the Mongol invasions. After the Trầns, the Lê dynasty would remain on the throne from 1428 until 1793.

In the fourteenth century, the Ngô-Đìnhs would be one of the first families to convert to Catholicism after receiving and meditating on the teachings of Father Odorico, a Franciscan missionary originally from Pordenone, Italy. Sent on mission around the year 1320, he arrived in Vietnam after having traveled throughout the Orient from India to China.[1]

The Ngô-Đình family introduced into Vietnam the worship of St. Anthony of Padua, another Franciscan priest, to whom they would faithfully conserve their devotion. After a long period of Christianization, the interdiction of the Cult of the Ancestors promulgated by the Church in the eighteenth century put an end to the development of Christianity and opened an era of terrible persecutions.[2] In interpreting it as an idolatrous cult, the Church committed an even more tragic error as the Cult of the Ancestors is the pillar of the Confucian tradition.[3]

Around 1870 the Ngô-Đình family paid its tribute in blood for their faith when a great number of its members perished in the arson perpetrated in their parochial church in Huế, the imperial capital and birthplace of the Ngô-Đình family.[4] Luckily, Ngô Đình Khả (1857–1923 or 1850–1925) was away when the tragedy broke out. His parents sent him to China and Malaysia to pursue his studies. He would be the father of Diệm and Nhu.

After this tough period of persecution, some of the surviving members of the Ngô-Đình family had chosen to assure their survival by keeping only the name Ngô, which was more widespread, and renouncing the middle name Đình, meaning "rectitude."[5] Only one branch of the family chose to keep the family name in its entirety. To this day, Ngô-Đình is a rare family name in Vietnam. It is therefore easily recognizable.

A man of good intelligence, of vast culture, and of great probity, Ngô Đình Khả founded a private school before entering the Court of Huế as a preceptor. He then became minister in charge of rites and finally Counselor to Emperor Thành Thái, to whom he always remained loyal.

In Asia, the role of the teacher is so respected that it supersedes even that of the father in the hierarchical ranking. As the highest-ranking mandarin (public official) at the Imperial Court in Huế, Ngô Đình Khả rebelled against the French colonialists when they stripped the emperor of his throne in 1907 and sent him into exile to Algeria where he spent

Portrait of Ngô Đình Khả, the father of President Diệm.

the rest of his life. Ngô Đình Khả submitted his resignation and thus renounced all his titles and perks.

Returning to his ancestral home, he led thereafter a life of retirement with modest financial means. He dedicated himself to agriculture,

By order of birth, the six sons of Ngô Đình Khả, with their mother on the upper righthand corner, President Ngô Đình Diệm in the center, and Nhu just below him on the right.

which he considered to be the foundation of human edification, and focused on the education of his children and that of his six sons in particular. He imparted in them the ideal of national independence through a rigorously disciplined life and a great love for the letters.

Remaining a Christian at heart and in practice, Ngô Đình Khả nevertheless did not disown the Cult of Ancestors which constitutes one of the most profound roots of Vietnamese spirituality. Every year he invited the non-Catholic people of the city to come to honor the memory of the deceased members of his family on the third day of Tết, that great Vietnamese festival celebrating the first day of the lunar year. At the end of this solemn ceremony, attended by the whole family clan, a great banquet was usually offered, which was also open to all the poorest people in the area. This familial practice was found to be in perfect harmony with the great festival of the dead, called Mass for the Deceased, which the Church has definitively set for November 2 in the liturgical calendar, following All Saints' Day traditionally celebrated on the first day of November.

This model of integrity and fidelity to the religious as well as traditional values of Vietnam, as exemplified by such eminent and respected a personality as Ngô Đình Khả, bears witness to the fact that one can be an authentic patriot and at the same time a Catholic.

That would not be the case for the fellow believers who "collaborated" with French colonialists. In the former Cochinchina to the south, many Vietnamese Catholics compromised themselves in the businesses they conducted with the colonial authorities. The natives contemptuously nicknamed those people "Da mihi terram" (meaning in Latin: Give me some land). In fact, on the pretext that they were fellow Catholics, French colonialists favored those Vietnamese Catholics by ceding or entrusting to them the most fertile lands in the country.

•

The sons of Ngô Đình Khả would each have a role to play in the emergence of their country's independence in the twentieth century.

After the First World War (1914–1918), the Vietnamese expressed their desire to be more involved in the affairs of the country. Albert Sarraut, who was appointed Governor-General of Indochina in 1911, gave them that hope in one of the official speeches he delivered in 1919. That hope was never realized.

It was then that the crisis of 1929 happened. Plunging the Western countries in grave economic, social, and political problems, the crisis did not allow those countries to support their colonies. Vietnam sank into widespread poverty. Pro-independence demonstrations were increasingly growing. In 1931, the League of "Việt Minh" (from the contraction of Việt Nam Độc Lập Đồng Minh, meaning League for the Independence of Vietnam) was founded. It was a rally of several nationalist parties. The most active would be the Indochinese Communist Party, with Nguyễn Ái Quốc (Hồ Chí Minh) as one of its co-founders in 1930.[6]

It was in this turbulent context that Ngô Đình Khôi, the eldest son of Ngô Đình Khả, governed the province of Quảng Nam. In that capacity, he was arrested together with Huân, his only son, in August 1945 by the Communist government of Hồ Chí Minh.[7] Neither he nor his son would return. The Communists shot them. It was many years later that their pitiable remains could be recovered.

•

The second son, Ngô Đình Thục, born on October 6, 1897, felt a calling to devote his life to God. After his formative years at the seminary, he was ordained a priest. Pope Pius XI appointed him the titular bishop of Vĩnh Long in 1938. In 1960, John XXIII appointed him Archbishop of Huế.

Primate of the Church in Vietnam, it was he who represented his country during the Ecumenical Council of Vatican II in Rome (1962–1965). Absent during the coup d'état of November 2, 1963, Monsignor Ngô Đình Thục would be unable to console himself either for his brothers' deaths or for his absence at their side on the fateful day. After years of living in exile in Italy, France, and Spain, he died in the United States on December 13, 1984.

•

Ngô Đình Diệm, born on January 3, 1901, was the third son. He was a brilliant student at the School of Law and Administration [École de droit et d'administration] in Hà Nội. He graduated at the top of his class in 1921. He worked at the imperial library of Hà Nội before embarking upon a career of public service, just like his elder brother.

Despite his reservations about collaboration with the colonial authorities, his family convinced him to put his exceptional administrative talents to good use. He was entrusted with numerous responsibilities like supervising about seventy villages around Huế, among other responsibilities, before assuming the governorship of the important Phan Rang region which included about three hundred villages.

To move around in the rugged topography of this region, Ngô Đình Diệm traveled on horseback or on foot. He acquired an in-depth knowledge of the rural world where he favored dealing with and resolving practical problems by direct contact with the peasants. Later on, when he became president of the Republic of Vietnam, he would devote an important part of his time visiting the forty provinces of the country. The ambassadors and other dignitaries, who accompanied him on his visits which lasted from dawn to late at night, would give eloquent testimonials on the fervent and respectful conduct of the population towards him.

His capable governance of the Phan Rang province, which has a large population of ethnic and religious minorities, led Diệm to be chosen in 1933 at the age of 32 by Bảo Đại, the reigning emperor of Vietnam, to become his minister of the interior.[8] This appointment of Diệm at such a young age was a prestigious one, because in Asia it is customary to entrust important positions to persons with more maturity in years.

After a few months, Diệm, a nationalist by conviction, understood that basically Bảo Đại did not intend to free himself of the French tutelage. He submitted his resignation and publicly denounced the absence of real power in the exercise of his mission. Faced with this open opposition, the French authorities threatened him with arrest and deportation. Diệm was forced to renounce any form of public life. Being a man of great faith and ascetic by nature, he deliberated on a possible religious vocation.

In September 1945, after his elder brother had met a similar fate, he was captured by the Communists and detained for a few months in the mountains of Tonkin, near the Chinese border. The conditions were so harsh that he fell seriously ill and had a brush with death. It was then that Hồ Chí Minh, well aware of Diệm's merits, attempted to convince the latter to join him in the struggle against the French. In spite of the pressure exerted, Diệm refused all collaboration with his interlocutor. He blamed the latter for the assassination of his beloved brother and nephew and for all the slander the Communists had spread about his family.

"Do you think I'm scared?" he asked Hồ Chí Minh.

With those words Ngô Đình Diệm put an end to the interview. The following day, the doors of the jail opened in front of him. He was free.

The recognition by Hồ Chí Minh of the authentic and courageous patriotism of the man who would become the president of South Vietnam would come a few years later. Hồ attested to it in a discussion with Ram Chundur Goburdhun, the Indian ambassador who chaired the Control Commission designated by the Geneva Accords.

Knowing that his life was in danger, Diệm undertook frequent travels abroad. He stayed in Asia, as well as in Europe and the United States, making sure to keep in touch with the Vietnamese he met. He thus wove an entire network—more particularly in Japan—of anticolonialist compatriots like himself.

In 1950, he made a stop in Rome for the Holy Year and left for Belgium. Then he arrived in the United States, where he stayed for a long time in a seminary at Lakewood in New Jersey. He was juggling the studies of history, theology, and philosophy, and always remained available to welcome those who wanted to see him.

At the beginning of the year 1954, which would prove so decisive for the future of Vietnam and its independence, Ngô Đình Diệm returned to Europe. He went to Belgium. On February 10, 1954, the feast day of Saint Scholastica, he attended the liturgical services of the Abbey of Saint Andrew in Bruges, a Benedictine monastery founded in the early twelfth century by Robert II of Flanders. He did not accomplish his devotions as a simple visitor; rather, he came to accomplish an act that committed his whole being and his future life. In the most absolute recollection, he came to offer his life, as an oblate, to God and to the Virgin Mary, to be their faithful servant. In order to underline his vocation of commitment to the monastic community, Ngô Đình Diệm added to his baptismal name, Jean-Baptiste, that of a second patron and protector, that of Odilon, who was the fifth abbot of the prestigious abbey of Cluny in 994. The future president of Vietnam had often confided to those close to him his desire to renounce the world and devote his life to prayer. However, only a few months later, he gave in to the urgings of Emperor Bảo Đại, joined by those of his brother Nhu, to devote himself to this small part of the world that was immense in his eyes, his native country.

Ngô Đình Nhu, born in Huế on October 7, 1910, was the fourth son of Ngô Đình Khả. His father died when he was still an adolescent. Eager to learn Latin, he went in quest of the priests who could teach it to him. He left for France in the 1930s to pursue the study of literature at the Sorbonne in Paris. He enrolled in the prestigious School of Charters (École des Chartes) and obtained a diploma of archivist paleographer in 1938.

The magazines of the time highlighted that he was the first Vietnamese to have trained in such a field. When he returned to the country, he was appointed to oversee the Imperial Archives in Huế, after having served as deputy director of the Library in Hà Nội.[9]

As a historian and a fine man of letters, he wished to write the history of his country without a colonial connotation. He was forced to abandon his project in 1946, when the Communists destroyed the Imperial Library of Huế in an act of arson, forever depriving Vietnam of its precious archives. To the tragic destruction of these ancient parchments was added the heartbreaking employment of those that had escaped the fire: The aggressors used them as wrapping paper. This terrible profanation in addition to other Communist abuses outraged him to the point of deciding to engage in a political resistance. Married a short time before and soon to be a father, Nhu gave up his family to go into hiding with others who were fighting for Vietnam's independence. For years he would live clandestinely.

From 1946 to 1954, he dedicated himself to setting up a resistance network that should allow the establishment of an independent and nationalist government when future opportunities arose. Nhu thus gained an in-depth knowledge of the terrain that would be very useful later on when he developed the "Strategic Hamlets" program of which he was both creator and director.

The two youngest brothers, Ngô Đình Cẩn and Ngô Đình Luyện, would also have functions to assume in the future republic. The first one would be responsible for the central region, while acting as one of the leaders of the Labor Personalist Revolutionary Party [Cần Lao Nhân Vị Cách Mạng Đảng] founded by his brother Nhu. Luyện, the last of the six brothers, would be entrusted with the post of Vietnam's roving ambassador to Europe. In mission at the time of the coup d'état, he would be, along with Ngô Đình Thục, one of the sole surviving brothers.

•

Trần Lệ Xuân, the future spouse of Ngô Đình Nhu, was born in Hà Nội on August 22, 1924, from a rich and noble family that introduced her to fine art, music, and dance. On the maternal side she hailed from the last imperial family, the Nguyễn dynasty founded by Gia Long. The emperors Minh Mạng (1820–1840) and Thiệu Trị (1840–1847) were respectively the grandfather and father of Emperor Tự Đức (1847–1883), whose elder sister was the great-grandmother on the maternal side of Trần Lệ Xuân. Further, this great-grandmother was the spouse of the first and only Imperial Censor in the history of Vietnam. Of this marriage the future Emperors Kiến Phước, Hàm Nghi, and Đồng Khánh were born.[10]

Lệ Xuân's father, Trần Văn Chương, was the elder son of the provincial chief of Nam Định, the most important province in the North. He became a famous lawyer and would often be called upon to play an important role, in particular when Bảo Đại appointed him minister of foreign affairs during the first attempt to build an independent Vietnam in 1945.[11] He accepted the post of minister of foreign affairs after having previously declined the post of prime minister. He considered himself too young for such a function.

Her family also paid the tribute of blood when her great-uncle Bùi Quang Chiêu, brother of her maternal grandmother, along with his six children, the youngest barely six years old, were assassinated by the Việt Minh.

Issued from a Confucian family and a Buddhist mother, Lệ Xuân converted to Catholicism when she married Ngô Đình Nhu on April 30, 1943, in Hà Nội. After the wedding ceremony, the young couple left the North to settle in Huế. Following the Second World War, Trần Lệ Xuân, now Madame Ngô Đình Nhu, was forced out of her house in Huế by the Communists. Deported to a zone under their control, she succeeded in escaping to Sài Gòn bearing Lệ Thủy, her three-year-old daughter, in her arms.

From 1947 to 1954, she lived in Đà Lạt, where she gave birth to her two sons, Ngô Đình Trác and Ngô Đình Quỳnh. She began to become acquainted with the central and southern parts of the country in addition to the northern region of her birth. There she discovered the different dialects then in use in those regions.

•

It was in 1954, after the defeat of the French at Điện Biên Phủ on May 7, that the three lives of Ngô Đình Diệm, his brother Nhu, and Nhu's spouse Lệ Xuân would converge. The union of their energies welded by the same demanding patriotism would mark the birth of the Republic of Vietnam and presided over its development.

•

CHAPTER 2

Birth and Development of the Republic of Vietnam, "Việt Nam Cộng Hoà"

During the Geneva Conference following the French defeat in Điện Biên Phủ, Emperor Bảo Đại was encouraged, in particular by the Americans, to build a team that would enable them to take over the affairs of the country. Vietnam wrote a new page of its history, and it was important that this team be made up of men of value and be recognized as such.

The emperor remembered Ngô Đình Diệm. If the French did not appreciate him for having resisted them, the Americans on the contrary saw in him a personality that would lead that resistance to the French and put an end to colonialism, which practice in principle the

Americans opposed. Moreover, Diệm was living in the United States at the time and the Americans thought they knew him well.

The French, making the best of a bad situation, did not however suspect Bảo Đại's loyalty toward them. On June 16, 1954, the emperor appointed Ngô Đình Diệm to be his prime minister. Diệm's return to Vietnam took place in July 1954, shortly before the end of the Geneva Conference. Bảo Đại was aware of the skills, moral and patriotic values, and integrity of the man he had appointed to the highest post. These values would predispose him to become a collaborator of quality in a government that must represent the unity of the country during this serious crisis situation following the French defeat.

Ngô Đình Diệm accepted this position. He and his brother Nhu had been raised with a love of their country and of its traditions, in accordance with the adage "Quốc gia hưng vong, thất phu hữu trách" (conscientious persons must take responsibility to improve the fate of their nation). Both being nationalists by conviction, Diệm wished that the nation be independent above all, while Nhu aspired to a reconciliation with that Western culture he appreciated through scholarly studies in France at the Sorbonne and the National School of Charters.

In that spirit of trust which they had maintained at different degrees, they hoped to benefit from a constructive dialogue with France. Did not France reiterate her humanistic ideals in the preamble of the 1946 Constitution at the founding of the Fourth Republic? With this display of will for liberty and openness she announced to her former colonies that she would know how to help their countries build their future and would definitively turn a page of a bygone colonialism.

After the Geneva Accords were signed [by France and Hồ Chí Minh's government] on July 21, 1954, it dawned on the Ngô-Đình brothers that, despite appearances to the contrary, France would neither be in favor of autonomy for her colonies nor aid them with sincerity to take that road.[1] In fact, she was obstinate in wanting to maintain her presence at all costs while many peoples concerned—in this instance Vietnam—were endowed with responsible leaders with a high level of competence.

This political myopia would have tragic consequences. In disappointment, the Ngô Đình brothers would mark their defiance toward France. If General de Gaulle, who would become president of France in 1959, seemed to have opted for a policy of neutrality about the future of the former Indochina, the French who wanted to stay put could not care less. Their well-secured interests prevailed over ideals. This antagonism did not give respite to the Vietnamese government. When the drama played out, the future of Vietnam would gradually vanish from the memory of the French.

It took no time for Ngô Đình Diệm, once installed in his leadership role, to discern the falsehood of his position. Blocked by France, he realized that he had little support from the emperor, who continued to play into the hands of the French. The emperor even seemed so uninterested in the future of the country that he spent most of his time in Cannes in the beautiful residence the French had provided.

Having analyzed the situation, and concerned about rectifying it as well as anchoring his country in a real independence, Diệm decided to put an end to this sort of sham government. Since he had officially received "full powers," he turned to the Vietnamese people. It was up to him to decide. He submitted a referendum to them so they could choose between Bảo Đại and him as the one who would lead them to the promised independence.

The referendum took place on October 23, 1955, and Ngô Đình Diệm received tremendous support from his fellow compatriots. They gave him 98 percent of their votes.[2] The victory was clear and indisputable. The electors knew as much about the nationalist patriot they had chosen as about their former emperor, who preferred to enjoy a peaceful and calm life which his country, barely coming out of the war, could not provide him.

Now Ngô Đình Diệm would have much more real elbow room to implement a democratic republic. The legislative elections of March 4, 1956, allowed the designation of a constitutional national assembly.

Ngô Đình Diệm, President of the Republic of Vietnam.

The president needed a trustworthy righthand associate, a patriot with as much resolve, honesty, and courage as him. The alter ego he was looking for he could only find in his own brother Nhu, who was asked to become his adviser. The two of them would buckle down to making the tremendous effort required in the development of their country in the independence it has just reached. At the outset, however, they had to confront very grave dangers. The religious sects and the Bình Xuyên signaled their hostility.

A letter from Ngô Đình Nhu dated April 20, 1956, to one of his fellow Chartists showed the complexity of the problem facing the two brothers caught between a colonial regime with its persistent intent on imposing itself and American assistance which was apparently more disinterested but yet to be tested:

> April 20
> My dear Benet,
> Thank you so much for the long letter of the 8th. This unity of thought is positively amazing between you and me on all the aspects of the problem of interest to us, whether it be the political realities or the men who participated in them, including my brothers, Mr. Khiem, or your compatriots. It is as if we have not left each other since 1949, and that we are working side by side in the same office under the benevolent inspiration of your Simone.[3] How happy I am to see such a communion of ideas and sentiments between you and me, being separated by thousands of kilometers. It is true that having overcome the Hinh crisis we are [present tense in the original!] about to embark upon the affairs of sects that could not present itself any more favorably.[4] Unfortunately, we are cornered between the lack of understanding of the French and the inexperience of the Americans: a difference in the appreciation of the opportunity to firmly and definitively break the feudal obstacle to free the poor Vietnamese people and rally them to us.
>
> The great thought of the President since he came to power is to break the two obstacles, iron circles that separated the Vietnamese people from the government [illegible word]. It is the national army and the "sects." We have won the first hand and hope to win the second one. Then the beautiful thing is the reelections that we are sure to win. Add to that the "nagging time" that did not allow us to meditate

along the road and to pursue the good old politics of compromise. The hour is therefore unique and decisive. If we fail in convincing the leaders of the Free World to help us neutralize the colonialists who support the feudalists against the national government, we will go straight to disaster. Because the disappointed Vietnamese people would finally abandon us. And the Asian bloc we have been working with in the last few months, that was starting to sympathize with us, will turn away from us. Isolated then from Asia, we will be at the mercy of the Viet Minh. Because we must not repeat the experience of 1945–1954 being supported only by the Western camp and isolated then in Asia, we are sure to be beaten by communism in Asia. We must have the help of the Vietnamese people and the sympathy of the Asian world so that Western support, once personally cleared by Pres. Diem, bearing the Asian label, can be useful. This concept is well understood by intelligent people who are conversant with affairs here, such as Messrs. Roux (at Foreign Affairs) and Risterucci (at Associated States). It must be worked out in such a way that instructions to that effect that are [illegible word] already in place be urgently sent to Sài Gòn.[5] General Ely is an honest man, unfortunately prone to anxiety and pessimism (see Hinh affair = army split in two, civil war if the President touches Hinh). [underlines in original] This general is some kind of Dr. "too bad" who sees everything in black or rather in red. Remember the wishes of the communists who sought to create an autonomous state in France at the time of the Liberation that the French government did not hesitate to suffocate in blood. You must sacrifice a few for the good of all.

Until now France hasn't had an Indochinese policy. The moment to have one is now or never.

To God, dear friend, and thank you for your advice and encouragement. I remain the same, except that my hair has started to turn white and with just cause.[6]

Confronted with the armies of the sects, the army under the president was supervised by French instructors who did not favor him.[7]

They longed for the return of France and of Emperor Bảo Đại. Ngô Đình Diệm faced with dogged determination the perils that hindered his march toward the unity of the country. He did not hesitate to expose his life to danger when he deemed it necessary. Trình Minh Thế, an energetic and experienced general, rallied decisively to the legitimate president of the young republic. This fervent anti-communist and separatist earned his stripes serving in the Japanese army. He was conversant with the patriotic nationalism of the president and wanted to support the president in the combat he led to victory.

The other grave hostility to overcome was the presence in Sài Gòn of those "river pirates," the Bình Xuyên, to whom Bảo Đại had entrusted the mandate of the local police in Sài Gòn, who terrorized the city instead of assuring its security.[8] They shamelessly operated a racket of gambling halls and nightclubs previously created during the time of the French. The capital of the country was under their rule as such. The insecurity was such that Ngô Đình Nhu was forced to keep his family, a wife and three children of young age, barricaded in one of the rooms of the palace. Murders were rife in the streets of the capital, and the spokesman for the president himself would be killed by the "river pirates." They sent his severed head to the president as a sign of defiance. It was urgent and vital to put them in a situation where they would cause no further harm.

After having overcome the armed bands of the Cao Đài and Hòa Hảo sects, Ngô Đình Diệm turned to confront the Bình Xuyên. On April 26, 1956, unable to tolerate further challenges by the group, Ngô Đình Diệm asked its chief Bảy Viễn to submit his resignation, which he refused to do without Bảo Đại's express order. The only thing left to do was to fire him. Two days later a pitched battle burst out in Chợ Lớn between the army and the Bình Xuyên, who retaliated with the bombing of the presidential palace, now newly baptized Dinh Độc Lập (Independence Palace).

The president then ordered a general assault against them. Most unfortunate were the events that followed. It was toward the end of this battle that Trình Minh Thế, the highly valued Cao Đài general, would be killed from behind by one of his men. Some attributed this low blow to the future author of the 1963 coup d'état, General Dương Văn Minh, who as second in command under the general would receive all the honors of the victory.[9]

At the peak of the battle, the American secret services consulted with the Vietnamese army while French secret services entered into a relation with the Bình Xuyên and secured their withdrawal from Sài Gòn. It was a great relief for the city's residents, who for a long time had suffered exacting demands from the Bình Xuyên, whose existence remained a burden for the government as they now joined anti-government rebels in the maquis. Despite the scant support from the city people, who kept a prudent distance before jumping on the bandwagon of victory, the president succeeded in restoring order and ridding the capital of those abusive bandits whose very duty was to maintain public order.

According to official documents, support from President Eisenhower's administration was only hesitantly given to President Ngô Đình Diệm pending verification on the ground of the latter's capacity to take the country out of the chaos into which it was thrown since the fall of Điện Biên Phủ. Those who would later accuse President Diệm's government of nepotism should have the intellectual honesty to recognize that very rare were those who at the time responded affirmatively to its request for assistance and collaboration. A great number of people who aspired to government positions waited until the situation cleared to bestow their commitment.

On September 27, 1956, the president finally obtained the departure of the last elements of General Ely's French expeditionary army. Having thus reinforced national independence, he could dedicate his efforts to the reconstruction of all the bases of the administration of the country after a century of colonization. In this semblance of peace, he had to pay extreme attention to what was going on in the countryside where pockets of insurrection were located and where the communist Việt

President Ngô Đình Diệm in conference.

Minh maintained their presence in flagrant violation of the Geneva Accords. The French opponents, on the other hand, were located mostly in the cities.

On October 26, 1956, one year after the referendum, the Constitution was enforced and the Republic of Vietnam (RVN) promulgated. Ngô Đình Diệm was the legitimate founder of that democratic republic. It was the end of the imperial monarchy and the end of the colonial period. By avoiding any provocations so as to keep the dialogue open, the republic strived to create order inherent to a country based on law.

The republic had to rid itself of colonialism while tragically being fully exposed to a global conflict that from then on pitted an aging colonialism against an emerging communism.

The French domination had caused a break in the Confucian system that assigned a crucial importance to education. All the best schools were concentrated in the cities while the countryside where most of the population lived was neglected and lacking in teaching staff. The president would set himself the task of remedying the resulting illiteracy. In the social hierarchical scale (of Confucianism), men of letters take precedence over farmers, soldiers, and traders. A great investment program was undertaken to open new schools and recruit and train teachers to be assigned to the most remote provinces of the country.

In 1900, the French administration in Indochina put an end to the writing of Vietnamese characters (chữ Nôm) and enforced the use of Latin characters (chữ quốc ngữ). That reform disoriented the Vietnamese. Across several decades, it has been difficult for them to access their archives. The shrinking number of men of letters underscored a decrease in erudition in the Vietnamese education system. The new generation now recognized the benefits of that reform which liberated them from the Chinese ideograms and facilitated their approach to so many other languages.

Ngô Đình Diệm promoted an agrarian reform that put an end to the agricultural exploitation of big plots of land, prevalent under a feudal system. The exploitation of plots larger than one hundred hectares would no longer be tolerated. These measures deprived him of the sympathy of many notables, including those within his own family.

New infrastructures were put in place. Those damaged by the war between the French and the Việt Minh were gradually repaired. The undertaking proved to be more daunting than anticipated as the country was under constant attacks from the [former] Việt Minh communists. If those with separatist or monarchist tendencies had left that movement to join the young republic, the remaining communist members gradually became the only force within the [remnants of] Việt Minh ranks. They were better trained to wage a maquis war, becoming more and more difficult to track down. Subversive propaganda leaflets were distributed among the population and terrorist acts of a rare violence aimed at neutralizing any spirit of defense. Indisputably, however, achievements were successfully realized.

In his book *Background to Viet-Nam*, Bernard Newman stressed that the Labor Code [of the RVN] was relatively progressive for that part of the world.[10] Trade unions as well as arbitration tribunals were instituted. Social security started to be developed. Public health services there were the best in East Asia. This was the reason why Lyndon Baines Johnson, vice president of the American administration at the time, once apprised of these performances, underscored the merits of President Ngô Đình Diệm. In May 1961, he paid tribute to him, calling him the new Winston Churchill of Asia. Many other governments in Asia even went so far as to portray him as the Miracle Man of Asia.

In their book *Legal and Policy Issues of the Indochina War*, professors John Norton Moore and Robert F. Turner of the University of Virginia School of Law quoted a few figures embodying the progress made by the Republic of Vietnam from 1954 to 1959:

> The number of pupils in primary schools rose from 400,000 to 1,243,918.
> The number of students in secondary schools increased by 400 percent.
> University enrollments multiplied by three times.
> Public health expenses increased by 40 percent.
> Textile production made a jump of 325 percent.
> Rice exports increased by 500 percent.[11]

•

Ngô Đình Nhu had substantially contributed, with his brother, to the positive balance sheet of the new republic. Assistant and political adviser to the president, he founded a political party that carried the traditional values of Vietnam: the Cần Lao Nhân Vị, meaning "Work and Human Dignity."[12] For rising generations he created a movement: the "Thanh Niên Cộng Hòa," which means "Republican Youth."

On these two lines of thought and action he wanted to structure the momentum necessary and conducive to the radical reforms that the government had to undertake. He would set out to provide each village with the necessary teaching and medical staff. Thus, he revived the very ancient tradition of self-government for the rural villages in Vietnam.

Close to his brother president with whom he would share his life until their deaths, Ngô Đình Nhu embodied the identity of a country in search of a modern development path respectful of its Confucian traditions. To be Confucian is to put one's words, actions, and thoughts in cohesion with mutual respect and be at the service of one another in the harmony that constitutes human life and its natural environment. This high-level requirement is conceived as a duty towards the human community. That path which is open to every person for his accomplishment is the Nhân Đạo.

Before French colonialism, the Confucian system allowed for democratic participation in the administration of the country. Public triennial competitions were open to all Vietnamese men, permitting each to demonstrate their capabilities and to be associated with the good governance of the country, in accordance with each one's own merits. A candidate who passed those very selective exams became a mandarin and could aspire to marry a noble young woman belonging to the Court of Huế. The exceptional character of this open and meritocratic process did not escape the attention of the West.

The attention paid to the Confucian roots contained in the Nhân Vị and the reference to Human Dignity that Ngô Đình Nhu promoted within the framework of his political actions enabled the government to be understood and respected by the rural population that had come out of 100 years of colonization and had greatly suffered from the war between the French and the Việt Minh from 1946 to 1954. It was Ngô Đình Nhu who had wished for and achieved that the preamble of the Constitution referred to that spiritual humanism to which he aspired for his country, and it was with that spirit that he created the Party of Labor and Human Dignity.

He would also institute another party called the National Revolutionary Movement [Phong trào Cách mạng Quốc gia] to which he assigned the mission of promoting and training an administrative body formed in the Vietnamese rather than the French fashion. This specifically Vietnamese formation, conceived in a martial mold, asked everyone to take charge of his own station in life and to fight against the three major obstacles that were Laggardness, Isolation, and Communism. It was a matter of adapting communal life to ancestral human values. A good mutual understanding is the best antidote for communism, which would end up disappearing. That would put an end to the hostilities.

The Nhân Vị, this path to transcendence on which the two brothers wished to engage the Vietnamese republic under their responsibility, was deployed in several dimensions:

Spiritual Dimension

To the two brothers, capitalism was a kind of materialism equally as atheistic as communism. It cannot satisfy Man, because not only is he matter but also spirit. Being transcendent, he cannot accomplish his purpose in life through material satisfaction alone.

Dignity constantly evolves within this space/time dimension and represents the center and goal of Nhân Vị, a wisdom that shows Man his way, the Nhân Đạo. In guiding his mode of action, it elevates him towards his Creator by the search for his full development in goodness through love and understanding of his fellow man.

Social Dimension

The repudiation of the family preached by the Communists is a cruel and Machiavellian perfidy aimed at exposing Man naked and powerless in the face of totalitarian communist machinery. That machinery would turn man into its own creature. The first line of protection for Man is his family, which must be healthy, happy, and prosperous, as the entire nation depends on this basic cell.

Political Dimension

The Nhân Vị guarantees to the individual all the dimensions of his path to Man that is the Nhân Đạo with all the liberties it entails.

Economic Dimension

Communal work is a solution to produce goods that are useful for the country. But man does not have to work like a drudge, and the work he provides in this communal effort must be of immediate benefit to the worker and not subject to confiscation by a domineering state. Those were the tenets of the movement "Work and Human Dignity" that Nhu wanted to institute.

Ill-informed or malevolent critics, who refused to make the effort to understand this path to a life of higher aspiration, would turn this quest, this profound necessity, into a travesty by involving a philosophy of personalism. It was a reductionist and superficial caricature behind which they would attempt to obfuscate the concepts of the two brothers.

The search for solutions based on authentic cultural roots and a policy open on wide human perspectives were therefore the essential characteristics of Ngô Đình Nhu's actions. He was preoccupied by what he termed the "intellectual underdevelopment" of the country which he thought was a more serious problem than the economic underdevelopment.

Through Nhân Vị, Ngô Đình Diệm and his brother set out to provide their compatriots with a truly improved existence, spiritually, intellectually, and materially. The economic progress that would benefit the South, which is by nature richer than the North, offered a singular contrast to the misery that reigned in the North, a misery aggravated by a long-drawn-out famine that would result in thousands of victims. The political leaders of North Vietnam becoming fanatical in Communist ideology were indifferent to the misery of their fellow citizens. To motivate their men to fight, the Communists had recourse to a lie. They painted such a false picture of the situation in the South that their men were shocked to discover that conditions there were much superior to their own.[13] Feeling cheated and manipulated, many would choose to desert despite warnings that they would be shot on the spot if they returned to their homes.

The war South Vietnam was waging against the North with the strong financial and logistical support of the United States—the overdriven, overabundant, and sophisticated war machinery at the Americans' disposal—would prove from day to day non-operational and inefficient in the face of guerilla warfare directed by the Communists. The Americans, who did not know how to integrate that guerilla aspect into their military tactics, wanted to intensify their strike force as opposed to Nhu who was intent on analyzing that style of combat in order to better adjust the dynamics of resistance and of offensive. He fine-tuned a novel response, that of "strategic hamlets," of which he was the creator and director. It consisted in leaning on the innumerable villages scattered throughout the country as well as giving them the means to protect themselves against the attacks aimed at them.

The principal victims targeted by the enemy were the province chiefs, teachers, nurses, and doctors sent by the government. They were often cruelly massacred. The terrorized population was to this point reduced to be so much at their mercy that they did not dare call the army to come to their aid.

Nhu empowered and trained the peasants in the defense of their space. He would provide them with weapons of first resistance. When an attack took place, they could defend themselves pending the arrival of the special forces by helicopters. The army became more efficient and mobile than a conventional army. Nhu put in place that large mobilization on a national scale that any simple person could understand and put to application.

From then on, the armed peasants lived in a protected space, surrounded by a moat and a bamboo fence erected by the inhabitants themselves. This system of "strategic hamlets" that combined self-policing surveillance and self-defense protected them from the actions by one-off terrorists who attacked isolated small towns that were unable to defend

Ngô Đình Nhu in 1962 or 1963.

themselves before. The policy restored morale to the populations that were no longer alone to face the terror communist commandos wanted to spread. These commandos were hampered in their operations, finding it more and more difficult to feed themselves on the spot. It was an operational and efficient way to deprive "the fish of water," to revisit an expression of Mao Zedong. Disappointment and desertion would increase in the ranks of the adversary because it was vital for them to find the food they needed immediately at hand. North Vietnam was so poor that it could not provide food for them.

With the strategic hamlets, the war was on the way to being won. Ngô Đình Nhu knew it. To his Charters School friends who were concerned about him and about Vietnam, he wrote that he thought he would soon win this "dirty war." The hitherto unpublicized letter we provide below was sent not long after Tết 1962 by diplomatic mail. It did not bear any postmark or date from the postal service.[14]

> Dear friend,
>
> I had sent a beautiful Christmas card and one for Tet to you and to the other friends who were kind to think of me. Probably our services celebrated Tet so much that they misplaced them.
>
> For the first time in many years, we have been able to celebrate Tet in a proper fashion. Thanks to the progress that we have succeeded in achieving in all fields in advance of the communists.
>
> I have become the father and the nanny of the "strategic hamlets," a system I have devised to solve the current Chinese puzzle. By that I mean the dual problem of democracy and underdevelopment. Thanks to this system we think we will soon win this dirty war.
>
> And you, do not you gripe anymore. You have done formidable things over there. You have made a new revolution with tremendous consequences for the coming world. Our parliamentarian mission over there has apparently broken the iceberg that separated our two people.
>
> My apologies for having written to you in red ink. It's what I have at hand. Besides, it is a propitious color. May it symbolize the future of the new relations between our two countries.
>
> To God. Take care.

During the spring and summer of 1962, American observers themselves emphasized that the war had taken a favorable turn thanks to the "strategic hamlets" program. The Special Forces coordinated by Nhu had inflicted severe losses on the enemy. On July 23, 1962, the same day of the signature of the peace treaty for Laos in Geneva, Secretary of Defense McNamara ordered the drafting of a plan for American disengagement from Vietnam as well as of long-term projects for reducing financial aid to the government of Sài Gòn.[15]

In this advantageous position of force, contacts were made in secret with North Vietnam to reinstate a peace process so that human lives could be spared. Ngô Đình Nhu was the promoter and the man in charge of this rapprochement attempt. Hồ Chí Minh himself gave an encouraging sign. For Tết he presented a symbolic branch of cherry blossoms to Ngô Đình Diệm. Nhu had proposed to organize a voyage to the North so his adolescent sons could discover that part of Vietnam they did not know.

The management of the war was so positive at this point that the Kennedy administration wanted to take all the credit and speed up the results. President Kennedy needed to reap a personal benefit after the Bay of Pigs incident and the erection of the Berlin Wall. Tremendous pressure was thus exerted on President Ngô Đình Diệm to accept an increase in the number of American advisers. With 16,000 men, America thought it could show the country's contribution to the war to best advantage. President Diệm appeared to be hesitant. He was then asked to kindly get his brother Nhu, deemed too independent, out of the country. Faced with the refusal of this request, the American administration decided to reduce the financial aid to its ally, yet on a full war effort.

This measure dealt a direct blow to the financing of the Special Forces attached to the strategic hamlets. It suspended food assistance programs such as powdered milk for children the Americans had themselves introduced to Vietnam. These measures were intended to turn the Vietnamese population against their government. Kennedy even went so far as to declare himself in favor of a change in politics and "personnel" in Vietnam. It was political interference aimed at strongly discrediting President Ngô Đình Diệm. The West had followed and trusted the Americans ever since they successfully intervened to put a victorious end to the Second World War.

On December 3, 1962, Roger Hilsman, director of the Bureau of Information and Research at the State Department, addressed to the Secretary of State a memorandum titled "The Situation and Short-Term Prospects in Vietnam." He reported:[16]

> The Vietnamese government has given priority to implementing a basic strategic concept featuring the strategic hamlet and systematic pacification program. It has paid more attention to political, economic, and social counterinsurgency measures and their coordination with purely military measures. Vietnamese security forces—now enlarged and of higher caliber—are significantly more offensive-minded and their tactical counter-guerrilla capabilities greatly improved. Effective [government] control of the campaign by the Vietnamese government has been extended slightly. In some areas where security has improved, peasant attitude towards the government appears also to have improved.

However, this memorandum specified that:

> Viet Cong influence has almost certainly improved in urban areas not only through subversion and terrorism but also because of its propaganda appeal to the increasingly frustrated non-Communist, anti-Diem elements. . . . There are also reports that important military and civilian officials, and dissidents outside the government, appear to be increasingly susceptible to neutralist, pro-Communist and possibly anti-American sentiments. They are apparently placing increased reliance on clandestine activities. . . . Hanoi can also be expected to increase its efforts to legitimize its "National Front for the

> Liberation of South Vietnam." . . . If security conditions continue to improve, Diem should be able to alleviate concern and boost morale within the bureaucracy and the military establishment.

The memorandum raised the possibility of a coup d'état: "The serious disruption of government leadership resulting from a coup would probably halt or possibly reverse the momentum of the government's counterinsurgency effort. The role of the United States can be extremely important to restoring this momentum and in averting widespread fighting and serious internal power struggle." (Might it then be inferred that this is an encouragement to launch a coup d'état?)

Whatever its worth, this memorandum at least had the merit of showing the efforts and progress of the Vietnamese government in its struggle against the Communists and to indicate the extent to which it was constantly harassed by the terrorist and subversive actions directed by Hà Nội, but also by a serious infighting struggle for power.

In the momentum of the anti-terrorist struggle led by the country, Nhu was focused on thwarting the subversive struggle in the field led by the enemy. He denounced the ideology of the Việt Minh and took away the luster of the "anticolonialist fight" with which they draped themselves offensively to influence and seduce the South Vietnamese. Nhu did not hesitate to call Việt Cộng those who would call themselves Việt Minh. From then on, the communist connotation would be clearly indicated by the word "Cộng." The enemy was therefore unmasked, so to speak. That appellation Việt Cộng found its way into the common language.

Finally, being aware that military action must be linked to political action, Nhu promoted in April 1963 the policy of Chiêu Hồi, translated as "Open Arms." By announcing that he would welcome all the Việt Cộng deserters like lost brothers coming back home, Nhu offered a wide-ranging amnesty. In some instances, he even instructed the military not to kill the enemy, only to destroy their logistics, and to leave an escape route so that they could be potential messengers of peace between Vietnamese brethren.

To make itself better understood, the government invoked in its speeches and directives the phrase "đồng bào" (same pouch), with the aim to signify to Vietnamese that everyone was born from the same mother. A legend recounts that the Vietnamese nation was born from a goddess mother who gave birth to a pouch containing 100 eggs. These eggs hatched into the first 100 Vietnamese. The term "đồng bào" expressed the profound idea of fraternity between fellow countrymen, much better than the word "fellow citizens" or "comrades" the Việt Cộng used. These orientations were founded on human fraternity, a concept not well understood by the American military advisers who would favor instead the body count of the enemy. Yet they have proven to be efficient. The flow of desertions swelled constantly.[17] Within a few months they went up to 10,000. Most of these deserters arrived famished, discouraged, and miserable. They recognized that it had become almost impossible to get hold of the population's food reserve because of the strategic hamlets. Their life of adventure in the jungle had become unbearable.

These deserting soldiers would prove very valuable and rich with information about the recruitment and terrorism the Communists had instigated. Mr. McNamara, US Secretary of Defense, also reported that at the beginning of October 1963 the situation of the loyal forces had remarkably improved. General Paul Harkins, commander of the US armed forces in Vietnam, stressed that there was a daily progress in the fighting spirit of the army.[18]

At the time of Ngô Đình Nhu's death, eight thousand villages out of the twelve thousand planned had been strategically reinforced. That was the most effective response to the thousands of assassinations and kidnappings perpetrated by Việt Cộng infiltrations every year in these villages in the countryside, where 80 percent of the total fourteen million people in South Vietnam lived at the time.

When the United States made Nhu disappear, they were no longer capable of pursuing the tactic of "strategic hamlets," which was so removed from their military culture. The US Army would bring in more than half a million Americans. It would invest in vain in heavier and heavier means for a frightening war that would end in total defeat twelve years later.

•

Mme. Ngô Đình Nhu took part in the politics led by the government in the development of the Republic of Vietnam. Elected a congress-woman, she was also the head of the movement "Phong Trào Phụ Nữ Liên Đới" (Movement for the Solidarity of Vietnamese Women) she founded. Through this movement based on the voluntarism of women, an important social work was born and would rapidly develop. Canteens, housing units, and professional workshops would multiply to welcome and accommodate those refugees who had come en masse from North Vietnam in 1954 and who had lost everything. Most of them were Catholics. They left their ancestral land when the country was divided along the 17th parallel and the Geneva Accords assigned the northern part of the country to the government of Hồ Chí Minh.

If there were almost one million to come to the south from the north, there were only [one hundred thirty] thousand communist partisans to go the other way, from the south to the north. This was the assessment made on the spot by foreign observers. People proclaimed with their feet that the government of President Ngô Đình Diệm was manifestly more attractive than that of Hồ Chí Minh.

Such massive influx had in no way been anticipated. French officials still in the country at the time had predicted that the partition of the country would cause a wave of two hundred thousand refugees. Due to a lack of accommodation, the families were first directed to the cement pipes opened on each end, a kind of drain, that would at least shelter them from rain and sun. The problems arising from the massive influx of refugees would be resolved within a few years. Such circumstances could have overwhelmed other countries that were better

Parade of the Solidarity Movement of Vietnamese Women, March 25, 1961.

equipped structurally than Vietnam and would present an insurmountable problem to its development.

The emblem adopted by the solidarity movement was the oil lamp of the wise Virgins of the Gospel. It built its works and made up for the shortcomings of a barely born state that did not have the usual social services. With ingenuity and foresight, the women of the movement set up all kinds of services and assistance. They intervened in a positive and realistic way in favor of the disadvantaged, orphans, victims of war, and the disabled. They opened dispensaries and drop-in centers for children.

Mme. Ngô Đình Nhu mustered all her energy to mobilize and support the voluntarism of the women. She appealed to a spirit of patriotic reconstruction that was well received by the population. A great number of initiatives were undertaken without public funds. State assistance did not originate in Vietnam, while individual and private charitable actions drew their force from the Confucian culture that emphasizes personal involvement with the community.

As an example, mention can be made of those popular restaurants that were open to everybody, including members of the National Assembly.

Mme. Ngô Đình Nhu delivering a speech at the cemetery for young girls assassinated by the Communists, March 27, 1961.

Co-payment rates were determined according to individual means, and the restaurants were managed to be financially self-sufficient. House visits by volunteers were regularly provided for the neediest and carried out to identify the needs. All this setup allowed for a joint responsibility of the public good that only a ridiculously malicious

Mme. Ngô Đình Nhu under the statue of the Trưng Sisters in Sài Gòn (the statue was destroyed in 1963).

foreign press would qualify as the "espionage networks of Mme. Ngô Đình Nhu."

The participation of about two million women from all social ranks was truly exceptional. For the first time these women felt they were called upon to become actors in a population where they were naturally in the majority but remained confined to a social and familial context that did not give them any public responsibility.

Mme. Ngô Đình Nhu launched a paramilitary women's movement as well, which was also founded on voluntarism. Every year it offered

Mme. Ngô Đình Nhu visiting one of the popular restaurants operated by the Solidarity Movement of Vietnamese Women, March 21, 1961.

to roughly one hundred thousand young women a structured training program featuring individual armed self-defense with the addition of medical training that would teach them the administration of first aid.

There were no plans to send them to the front, only to make sure that additional mobilization would be available when necessary. It was a matter of willful participation in the face of a subversive war that could

Mme. Ngô Đình Nhu traveling with her delegation.

not be won without an individual awareness before it could become collective.

To set an example, her eldest daughter Lệ Thủy enlisted in the movement at the age of 16. She demonstrated her sharpshooting ability in national parades and graduated as a major of her class. Rightly so, Mme.

Ngô Đình Quỳnh, Mr. and Mme. Ngô Đình Nhu, and Ngô Đình Trác attending a concert given by the young women of the Women Paramilitary Movement to which Lệ Thuỷ belonged, Sài Gòn, 1963.

Mrs. Ngô Đình Nhu, in the company of her husband, salutes members of the Women Paramilitary Movement, Sài Gòn, 1963.

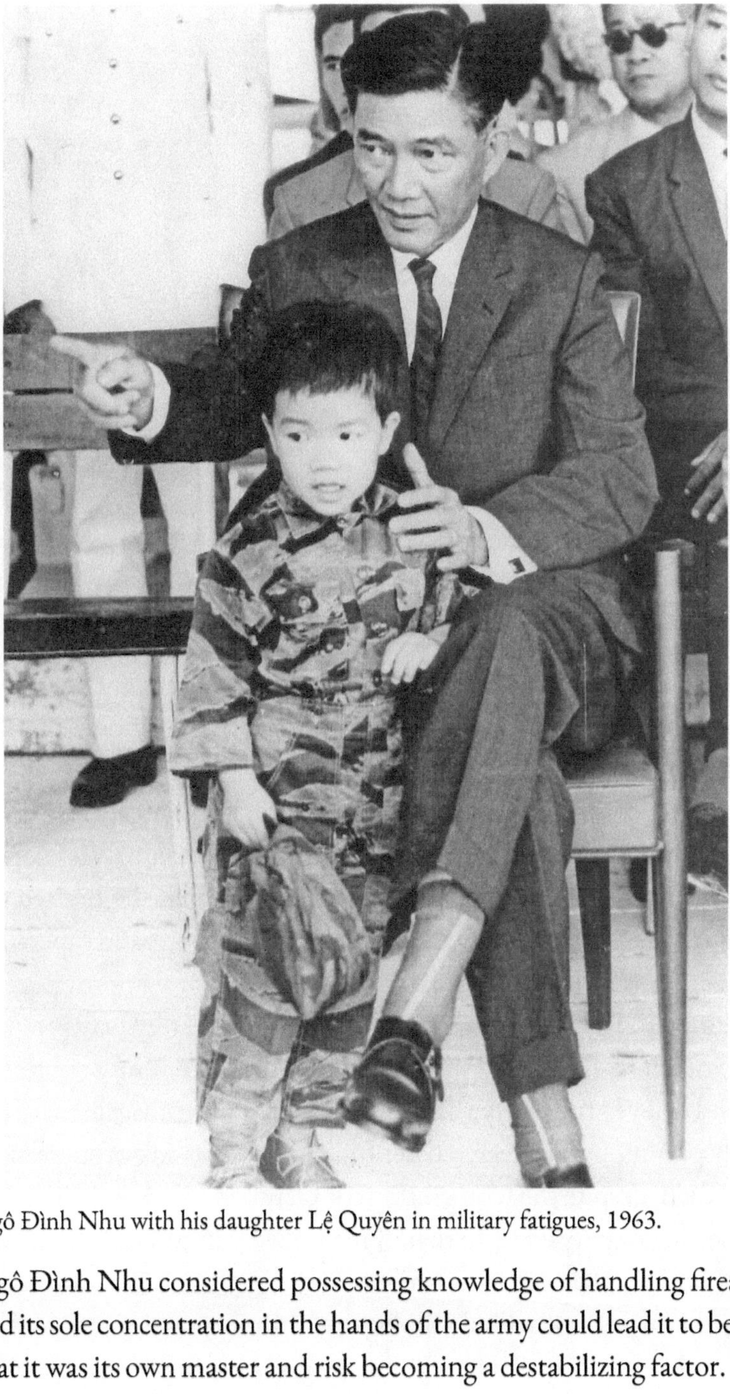

Ngô Đình Nhu with his daughter Lệ Quyên in military fatigues, 1963.

Ngô Đình Nhu considered possessing knowledge of handling firearms and its sole concentration in the hands of the army could lead it to believe that it was its own master and risk becoming a destabilizing factor. This

Lê Thuỷ (standing) in paramilitary garb. On the right is her father Ngô Đình Nhu, 1962 or 1963.

was what happened to Vietnam upon the death of President Ngô Đình Diệm. The country had no other alternative than to endure the dramatic conflicts between the generals.

Another contribution of Mme. Ngô Đình Nhu must be expressly recalled and highlighted. It is the legal emancipation of Vietnamese women. This goal was at this point so essential that she drafted the Family Code herself with the help of a group of lawyers and experts. In 1958, she submitted it to the Legislative Assembly for approval and it was adopted. For the first time, the principle of equality between men and women was legislated in detail. The woman became a subject of law and enjoyed full parity with her husband in the management of the family patrimony. She received her full place in the rank of succession. Until then, despite the Constitution of October 26, 1956, which proclaimed her dignity equal to that of men, a woman was still submissive to her husband who acted as her tutor.

In the new Family Code, polygamy, still in practice among rich families, was abolished. The legitimate family issuing from a marriage was fiercely defended in a country that tolerated concubines. Until then, in case of divorce ruled with no fault on her part, a woman could be excluded from the family and lose all her rights to the patrimony. The Vietnamese woman was thus reduced to the role of an "incapable minor."

That condition of the Vietnamese woman made Mme. Ngô Đình Nhu profoundly indignant. She speeded up the drafting of the Family Code without waiting for the general overhaul of the Civil Code that must unify the various legislations in force in the three major parts of North, Central, and South Vietnam.

As the president of the Republic of Vietnam was unmarried, it was therefore she that he asked to play the role of First Lady to receive representatives from other countries.

From 1958 to 1963, on official visits of foreign delegations, Mme. Ngô Đình Nhu never hesitated to mention the Family Code to developing countries that had not yet been concerned with promoting the dignity of women. She would likewise call attention to it when she represented her country during her four tours around the world. Therefore, whenever practical, she defended the emancipation of women and the role played by families. These lines of force that for her were foundational and necessary mobilized her for her country just as much as her fight against communism.

She was one of the first women to have a driver's license in a country with few cars in circulation. And she took it to heart to give other women the chance of being at the helm of their own destiny.

•

Magazines and photographic reports produced in Vietnam at the beginning of the 1960s bore witness to the economic and social progress achieved when Ngô Đình Diệm was heading the country.

On the military side, the unpublished letter from his brother Nhu, reproduced above and published in Appendix 4, revealed that the "dirty war" against the Việt Cộng was about to be won thanks to the success of the "strategic hamlets." The reports from the US administration we have cited testify to the fact that this country, at maximum effort, was in the process of moving closer to its objective. This undeniable progress, achieved thanks to the energy of an entire people confident in their leaders, would be brushed aside with the back of a hand. In a gesture of startling irresponsibility that did not ensure any future or any alternative solution, as the events would later demonstrate, the American government would crush everything that had been achieved. It decided to eliminate President Ngô Đình Diệm as well as Nhu, his brother and counselor.

It was not from the Vietnamese people attached to their leaders that the plot would originate, but from the generals who wanted power for themselves while being incapable of exercising it later. Susceptible to honors and money, manipulated by the Americans but also by well-camouflaged Việt Cộng spies, they would be pawns in the game of dupes that set in.

•

CHAPTER 3

The Coup d'État

During the month of August 1963, the president and his brother Nhu got wind of what was going on behind their backs. They discovered that the Americans had put in circulation secret funds to incite the generals to mount a coup d'état against them. They decided to convene the generals at the Presidential Palace to let them know that they were aware of that American attempt to overthrow them and of the dollars in circulation to buy consciences and finalize a coup. All the generals were present. The Ngô Đình gave an order and called on the generals' sense of duty in the face of a subversive war that continued to threaten their country and toward the people they were tasked to protect. The generals regrouped into the obedience of the army.

The two brothers would mention this attempt at conspiracy against them to two journalists they met successively a few days before their assassination. They were Marguerite Higgins and Suzanne Labin, who knew Vietnam well because of having often crisscrossed it.

Kennedy had his ambassador Frederick E. Nolting Jr.—deemed too close to President Diệm—recalled and replaced by Henry Cabot Lodge, resolutely hostile to the Vietnamese government he found uncooperative and viewed as too backward-looking. Lodge, who was steeped in certainty, did not imagine that President Ngô Đình Diệm could have his own opinions when it came to the policy to follow in the defense of his country, and that he would not simply and purely bow to the instructions of his (American) supervisors.[1] Under such circumstances, there could only be total disagreement between the two men.

Lodge, the new US ambassador, landed in Sài Gòn on August 22, 1963. Less than 48 hours after his arrival, he wrote a telegram to the State Department declaring that the general officers, in the most important positions of command in the Sài Gòn area, remained faithful to Diệm and his brother. Lesser known was the loyalty of the other general officers. Under these circumstances, for the United States to support a coup would be tantamount to "shooting in the dark."[2]

On August 31, 1963, a telegram from Lodge indicated that the plotting generals had given up their plan. The United States found itself at a dead end.[3] As the study by the Pentagon made clear, by the end of August, Washington had run out of policy! On that same day, in the absence of President Kennedy, the members of the National Security Council met.[4] The atmosphere was dominated by a sense that the "administration was adrift."

For lack of a clear solution, they headed back to a replay of support for Diệm. Dean Rusk [US Secretary of State] insisted on the necessity to base American politics on two ideas: "That the Americans would not withdraw from Vietnam before the war is won, that they would not get involved in a coup d'état of any kind." McNamara supported this point of view and Johnson himself wholly approved this thesis.

The reading of the Pentagon Papers is very enlightening about what the observers called the drifting of their administration. Let's briefly recap the explosive affair of the "Pentagon Papers." On Sunday, June 13, 1971, *The New York Times* started to publish confidential documents that Robert McNamara had ordered assembled since June 1967 to form a report on the ultrasecret history of the US action in Indochina. The theft of what was to be called the "Pentagon Papers" and their leak to the press made President Richard Nixon flare up with indignation. He attempted to block the publication of those documents. The process was moving at a very intense and sustained pace, and on June 30,

1971, the US Supreme Court granted *The New York Times* and *The Washington Post* permission to publish those secret documents. The Supreme Court ruled that the people's right to free and complete information was guaranteed by the First Amendment of the Constitution, and that no consideration, however legal—in this instance, the fact that those documents had been stolen—could prevail over that right.

The title of chapter 4 of those files is "The Overthrow of Ngô Đình Diệm." The comments by [*New York Times* reporter] Hedrick Smith were as follows: "The secret study by the Pentagon on the war in Vietnam reveals that President Kennedy was aware of the plans of the military coup d'état of 1963, and that he had approved them." That study specifies that, "Beginning in August of 1963, we variously authorized, sanctioned, and encouraged the plot of the Vietnamese generals and offered full support for an eventual alternate government. . . . The part we played in this coup d'état can only reinforce our responsibilities in Vietnam and the commitment of the United States."[5] The notes and reports gathered in the Pentagon files showed, however, that there was no unanimity on the part of the Americans to judge and condemn the actions of President Diệm.

In the quest for a precise position to assume, Kennedy decided to send a mission to Sài Gòn, tasked with making a new evaluation of the situation. It was entrusted to two men, Brigadier General Victor H. Krulak, an anti-guerilla specialist at the Pentagon, and Joseph A. Mendenhall, former political counselor at the Sài Gòn Embassy. When they came back from South Vietnam, they presented two diametrically opposite views to President Kennedy. The Pentagon files gave us the reaction of Kennedy: "You two, are you sure it was the same country you had visited?"[6]

Kennedy was very annoyed that the result of this mission did not help him make up his mind. On September 23, 1963, he sent out a new mission. This one was entrusted to two of his close and eminent advisers: Robert McNamara, defense secretary, and General Maxwell Davenport Taylor, Chairman of the Joint Chiefs of Staff. In the report they prepared on October 2, 1963, they noted that the military campaign has achieved significant progress and continued to evolve in a good way.[7] They proposed to their president various measures, among which was the expansion of the fortified Strategic Hamlets program, especially in the Delta.

The results they had observed allowed them to entertain the idea that the "bulk" of the troops could be repatriated toward the end of 1965. The report also provided for economic retaliatory measures to force Diệm toward instituting political reforms. A strict surveillance would allow them to see to what extent he would renounce the repressive measures. At this stage, the observers did not entertain any change in government whatsoever, while adding that US policy must be to urgently identify those people capable of providing an alternate solution, as soon as it was outlined, and to establish contact with them.

What conclusion is to be drawn from such a report? The president of Vietnam found himself in a situation of supervised freedom, despite the satisfactory military results. His repressive politics were criticized despite an awareness of the subversive Communist infiltrations into the country. Terrorist actions continued to be led by the Việt Cộng commandos. Why then imagine that the president of a country under a constant threat could think of alleviating the means of surveillance and repression?

As things stood, with the consent of Kennedy, McNamara and Taylor announced that 1,000 men would leave Vietnam at the end of 1963.

Two contradictory documents gave an inkling of the ultimate and still indecisive situation confronting Kennedy, who was asked to take the last step while still wavering between the advice of the pro-Diệm and anti-Diệm advocates.

On October 30, 1963, General Paul Harkins, commander of US armed forces in Vietnam—and therefore in a better position to assess the military situation—sent a note to General Taylor. Harkins wrote,

> [O]n the basic guidance that no initiative should now be taken to give any active covert encouragement to a coup, . . . I am inclined to

> feel that at this time the change should be in methods of governing rather than complete change in personnel. . . . In my contacts here I have seen no one with the strength of character of Diem, at least in fighting communists. Clearly there are no Generals qualified to take over in my opinion.
>
> I am not a Diem man per se. I certainly see the faults in his character. I am here to back the 14 million SVN Vietnamese in their fight against communism and it just happens that Diem is their leader at this time.

As for the positions of the armed forces, the general added that the Vietnamese government "is a way ahead in the I, II and parts of the III corps and making progress in the Delta."[8]

On the other hand, Ambassador Lodge sent a note to McGeorge Bundy, [US National Security] Adviser to Kennedy, declaring:

> My general view is that the United States is trying to bring this medieval country into the 20th Century and that we have made considerable progress in military and economic ways, but to gain victory we must also bring them into 20th Century politically, and that can only be done by either a thoroughgoing change in the behavior of the present government or by another government. . . . We should continue our present position of keeping hands off but continue to monitor and press for more detailed information. . . . As to requests from the Generals, they may well have need of funds at the last moment with which to buy off potential opposition. To the extent that these funds can be passed discreetly, I believe we should furnish them, provided we are convinced that the proposed coup is sufficiently well organized to have a good chance of success. . . . We have a commitment to the Generals from the August episode to attempt to help in the evacuation of their dependents. We should try to live up to this if conditions will permit.[9]

Thus, Lodge recognized the considerable progress in military and economic areas that Vietnam had achieved, but he remained totally unyielding to the personality of Diệm he found to be outmoded in his attachment to the traditions of his country. It was Lodge's wish to launch Vietnam toward modernity American style. With Diệm this was impossible; he must therefore be suppressed, no matter the consequences, which the American ambassador himself was not capable of bringing himself to analyze, as the unfolding of events would later demonstrate.

Lodge's determination would force the hand of President Kennedy. Hesitant until the last moment, Kennedy did not oppose in any formal way the putsch that he allowed to develop. From that time on it was too late to stop. Two days later, it was launched. The funds had been distributed; the portion reserved for the generals who chose treason was ready.

For the success of this coup d'état the Kennedy administration relied on the services of Lucien Conein.[10] A lieutenant colonel in the US Army, he was working for the CIA at the time. French by birth, Conein could easily talk with the Vietnamese generals who received their military training from the French and spoke little or poor English. He incited them to betray their president. He had at his disposal the financial means to bribe them. He knew how to convince them, thanks to the meetings of Lodge, that in case the coup d'état failed they would be protected by America, but if successful they would have gained power.

"He was the indispensable man," said Lodge in the October 25 telegram he addressed to McGeorge Bundy. Lodge added, "I have personally approved each meeting between General Don [Trần Văn Đôn, one of the three principal conspirators] and Conein who has carried out my orders in each instance explicitly."[11] As the official documents revealed, after receiving the green light from the ambassador, the CIA collaborated closely with the generals even to the point of offering them important information on weapons and billeting locations of the troops that supported Diệm.

In those last days of October, the atmosphere was heavy and somber in Sài Gòn. Ngô Đình Nhu thought of his wife and daughter who had gone away to defend the flags and values of Vietnam. He also thought of his three other children. He summoned Trác, who was not yet sixteen. Trác was the heir to the lineage of all the Ngôs since the three elder Ngô brothers had no progeny. In a few words, he explained to his son that the future might reserve serious surprises and he expressed the desire to see him spend the All Saints' holidays far from Sài Gòn in their Đà Lạt resort with his younger brother and his four-year-old sister.

"Here is some money, go! If misfortune comes to me, I will entrust your two sisters to you. Always remember that you are responsible for them."

Then he saw his children off. No doubt he also entrusted them to God Almighty.[12]

Toward noon on November 1, the generals and colonels met at the Joint Chiefs of Staff headquarters to attend a luncheon organized by General Trần Thiện Khiêm. When everybody was in their seats, General Dương Văn Minh stood up to announce the launching of the putsch and demanded allegiance from all. Everyone applauded except Colonel Lê Quang Tung who was the Commander of Special Forces and the Presidential Palace Guards. He addressed the assembly with these few words: "Just remember who has given you your stars!" He was arrested on the spot and executed that same evening with Lê Quang Triệu, his brother.

Nguyễn Hữu Duệ, the deputy commander of Presidential Palace Guards, telephoned President Ngô Đình Diệm to tell him he was ready to launch a lightning attack on the Joint Chiefs Headquarters using his forces combined with armored vehicles. If the attack was launched right at that moment, there would be a good chance to capture all the rebels before their reinforcements arrived. Ngô Đình Diệm refused to authorize the attack that would cause blood to flow between fellow compatriots and told his interlocutor that he preferred a discussion to learn what the coup leaders actually wanted from the government.

Around 5 p.m., Dương Văn Minh, the coup leader, telephoned Ngô Đình Nhu, saying that if he himself and the president did not surrender, the palace would be destroyed by cannons and bombed by the Air Force. But at 5 p.m. no general wanted to take the initiative for this attack.

At nightfall around 8 p.m., Lodge telephoned President Diệm to let him know that if he surrendered, he could help him head overseas to the destination of his choice. The president replied that he would remain in his country until the end and that he was ready to die at his post out of loyalty to and for the honor of his people.

General Đỗ Cao Trí, the commander of the First Military Region in Huế, as well as General Nguyễn Khánh, the commander of the Second Military Region in Pleiku, jointly presented to the president their plan to send their troops to quash the coup d'état. General Huỳnh Văn Cao, Commander of the Fourth Military Region in Cần Thơ, gave the 7th Army Division and all the forces of his region the order to advance toward the southern bank of the Mekong River. Nguyễn Khánh proposed to President Diệm as well as to his brother to have them driven to Pleiku pending the arrival of the troops that would take a few days owing to the distance traveled. But the president refused to flee as much as he had to allow fighting between South Vietnamese units.

Later in the night, at the insistence of his brother Nhu, Ngô Đình Diệm ended up agreeing to leave the palace in the car of Cao Xuân Vỹ, general director of Republican Youth, a movement founded by Nhu. The president was seated in the front next to Cao Xuân Vỹ. Nhu settled in the back with Đỗ Thọ, the orderly officer of the president. Once he arrived at the destination, the president had orders dispatched to the defenders of the palace not to fight to avoid bloodshed. When Colonel Nguyễn Văn Thiệu launched the attack on the palace, the defenders would after all resist. They would not stop shooting until they ran out of ammunition.

The president and his brother spent the night at the house of Mã Tuyên, a Chinese-born Vietnamese in charge of Republican Youth in Chợ Lớn. Early on the morning of November 2, 1963, the Ngô Đình brothers received Communion and participated in the Mass at the Church of Saint Francis Xavier in Chợ Lớn. It is a feast day for the Catholic Church, on which one prays for all the dead after having honored the previous day of November 1 the memory of all the saints of Christianity.

At the end of the Mass, Ngô Đình Diệm asked the officiating priest to call General Trần Văn Đôn, who was unaware of the president's whereabouts. The president proposed to the generals to meet that same morning. He remained convinced that he could bring them back to reason by appealing to their patriotism. The country was on its way to winning the war against communism; this rebellion was an act of total irresponsibility. Generals Trần Văn Đôn and Trần Tử Oai asked for a room to be prepared to properly receive the president and his brother with dignity at the Joint Staff Headquarters. General Mai Hữu Xuân was given the task of picking them up. He was accompanied by Major Dương Hữu Nghĩa and Major Nguyễn Văn Nhung, Dương Văn Minh's bodyguard. Before they left, General Dương Văn Minh gave a signal to General Xuân. He raised two fingers of his right hand. It was the order to kill the two brothers.

Diệm and Nhu waited in front of the Church of Saint Francis Xavier while talking to the priest. They saw the arrival of a Jeep and an armored personnel carrier. Mai Hữu Xuân told them that he came to arrest them and opened the door of the armored vehicle. When Nhu opposed his brother's having to go into such a vehicle, their captor informed them that it was to better assure their own security.

During the drive that took them to the Joint Staff Headquarters, the two brothers were killed by several bullets and stabbings administered by Nguyễn Văn Nhung. Wanting to deny the assassination thus perpetrated, the latter would attempt to feign the suicide of the two brothers while he killed them with their hands tied behind their backs. There was consternation at Joint Staff Headquarters at their massacre.[13] Kennedy himself was upset by these deaths he had not expected.

A few days later, General Minh would have Nguyễn Văn Nhung, his henchman, executed.[14]

It was on the morning of November 2, 1963, the Day of the Dead, that Ngô Đình Diệm was assassinated along with Nhu, his favorite brother. One can only wonder at this strange coincidence, ultimately a strong sign of destiny, if one is willing to remember the patron saint that Ngô Đình Diệm had chosen when he became an oblate on February 10, 1954. This second name that he chose for himself gives to the life of the president, and to his death, a very particular dimension. Odilon! It is he who, among other remarkable works, was the initiator of this feast of the dead that is celebrated the day after All Saints' Day, on November 2. Odilon celebrated this feast for the first time on November 2, 998. Leo IX (pope from 1049 to 1054) approved this initiative, and the custom then arose throughout the Church of saying a Mass for the dead on November 2. It became universal and was integrated into the Roman liturgy in the 13th century. How can one not be struck by this intervention of providence, which seals this day of November 2, instituted by Saint Odilon, by inscribing in it the heroic death of Ngô Đình Diệm, who had chosen him as patron saint? Providence thus seems to emphasize and gratify this fidelity of the Ngô Đình family to this feast of the dead which it always marked with great solemnity without forgetting—but on the contrary by uniting it—his Cult of the Ancestors to which it was equally faithful.

Running parallel to the dismantling of the government of President Ngô Đình Diệm and the ineptitude of the junta attempting to replace it, the Communist armed forces would strive to rally the South Vietnamese to drag them into their struggle against this new colonialism hiding under American imperialism. That accusation of South Vietnam's alliance with America being a colonial relationship was a primary method by which the Việt Cộng sowed doubt about President Ngô Đình Diệm's nationalism. The alliance with the Americans was certainly more visible than that of the North Vietnamese with the Chinese Communists. Without the intervention of the Chinese Communists—and of the Russians—on North Vietnam's side, the Republic of Vietnam would certainly not have needed the Americans as much for its defense.

It was the same General Dương Văn Minh who would be called in 1975 by the Communist National Front for the Liberation of South Vietnam (NLF). It was he who sped up the departure of the Americans. He would surrender without offering any resistance when the Communists arrived in Sài Gòn and delivered the country to the invaders. A shameful end for someone who bore the principal responsibility for the treason of his chiefs, in their assassination and in the fall of his country into chaos.

On November 5, 1963, General de Gaulle, then president of the French Republic, had an interview with Charles Bohlen, the US ambassador to France. During this interview, General de Gaulle expressed his views on the events in Vietnam as follows:

> It was you who pushed President Diệm and his team, and we could not be too proud about it. And you weren't successful. I do not believe that what you are planning to do in Vietnam by way of direct intervention into that country could be successful. It is a shame for America that President Diệm and Mr. Nhu have been assassinated. Those who have replaced them will undoubtedly not have a better success. Our own experience has taught us that those who wield power by virtue of foreign intervention are doomed to fail. That failure is more certain when they are assigned the task of waging war. We will see how the situation will develop, but we do not believe at all that it will evolve favorably. My personal feeling is that it would have been wise not to get involved in the affairs of Vietnam, as it had been decided in Geneva in 1954. Obviously, this remark applies to the Communists, but it applies to you as well. I fear that you will be caught in the quagmire of a vain undertaking from which it will be more and more difficult to get out.[15]

After Ngô Đình Diệm's death, there were as many as eight successive governments in two years. Despite the full American support secured, none of these governments could demonstrate their aptitude or their authority to lead the country. Everything the Ngô-Đình had built in ten years was destroyed. All the parties and movements were shut down. The collaborators who remained loyal were killed or imprisoned. Forty-one province chiefs were replaced. Those who fought for the independence of the Republic of Vietnam were disappointed by the disorder that prevailed in their country. A great number of them came around to joining the Communists so that they could continue their fight for independence. The Communist army of the maquis would become a strong revolutionary army united in the name of the country. It would confront the arrival of new American troops, becoming larger and larger in 1964 under President Lyndon Baines Johnson.

To please the Americans and attract the favor of world opinion, the generals did not hesitate to make their appearance in nightclubs and dance the twist. It would not take long for the Vietnamese to notice this new lifestyle that was so remote from the austere government of Ngô Đình Diệm, who had tea served at official receptions instead of expensive champagne. The sober lifestyle of the president was legendary. He led a monastic existence, spending his one Christmas Day off with the troops at the front.

As for Mme. Nhu, it is said that she was one of the seven richest women in the world, with fantastic properties across the globe. A simple duty to objectivity has obliged us to recall that in exile only the income she could derive from interviews allowed her to meet the needs of her four dependent children.

After Kennedy's assassination, the Johnson administration was confronted with a resurgence of attacks by the Việt Cộng, who were thrilled by the murders of the Ngô Đình. Nguyễn Hữu Thọ, president of the National Front for Liberation, declared to the Australian journalist Wilfred Burchett that "the fall of the Ngô Đình was a gift from heaven for us."[16]

•

CHAPTER 4

Another Look

Notwithstanding what was written above, a reader who opens a book today invoking the history of the Ngô Đình will no doubt find stories limited to the "persecution of the Buddhists" or to their "dictatorial, bloodthirsty, and corrupt regime." At best, it would be said that President Ngô Đình Diệm did not respect the Geneva Accords by discarding the decisions reached there to carry out general elections throughout the country.

Concerning those totally unfounded allegations, here are some facts and logical information that can be easily verified:

With regard to the Geneva Accords of July 1954 that stipulated the division of Vietnam into two parts, recall that they were only signed by the French government and the representatives of the Democratic Republic of Vietnam (DRV), the future North Vietnam of Hồ Chí Minh. These Accords were officially denounced by the Republic of Vietnam, by the future South Vietnam of Ngô Đình Diệm, and by the United States that was party to the Conference with China, the Soviet Union, and Great Britain.

That part of the Accords dedicated to the elections that should have unified the country in 1956—and contained in the final declaration—was never signed. That part did not constitute a binding accord on the commitment of the signatories.

However, when the time came for the elections to take place, the

Republic of Vietnam immediately responded in a positive manner to the propositions of the North but asked for guarantees that the elections could be conducted under conditions of total security and transparency. Aside from newspapers published in the South, nobody in North Vietnam or in the rest of the world stated the respective positions of the two states and put the onus for not carrying out those elections on South Vietnam, whereas it was the Communist authorities who did not follow up on the propositions of the South by interrupting the discussions.

On the other hand, the continuing infiltrations and acts of terrorism led by the Việt Cộng against South Vietnam represented among the most obvious violations of the Geneva Accords. On several occasions they were even denounced by the Control Commission of the Geneva Accords, presided over by an Indian national with two participating members from Poland and Canada to show that both the Communist bloc and the Western bloc were duly represented.

The Communist objectives for hegemony were so patent that they would manifest again with the non-observance of the Paris Accords of 1973, despite the Nobel Peace Prizes lugubriously awarded to the negotiators of the Paris Peace Accords, to Henry Kissinger on the American side and to Lê Đức Thọ on the North Vietnamese side. These Accords would be once again violated by North Vietnam, which invaded the South two years later in 1975, taking advantage of the Americans being embroiled in the Watergate scandal.

As for the so-called Buddhist crisis, history has demonstrated a mystification that was largely set up against President Ngô Đình Diệm who was not fooled. Mme. Ngô Đình Nhu was quick to realize that this was only a subversive gust of wind blown from opponents of all stripes: Americans, French, Vietnamese, and Communists. Before the first self-immolation by a bonze in 1963, which the world press quickly seized upon, there had been no denunciation of any persecution whatsoever leveled at the Ngô Đình government, which had been in charge of the country since 1954.

It is still often not understood that to become a bonze, one needs to simply have one's head shaved and dress in a saffron-colored robe, without any other formality. The infiltrations were therefore easily carried out. They were practiced adroitly with pathetic results. Their authors were well aware that the images of bodies burnt alive would cause such emotion in the West that it would lose its ability to think critically.

After May 1963, the media frenzy led by some with the blindness of the others accused the "Catholic" Ngô Đình government of all sorts of crimes by concealing numbers that were indisputable: During the presidency of Ngô Đình Diệm, there had been an unprecedented development of Buddhism, with the building of 1,275 pagodas. The Xá Lợi pagoda that proved to be one of the most subversive was built with a donation of 600,000 piasters from President Ngô Đình Diệm. There were also 1,295 pagodas restored, meaning an explosive 200 percent increase in the numbers of pagodas. On the Catholic side, there was no such explosive increase but a steady increase of 30 percent in the number of churches.

Of the eighteen government ministers, only five were Catholic. Of the thirty-eight governors in the country, twelve were Catholic. Furthermore, three generals out of nineteen were Catholic. Of the 113 members of the National Assembly, 75 declared they were Buddhists. The vice president of the republic and even the governor of Huế, where the first unrests took place, were Buddhists. No full-blooded dictator would put himself in such a minority position in his own government as well as in the representation of his own government by welcoming those whom he would intend to persecute. As Ngô Đình Diệm pointed out to a journalist who queried him on the subject: "After nine years as president I must be crazy to think about persecuting [Buddhists] at a decisive moment in the war we are waging. But I am not crazy!"

The *casus belli* used as an excuse was a government circular demanding that precedence be given to the national flag over any religious emblem. To deal with an incident with worrying consequences, the president instituted a committee charged with bringing it to closure once and for all. When the committee representing the government and the Buddhists signed a "Joint Declaration" on June 16, 1963, the issue was immediately settled. The Buddhists were satisfied.

The end of this Buddhist affair blocked the subversive goals of the activist (Venerable) Thích Trí Quang. A so-called bonze but communist above all, he had created a movement called "Phật Giáo Cấp Tiến," meaning "Radical Buddhism."[1] He rallied all the opponents to his side. In Sài Gòn a very old bonze was taken out of a car, supported at the shoulders. Two "friends" who would never be seen again dragged him to the center of a city square. The appearance of this poor man who was dragged in that fashion without any reaction even at the approach of fire led people to think that he was drugged. Other immolations by fire followed. It was then that President Ngô Đình Diệm reacted by ordering the search of the pagodas where the police had observed unusual activities. There they found all kinds of weapons.

On August 28, 1963, the military governor of Sài Gòn gave a press conference with the exhibition of everything that had been seized in the pagodas: knives, guns, bombs, and even a mortar and a very imposing mass of propaganda materials: tracts, flyers, brochures, and detailed instructions to widen their hold on the masses, etc. The venerable bonze Thich Tien Hoa who was president of the National Buddhist Association, a very old Buddhist association, declared that "there was enough of an artificial agitation."[2] He invited the honest Buddhists to "recognize that they had never been persecuted." He denounced the leaders who only pursued political objectives and announced he would be in charge of the management of all the pagodas. Of the 4,000 existing pagodas, the twelve that had been closed were reopened again. In Sài Gòn, 250,000 people came out in the streets, at the appeal of the "Republican Youth," to show their support for President Ngô Đình Diệm.

In a bitter letter dated September 2, 1963, two months before his death, Ngô Đình Nhu observed to his Chartist friends the reality he had to confront:

Personal
Dear [*lady*] friend,
My apologies for giving you so much worry. I detest those journalistic hacks with their love for sensationalism and their mercantile cupidity because they deprived you of sleep. At the bottom of it all there are three times nothing more than the conspiracy of the Americans and the communists against South Vietnam, because Vietnam simply wants to be itself, and nothing else, neither americanized nor communist. Hence that Buddhist affair they have set up against us. We are obliged to settle it once and for all by breaking the circle of magic and terror they have installed in 5 pagodas out of the more than 4,000 pagodas throughout the country. In these pagodas they use all the means, including terrorism to hypnotize certain minds, aiming at throwing them to the fire after alerting the American television networks which pay a good price for this unique spectacle of the twentieth century. Since the state of siege, that is August 20 until now, there have not been any more suicides by monks. [underlines in original] It is the proof that, once liberated from the secret Americano-Soviet organization (terrorism, drugging etc. . . .), the monks can resume their normal life: the affair is closed. However, the conspirators, thwarted in their plans to install at the head of the country another Bao Dai, wanted to create a student movement as in Korea or in Turkey but we have smothered them in their eggs. All these so-called students were placed in a military training camp, which they got out of after two days to get home, completely rehabilitated. They had been manipulated by Americano-Soviet propaganda and terrorized by secret gangs. We know they have put 20 million dollars into this affair. They did not leave us alone because they must justify these enormous expenses to their chiefs. They must have put a lot in their own pockets, and now they are afraid for their skins.

I am telling you all this neither to drug you up nor to appease you but because I want to talk to you as so loyal and sensitive a friend, in all sincerity. If my poor country was not in grave danger, I would

> drop everything, if only not to cause you heart attacks because of me.
>
> This is all to say how much I am touched by your affectionate friendship, and also how much in the grave dangers I encounter at each instant your thought is for me a consolation and a precious encouragement. I am not making fun of the prayer you sent me. I will always wear it on me, not out of superstition, but because it represents the presence of your thought in me amidst the dangers that you have harshly experienced yourself when you were in the Resistance.
>
> Your Ngô Đình[3]

The ad hoc United Nations commission, in charge of the investigation into the Buddhist affair at the urgent request of President Ngô Đình Diệm, conducted its work from October 24 to November 3, 1963. It registered 116 testimonies and interviewed seven government representatives and forty-seven witnesses, of which there were four bonzes who were supposed to have perished by fire according to denunciations received by the Commission.

As presidential adviser, Ngô Đình Nhu had declared to that same commission, "The government has no interest whatsoever in imprisoning people when national security is not at stake. Of the more than 200 monks who were kept under surveillance, only some 10 of them were imprisoned for subversive activities after being tried by a regular court."

The Commission reached the conclusion that in fact there were no persecutions against Buddhists. On December 7, 1963, the Commission consigned to the United Nations' General Assembly its 234-page report, but the United Nations did not publish these conclusions.

Below is a passage written by Fernando Volio Jiménez, a Costa Rican member of the Commission:

> The accusations leveled by the United Nations' General Assembly against the Diem government have not stood up to an objective inquiry. There have been neither discriminations nor religious

> persecutions. . . . There is no other way to judge the facts. The frictions between a small fraction and not of the totality of the Buddhist community against the Diem regime were exclusively of a political nature. The majority of the Commission concurs with me.[4]

The UN Commission included delegates from Afghanistan, Brazil, Ceylon (now Sri Lanka), Costa Rica, Dahomey (now Benin), Morocco, and Nepal. Its conclusions were part of the United Nations Archives. In February 1964, this report, which had been put under wraps, was discovered and published by the Senate Subcommittee on Security. There has been almost no trace in the media and in history books of this important work that has never been referred to except by Mr. Trương Vĩnh Lễ or by other reporters more concerned with the truth such as Suzanne Labin or that famous journalist Marguerite Higgins who deserved the Pulitzer Prize for her eminent professional qualities.[5] The professors John Norton Moore and Robert F. Turner of the University of Virginia School of Law also quoted the testimony of the Costa Rican member of the UN Commission in [one of their books].[6]

Mrs. Higgins had visited Vietnam ten times, through diverse missions in the most remote provinces. In her book *Our Vietnam Nightmares*, she noted her observations and analyses on the purported arrests and detention of the Buddhists.[7] "Nobody would believe you," Trí Quang predicted to Higgins, when she was blaming him for the series of Machiavellian actions that had nothing to do with the Buddhist philosophy. She did not hesitate to denounce the subversive and destabilizing works of the false bonze, Trí Quang, whose connections with the Việt Cộng were discovered much later.[8] Ambassador [Henry Cabot] Lodge granted him political asylum in the fall of 1963 to protect him from the well-founded accusation of "incitation to suicide."

It is worth emphasizing that it was the same American embassy which, after the coup d'état of November 2, 1963, that had cost the lives of President Ngô Đình Diệm and his brother, refused to give political asylum to their younger brother Ngô Đình Cẩn. In charge of the care of his aging mother in Huế, Cẩn found refuge with the Canadian Redemptorists of whom he was a benefactor. In order to provide him the guarantee of a better protection, they called upon the American Consulate in Huế which contacted the American Embassy in Sài Gòn. The latter declared it would guarantee the security of Cẩn upon his arrival in Sài Gòn. When he got off the plane, Cẩn was handed over to the rebels. With no more public function and being gravely ill, Cẩn was shot on May 9, 1964, without being able to defend himself, on the explicit request of Trí Quang. Protected by the Americans, thus becoming untouchable, this false bonze exerted a baneful influence before his true intentions were alas too belatedly foiled.

As could be predicted, the media gave a wide amplification to an expression used by Mme. Nhu when she referred to the "barbeque" of monks. It is worth emphasizing that the expression was the same one used by some American photographers among themselves, looking for a scoop when they casually addressed the so-called chief monk, to ask where and how the next "barbeque" would take place.[9] It is important to note that the journalists were informed of these events sufficiently in advance to have the time to position their cameras and do their work. Moreover, to make sure that this atrocious event would be filmed to the end and in the best conditions, accomplices of the so-called bonzes formed a crowd to prevent any intervention by the emergency services and the police.

In the five weeks that followed the coup of November 1, there were as many as six attempts at self-immolation by the so-called bonzes but this was no longer of interest to anybody, and the media did not talk about it. All this really pointed to an obviously scandalous manipulation of the media.

•

[President Lyndon] Johnson, who was opposed until the last minute to the recommended coup d'état supported by the other wing of the

Kennedy administration, inherited the situation and committed to it all the military means available to him.

In 1968, there would be 536,000 American soldiers in Vietnam. The general mobilization ordered in the South of Vietnam would raise to 820,000 men the strength of the Vietnamese army. In 1970, it went up to 986,000.

[Richard] Nixon, who was elected in November 1968 to the presidency of the United States, assumed his functions in January 1969. He was seeking to obtain peace. On January 23, 1973, the Paris Accords were signed, and a ceasefire was established. More than 55,000 American soldiers would be dead by the time the Communists seized power.

It was under the pretext of winning the war more speedily that the coup d'état against the two Ngô Đình brothers was engineered. From that fatal date of November 1963 to July 2, 1976, thirteen years elapsed in a war becoming more and more murderous that did not serve any other purpose than to totally destroy a country and cost thousands and thousands of human lives.

Everybody remembers the image of that ambassador, perched on the roof of the embassy, a rolled American flag under his arm, hurrying to climb into the last helicopter. "What good is this American military might, if it's only to run away with it?" Mme. Nhu pointed out during an interview with NBC News in New York, the day after April 30, 1975.

A few days earlier, on April 17, 1975, the Khmer Rouge came into Phnom Penh, in Cambodia.

On April 30, 1975, the Việt Cộng penetrated into Sài Gòn.

On November 29, 1975, the People's Democratic Republic of Laos was proclaimed, and King Sisavang Vatthana abdicated.

July 2, 1976, marked the official reunification of Vietnam. The Socialist Republic of Vietnam (SRV) was founded.

In 1976, former Indochina in its entirety came under the control of the Communists.

•

In light of these indisputable facts, how can one explain the campaign of lies and slander that was directed against the Ngô Đình brothers and the thick silence that has settled in since then and continues to hide the truth?

Innumerable proofs have established that the silence had been imposed. It appears to us that the following is of particular significance: In June 1964, Mme. Ngô Đình Nhu and her daughter Lệ Thủy, who was almost nineteen, were invited to come to the United States for a press tour, the Truth Rally. These public opinion groups would have liked to have access to a different version of the facts than what was officially advertised. The year 1964 was the election year for a successor to President Kennedy.

Citing "reasons of national security," the American authorities refused to give entry visas to Mme. Ngô Đình Nhu and her daughter. Both were thus prevented from coming to the United States. They could not respond to the legitimate desire of those opinion groups who wanted to inquire for themselves.

Surely more perplexing is the danger the arrival of these two women on the territory of the most powerful nation in the world could cause to its security. Since that is impossible to believe, what remained tangible is a well-imposed silence.

This was also the case regarding the "Special Issue" on Vietnam in 1985 published by various press agencies ten years after the Communist takeover.

Magazines as prestigious as *Newsweek* have refrained from making public the only enlightening interview that Mme. Nhu had accorded them. On the other hand, these magazines would publish a plethora of articles, including those written by personalities that had nothing to do with Vietnam.

•

Terrorism has manifested itself in the West during these last decades. Nobody dared to challenge the right of governments that were facing this violence to conduct interrogations and searches necessary to the security of their populations, not even the right to meticulous searches at airports. And yet nobody can allow themselves to consider these governments as police states or dictatorships.

The Ngô Đình government was not entitled to the same understanding.

The press, like intellectuals and politicians of all stripes, imbued with self-importance and ideological pretensions, pontificated on the necessity of Vietnam opening to democracy, whilst being confronted with a subversive war using terrorist means.

Millions of youths protested this war they did not understand at all. Many sided naively with the little Vietnamese people embodied by the old uncle Hồ against the American Goliath.

If there had not been the sacrifice of those millions of boat people, toward the end of the 1970s and the beginning of the 1980s, jumping into the sea to flee a Communist regime of terror, perhaps the myth of the Việt Cộng liberator and nationalist would still survive until today.

When Communists seized South Vietnam, they would sow desolation, burn schools, massacre professors and doctors, blow up bridges, destroy roads, and take the country to years of backwardness. The West and the media would cover up the violence, destruction, and massacres with silence until the poignant drama surfaced of the thousands and thousands of Vietnamese who jumped into the sea.

The Ngô Đình brothers had lived through their Gethsemane on the night of November 1 going into November 2, 1963. They knew how to respond to events and betrayal by a testimony of their virtues as men of government and as Christians.

The dead cannot be brought back to life, but at least they are owed Justice and Truth in facing the facts of reality. To persist in not doing so is to end up having to share the responsibility with those who caused their death and the disaster in Vietnam.

It was a moral complicity the world and even the Church can no longer afford.

•

APPENDIX 1

Madame Ngô Đình Nhu's Prophetic Vision[1]

To convince me of the necessity to write my memoirs, I had to go through what I was authorized from Above through an amazing vision. I am reporting it here as I have received it because it is lighting the path that was mine and that I would not have been capable of explaining with my only means:

One day I saw myself on a road, my Beloved Savior and Master by my side, in a setting I had never seen before even as an image.

The road was very dry, under a summer sun, in a deserted landscape where no note of color, of flower, of leaves even, could be found, as everything had the color of dry sand. As usual both of us were alone.

The predestined "very little one" that I am was only a presence, nothing precise. Tranquil and quiet he walked next to his Master, so carefree as to seem hardly to have existed. The landscape remained completely deserted as they were marching this way together for a good while, so it appeared.

No plant, no flower, no leaves. There was nobody and no indication that any presence whatsoever could materialize in this desolate place. The curious thing, however, was that they arrived at a gigantic banyan tree, like nobody has ever seen before. Although its visible roots were arranged in compartments void of any life, nothing appeared to be totally desolate. The pair just stood in front of this banyan tree by the roadside.

The predestined "very little one," a simple evanescent presence barely defined next to his Master, was looking, like Him, at a vehicle arriving quietly. It was the kind of vehicle never seen before anywhere. The undercarriage seemed to be made of robust wood; it rested on six strong wheels that correspond to that means of locomotion called automobiles. Nobody was driving it. It rolled by itself noiselessly and stopped in front of the two hikers who seemed to be expecting it. The front door to the left of the (absent) driver opened. The predestined "very little one" slipped behind the empty driver's seat. The car started abruptly again, driverless as before.

The little passenger who did not expect to be alone on board leaned out of the open window behind the invisible driver. Of course, only his bust made it through and he was facing the Lord, still at the same place, motionless. He just raised the Eucharist to the level of the face of the "very little one" who did not understand it that way. His presence carefree as usual until now, evanescent even, suddenly revealed himself to be nothing less than that of a woman, myself in flesh and blood. Pitifully panicking. Oh, how much!

Then suddenly nothing was to be seen anymore.

Instead of that evanescent presence that was mine next to my Lord since the beginning of my journey, so special, I found myself this time by His side but in myself.

Was it what I had to understand of the Eucharist that was leveled at my eyes by my gentle Master and Savior to bring me back to myself and bring me into existence?

Incidentally, this had happened to me before in front of Him, to discover myself under different aspects, be it as a simple three- or four-year-old child, playing alone and quietly under His tender gaze in that very room I now occupy.

The driverless car continued on its way.

I did not see myself with half of my body outside the window, but quietly sitting instead on a long bench behind the always absent driver. I was just next to the door with the upper glass portion, next to the Lord, on His right. I was holding tightly against me on my lap one of those thick cushions made of royal blue satin, embroidered with Vietnamese motifs. That cushion so characteristic of Vietnam was the unique identifying element amidst the anonymity of all the rest.

To me it meant the divine support of our country.

And there! Marvel of Marvels, that cushion was nothing less than the pillow on which was resting the head of my Gentle Savior with His eyes closed. He was relaxing, all stretched on the little wooden bench. He had thus allowed me to be present at His side. Stretched on the bench He rested his Holy Head on the pillow I was holding between my arms. And I with my left arm to wrap around his Divine bust resting on my lap. It was a moment of absolute contemplation, so close to the Holy Face, lovingly surrounded by the arms of a mere mortal, my right one around the comfortable pillow, my left one delicately wrapping around the chest of my Beloved Savior. That lasted all the time I was granted.

Being a woman of Vietnam, I did not refrain from showing my tenderness in that natural way of mommies for their cherished babies without being interrupted by anything during this whole period of ecstatic contemplation I was allowed. I did not refrain from tenderly embracing the Holy face in the manner of moms in their homes. What a delight then to be able, with my eyes half-closed, to smell each part of the Holy Face with His eyes closed out of fatigue. It is an ecstatic pleasure that those who ignore the Vietnamese kiss cannot know. Did Saint Mary Magdalene know it when she felt amorously carried toward her Divine Lord? In this regard, it's time to rectify this common error that represents Mary Magdalene as a "prostitute." She was the very spoiled daughter of an old family of great renown, and had lived her life as she well pleased, in the style of liberated women of the present time. This reinstatement of the truth is presented to us by Maria Valtorta in her ten books that His Holiness Pie [Pius] XII justly considers a masterpiece. The man-woman relationships from which sexual contact is banned cannot be more than what they are. The possible frustration that could result from it is, on the contrary, unknown in the expansion of love when it can be expressed by the Vietnamese kiss like a mother for her child, for as long as it is allowed. But it seems that the adult has never thought about this exchange that comes only naturally from the ecstasy of the mother in the presence of her most cherished child. She indulges delectably and wholeheartedly in the pleasure of smelling as soon as she can. That is to say this Vietnamese privilege even toward the Lord during this time of adoration that I was allowed for Him in His heavenly divine love. Divine right no woman would refrain from since she is used to this expression of love so appropriate for Vietnam. The predestined "very little one" could only connect his march, his path to his encounter-adoration with Him, being held by the hand of his Master Savior. We cannot then wonder about the performance of a being when he is so fulfilled and how he has come to not wanting anything else.

Hence the intuitive power accorded from High above on the intangible, a gift granted by the Lord to whomever seeks Him as He lets Himself be found.

This is how the adoration toward her Master permitted to the predestined "very little one" of the Lord, who is only a typical traditional woman of Vietnam, was revealed. Wrapping with my right arm the Divine Head at rest, eyes closed, on the thick pillow placed in my arms, I was thus indulging delectably, in the ecstasy to smell, touch by small touches each part of the Divine Face without missing anything.

To my knowledge, it was the very first time that such an expansive fondness was permitted by the Lord. He let Himself relax in the arms of His predestined "very little one."

And He, for the same first time, lowered His height toward this toddler to give him the Vietnamese kiss in the hollow of the neck. As if the strength of the first surrender held all the others.

This amazed tenderness which allowed the predestined "very little one" to express himself thus to his Lord is to be noted as a privilege which allows me, of course, to make it known and so to confirm the imminent miraculous return of the Lord to Vietnam itself.

This imminent return has been announced since 1988 by the Schools of Divine Radiance that He aroused in the world from Switzerland.[2]

Hence this great expectation where Vietnam counts. I cannot but say it more clearly.

All that the predestined "very little one" has endured since his birth authorizes him, in the name of the merciful love of his Divine Master, to appeal to Him, to settle everything in the brevity of the shared time, just by enlightening others on what it takes. What in fact is Almighty Mercy if it does not make people understand, in the brevity of the allotted time, what simple Justice is satisfied with? Why pay a high price for what can be had at the lowest price thanks to the Almighty Loving Power of the Lord?

How would I have come to the endless love for my Sweet Savior if He hadn't gotten everything from me by making me understand first at the lowest price? It could be objected to me that in the end He only got everything from me after he did make me pay at the highest price! But for what other reason than that it was only at this overwhelming price that my intelligence opened up.

The rules of the Game are not changed, nevertheless.

•

APPENDIX 2

The Church and Viet Nam

An additional note is in order regarding the relationships that were woven between Vietnam and the Church that date back almost seven centuries. It was around 1320 that the Franciscan brother, Odorico, native of Pordenone, Italy, was sent as missionary to the East, from India to China via Vietnam.

In the following centuries, Dominicans and Jesuits went in their turn to these distant lands. In 1582, Father Matteo Ricci, founder of the Jesuit missions in China, arrived in Asia. He was passionate about the culture and civilization of the countries through which he traveled. Very quickly, he understood that the Christian religion must consider certain transcendent practices deeply ingrained in the Confucian rites.

Thus, Father Ricci left to all those who decided to follow the path of Christ the choice to use their own terminology. They could, therefore, invoke God using their usual terms like "The Sovereign from Above" or "Heaven." The Jesuit also discerned that the rite of the "Worship of the Ancestors" practiced in Asia has nothing to do with any idolatry but is, on the contrary, a manifestation of filial love and of the legitimate respect that we owe to our ancestors. Respect and love that the Church itself practices when celebrating the feast of the dead which follows the great feast of All Saints' Day of November 1.

The Jesuits in Beijing received permission to celebrate the Mass in Chinese. They published a missal in Chinese. Christianity was developing in Asia because the Orientals found, in that loving transcendence to which Christ calls all men, many truths which they themselves had sensed. Father Ricci died in 1610 and his apostolate was continued by his Jesuit successors.

Alexander de Rhodes, also a Jesuit, arrived in Cochinchina in 1625. He stayed there for a while then went up to Tonkin and settled in China in 1630. He remained there for ten years before returning to Cochinchina. An edict compelled missionaries to leave. Some twelve thousand Christians remained without priests. A few months later, Alexander de Rhodes returned to Tourane. Thanks to the tolerance of the Prince of Huế, he was allowed to stay two years in the country before being expelled in 1645. Coming from Provence, a man of great culture, gifted for languages, he learned Vietnamese and spoke it perfectly. In 1651, he published a first catechism as well as a dictionary in Quốc Ngữ, that is to say the Vietnamese language written with Roman characters. Vietnam is the only country in [East] Asia whose language can be written with Roman characters. Its traditional characters will remain in use in literate circles familiar with the arts of calligraphy.

The hostility that Asia had begun to show towards Christianity, and which earned Alexander de Rhodes his expulsion from Vietnam, was attributable to the influence of the Franciscan, Dominican, and Augustinian orders who were unanimous in condemning the cultural tolerance of the Jesuits with regard to certain Confucian rites including those linked to the Cult of the Ancestors. This disastrous incomprehension would reflect on Pope Innocent X. On December 12, 1645, the head of the Church issued a pontifical decree that equated the Confucian rites to superstitious practices and condemned them. The Pope, who never traveled as far as Asia, had no way to question what these returning missionaries told him and who sent him this pressing information.

The Jesuits could not bring themselves to accept this decree founded on an erroneous approach to Confucian rites.

They dispatched one of their own, Father Martini, to the Pope to shed more light on the nature of these rites misinterpreted by other missionary orders. In 1656, Father Martini obtained from the new Pope, Alexander VII, another decree which tolerated the homage to Confucius as a "purely civilian and political worship." Three years later, in 1659, the Pope went even further when he gave his instructions to François Pallu and Pierre Lambert de la Motte, founders of the Society of Paris Foreign Missions. He advised them as follows:

> Never press, do not in any way persuade these people to change their rites, their customs, their manners, unless they are obviously contrary to religion and morality. What could be more absurd than transporting France, Spain, Italy or some other countries of Europe to the Chinese? Do not introduce our countries to them, but faith, this faith which does not reject or injure the rites or the customs of any people, provided that they are not hateful but, on the contrary, wants us to keep them and protect them. . . . So never put the uses of these peoples in parallel with those from Europe; on the contrary, hurry up there to get used to them.[1]

Things were thus put back to their order as they should be, and evangelization could resume in Vietnam.

In 1668, the first ordinations of indigenous priests took place.

Jesuit Father Dominique Parrenin left for China accompanied by a group of six religious, mathematicians and astronomers that the Emperor of China had requested from Louis XIV. They arrived in Canton in 1699. In 1701, he consecrated a treatise to the study and analysis of the "Cult of the Ancestors." There he developed the concept of familial piety which permeates this cult.

In 1693, contrary to the prescriptions of Pope Alexander VII, Msgr. Maigrot, apostolic vicar at Fụjien (province in the southeastern part of China, located opposite the island of Taiwan) took it upon himself to ban Confucian rites.

In 1704, under his influence, Clement XI walked back on the open-minded spirit that had been manifested and recorded by decree fifty years earlier. He again condemned the evangelistic methods of the Jesuits. The papal legate, Thomas de Tournon, who was sent there accumulated so many blunders that he was expelled by Emperor Jiangsi. Annoyed, he obtained a new papal condemnation of Chinese rites; it would be the papal bull "Ex Illa Die" of March 19, 1715.

The emperor, outraged, banned the preaching of Christianity and expelled all missionaries except the Jesuits, who would ultimately have to give in to the Vatican when Benedict XIV pronounced the "Ex Quo Singulari Providentia" bull on July 11, 1742.

A strong brake will weigh on the expansion of Christianity and, worst of all, the persecutions would begin. They were terrible.

Then came a very amazing story that would unite France and Vietnam through the Church.

A priest, Pierre Pigneau de Béhaine, bishop of Adran, arrived in Cochinchina in 1774. He met the young Nguyễn Ánh who was grappling with a tragic situation. Nephew of Emperor Dụ Tông, he was twelve years old when three brothers of the village of Tây-Sơn put themselves at the head of a large number of rebels, attacked the authorities, and killed his uncle and all the contenders for the throne. Miraculously, Nguyễn Ánh was the only one to have escaped the massacre. Forced to hide, he took refuge in Siam. Touched both by the distress and the qualities he sensed in this young man, the bishop of Adran intervened to obtain his support from France so that he could regain his kingdom.

By the Treaty of Versailles, signed on November 28, 1787, King Louis XVI agreed to help Nguyễn Ánh. In exchange, France received the promise of a commercial monopoly in Cochinchina. With three armed vessels as well as support from military and technical advisers, Nguyễn Ánh managed to recover in 1788. The following year the French Revolution broke out. While the King of France could no longer act, some French nobles maintained their support for the young Vietnamese chief. He triumphed over the Trịnh dynasty and that of the Lê.

Victorious, he entered Huế, which he chose as capital in 1801. He imposed his authority in Tonkin. His power extended to Cambodia and Laos under French protectorate.

Nguyễn Ánh achieved the union of north and south Vietnam which had been separated for sixty years. The Vietnamese kingdom was now made up of Cochinchina, Annam, and Tonkin.

This was a huge event. In 1802, he became the emperor of all Vietnam under the name of Gia Long. The French nobles who helped him in his work of reconquest received the title of senior Vietnamese mandarins.

Undeniably, there has been a happy alliance between Vietnam, the Church, and France. Gia Long ended the persecutions by issuing edicts of tolerance such as this one:

> Catholics are as citizens of greater Viet-Nam like our other subjects. Forcing them to practice a religion contrary to their belief would be a mistake of great injustice. For me, it would be displeasing to our Heavenly Father to violate that spirit of fairness that he instilled in me.

The bishop of Adran died in Sài Gòn on October 9, 1799, at the age of fifty-eight. Emperor Gia Long died in 1820. His son Minh Mạng closed the country to strangers and began to persecute Christians for "destabilizing" the old order. In January 1833, he issued an edict of persecution and ordered his mandarins to force the Christians of their territory to renounce their belief and raze their places of worship.

Thiệu Trị succeeded his father in 1841; there was a lull because he feared a French intervention in favor of the Christians.

Tự Đức succeeded him in 1847, and the first twelve years of his reign were a period of intense persecution because the emperor wanted to have not only political but also moral and spiritual unity for his empire.

According to the sources of the Foreign Missions of Paris, ninety thousand Christians suffered for their faith in the Empire of Vietnam during the nineteenth century. Most were lay people, men, women, and children. Not all of them died at hangmen's hands, but many of them were excruciatingly martyred. Emperor Tự Đức created the torment of one hundred wounds: the executioner tore one hundred pieces of flesh from the Christians who were still alive; it was a terrible sight. People from entire Christian villages were deported to unsanitary regions.

In order to aid the massacred Christians, France sent an army in 1862. It invoked the treaty of 1787 to justify its intervention on the "protectorate" that it considered to have on Cochinchina by the trading posts it had established there. The intervention was received without enthusiasm by Christians and missionaries. This was the start of French colonization. Europe's era of colonial expansion was in full swing.

Besides the business carried out with respect to the interests of any given body, each one pursues his material and spiritual life in accordance with the education received and the surrounding environment. The Vietnamese Catholic Church experienced her own growth. In 1933, Pope Pius XI consecrated the first bishop of Viet-Nam, Msgr. Nguyễn Bá Tòng.

He then addressed these prophetic words to the new bishop: "Go back to Vietnam, your country. Continue the missionary apostolate, because Vietnam has a great vocation and a great mission: it is the eldest daughter of the Church in the Far East."[2]

On December 8, 1939, at the celebration of the Immaculate Conception, Pope Pius XII decreed that the Christians of Asia be allowed to practice their ancestral rites.

Not quite ten years later, on October 1, 1949, Mao Zedong proclaimed the People's Republic of China in Beijing. It was the triumph of communism. Soon all cults, whether Confucian or Christian, were prohibited.

On June 19, 1988, Pope John Paul II proclaimed to be saints 117 Christians who were martyred in Vietnam. Among them were 96 Vietnamese priests and lay people, 11 Spanish Dominicans, and 10 French priests from the Foreign Missions of Paris.

If there were greedy colonialists with un-Christian behavior, there were also beautiful figures and consecrated souls from the West who gave the best of themselves to Vietnam. We think here of Jean Cassaigne, also called "the leper bishop." He was born in France on January 30, 1895, in Grenada on Adour, in the Landes, and died on October 31, 1973, at the Di Linh leper colony (formerly called Djiring) in the high plateaus in the northeast of Sài Gòn, where the mountain people lived. Jean Cassaigne, after being sent as missionary to the mountains in January 1927, had received against his will the order to assume the office of bishop of Sài Gòn in June 1941. Affected by leprosy, which he had treated for so long among the Montagnards, he chose to die at the leper colony of Djiring with this mountain population who had welcomed him from the start of his mission and whom he cared deeply about. The Holy See appointed Msgr. Hiền to be his successor in Sài Gòn in November 1955.

Another endearing figure of the Christian faith is embodied by the young Joachim Nguyễn Tấn Văn, also known as Marcel Văn, who died on July 10, 1959, at the age of 31 in a communist reeducation camp in the north of the country. Sainte Thérèse of the Child Jesus, to whom he had entrusted his spiritual life, gave him the mission to continue, with her, to embody the love of Christ in Vietnam. She loved this country. Her monastic order had planned to send her to the Convent of Carmel in Hà Nội, but her too fragile health forced her to give it up. Despite his hatred of the French, Marcel Văn learned with Sainte Thérèse to pray for them so that the friendship rediscovered between the two peoples might bring about unity between East and West. In 1925, Pope Pius XI, in canonizing Sainte Thérèse, proclaimed her patron Saint of Missions along with Saint Francis Xavier.

Shortly before dying, Marcel Văn left one last message: "And here is now the last word that I leave to souls: I leave them my love and with this love, however small, I hope to satisfy the souls who want to become very little to come to Jesus. This is one thing I would like to describe but with my little talent, words fail me to do so."

Văn's cause for beatification was introduced on March 26, 1997, in the diocese of Belley-Ars, as Confessor of the Faith.

John Paul II again manifested his warm support to the Church of Vietnam on the eve of the 200th anniversary of the apparitions of the Virgin Mary in La Vang. On December 16, 1997, he wrote to Cardinal Paul Joseph Phạm Đình Tùng, Archbishop of Hà Nội and President of the Episcopal Conference of Vietnam:

> At the beginning of the jubilee celebrations for the 200th anniversary of the Virgin Mary's apparitions in La Vang, I warmly join in the joy and thanksgiving of the Bishops of Viêt-Nam and the members of their Dioceses.
>
> In this shrine, so dear to the heart of Catholics in your country, it is a message of hope among spiritual and physical tribulations which the Mother of the Lord gave to her children in 1798, announcing to them: "Have trust, be willing to suffer hardship and sorrow. I have already granted your prayers. Henceforth all those who come to pray to me in this spot will see their wishes fulfilled." For two centuries this message, still current, has been fervently welcomed in La Vang. Despite the great trials which have marked it in the course of its history, it has now become a national Marian centre which has been able to keep alive the tradition of pilgrimages. Many people, of all origins and all conditions, come here privately to entrust their troubles and hopes to their Mother in heaven. Bishops, priests, religious and lay people like to find in her the welcoming presence of the One who gives them the courage to bear an admirable witness of Christian life in circumstances that are often difficult. I bless God who never abandons the people who seek him and who, with the motherly assistance of the Virgin Mary, continues to guide them, in days of happiness and of adversity.
>
> I hope that the faithful who will come to pray to Our Lady of La Vang at her shrine during this jubilee year and those who will invoke her in other places will find a new apostolic impetus

for their Christian life and receive comfort and strength, to face life's trials. I invite them to see in Mary the Mother Jesus himself gave to men, who leads them towards her divine Son. Having lived her condition as a disciple of the Lord perfectly, she calls Christians to progress on the path of a fervent life in accordance with the Gospel. May she make them pilgrims of steadfast faith in the person of Christ, the one Saviour of humanity, pilgrims of hope, waiting anxiously for the hour of God, for the harvest of the seed already scattered on the ground, pilgrims of charity living their vocation of unity, fraternity, and service amidst their brothers and sisters whose life they share!

Now that we have entered the second preparatory year for the Great Jubilee of the Year 2000, dedicated to the Holy Spirit, I urge the Catholics of Viêt-Nam to contemplate in Mary a humble human woman who allowed herself to be led by the inner action of the Spirit. In intense and deep union with God, she obeyed his call with total fidelity. May everyone discover in her a woman of silence and attentiveness, who cherished in her heart the loving presence and sanctifying action of the Lord's Spirit which he enabled her to perceive! Never letting difficulties discourage her, she gave full expression to the longing of the Lord's poor, a radiant model for those who put all their trust in God's promises.

As in my heart and in my prayer I join the many pilgrims of La Vang, I ardently invoke the Mother of Christ, the Mother of men, for the entire people of Viêt-Nam and for the Christian communities, originally from here, who now live abroad. May they put their trust in the Virgin most holy who maternally accompanies them on their earthly pilgrimage! Wherever they live, may they be faithful and generous disciples of Christ, witnessing to God's infinite love amidst their brothers and sisters!

On this happy occasion of the second centenary of the apparitions of the Blessed Virgin, I send you, Your Eminence, my affectionate Apostolic Blessing which I willingly extend to the Bishops, to the priests, and to those preparing for the priesthood, to the religious and to all the faithful of Viêt-Nam and the diaspora.

IOANNES PAULUS PP. II

On August 15, 2012, on the solemnity of the celebration of the Assumption of the Virgin Mary, the president of the Episcopal Conference of Vietnam, Msgr. Pierre Nguyễn Văn Nhơn, the representative of the Holy See in Vietnam, Msgr. Leopoldo Girelli, the archbishop of the place, Bishop Etienne Nguyễn Như Thế, in the presence of sixteen bishops, of a hundred priests and more than 200,000 pilgrims, went to Notre Dame de La Vang.

They posed the twenty-seven first stones of the construction of the future basilica in replacement of the previous war-ravaged one. These stones symbolize the twenty-six Vietnamese dioceses. The twenty-seventh stone represents the participation of the entire Catholic Vietnamese diaspora in the world.

It was in La Vang, at the height of the persecution against Catholics, that Our Lady had appeared in 1798, to protect the Christians who had taken refuge there in their flight. For over one hundred years, the Vietnamese have been coming there in pilgrimage.

Jacqueline Willemetz

APPENDIX 3

Statement by Senator Thomas Dodd addressed to the Subcommittee to Investigate the Administration of the Internal Security Act and Other Internal Security Laws of the Committee on the Judiciary, United States Senate, United States (1964)

[COMMITTEE PRINT]

88TH CONGRESS 2d Session } SENATE

REPORT OF UNITED NATIONS FACT-FINDING MISSION TO SOUTH VIET-NAM

PUBLISHED BY THE SUBCOMMITTEE
TO INVESTIGATE THE ADMINISTRATION OF THE
INTERNAL SECURITY ACT AND OTHER
INTERNAL SECURITY LAWS

OF THE

COMMITTEE ON THE JUDICIARY
UNITED STATES SENATE

Printed for the use of the Committee on the Judiciary

U.S. GOVERNMENT PRINTING OFFICE
27-440 O WASHINGTON : 1964

COMMITTEE ON THE JUDICI...

JAMES O. EASTLAND, ...ssissippi, *Chairman*

OLIN D. JOHNSTON, South Caro... a
JOHN L. McCLELLAN, Arkansas
SAM J. ERVIN, Jr., North Carolin
THOMAS J. DODD, Connecticut
PHILIP A. HART, Michigan
EDWARD V. LONG, Missouri
EDWARD M. KENNEDY, Massachusetts
BIRCH E. BAYH, Indiana
QUENTIN N. BURDICK, North Dakota
...RETT McKINLEY DIRKSEN, Illinois
...MAN L. HRUSKA, Nebraska
...NNETH B. KEATING, New York
...IRAM L. FONG, Hawaii
HUGH SCOTT, Pennsylvania

SUBCOMMITTEE TO INVESTIGATE THE ADMINISTRATION OF THE INTERNAL SECURITY ACT AND OTHER INTERNAL SECURITY LAWS

JAMES O. EASTLAND, Mississippi, *Chairman*
THOMAS J. DODD, Connecticut, *Vice Chairman*

OLIN D. JOHNSTON, South Carolina
JOHN L. McCLELLAN, Arkansas
SAM J. ERVIN, Jr., North Carolina
ROMAN L. HRUSKA, Nebraska
EVERETT McKINLEY DIRKSEN, Illinois
KENNETH B. KEATING, New York
HUGH SCOTT, Pennsylvania

J. G. SOURWINE, *Counsel*
BENJAMIN MANDEL, *Director of Research*

II

U.S. SENATE,
COMMITTEE ON THE JUDICIARY,
FEBRUARY 17, 1964.

Hon. JAMES O. EASTLAND,
Chairman, Senate Subcommittee on Internal Security,
Washington, D.C.

DEAR MR. CHAIRMAN: In early September of last year, at the height of the Buddhist crisis, 16 governments filed a statement with the U.N. Secretary General charging that the Vietnamese Government had been guilty of a "serious violation of human rights." In response, the government of President Diem had invited the United Nations to send over a factfinding mission, and had pledged itself to give this mission its complete cooperation. The General Assembly decided to accept this invitation and on October 11 a factfinding mission was set up consisting of the representatives of Afghanistan, Brazil, Costa Rica, Dahomey, Morocco, Ceylon, and Nepal.

The Mission's report on Viet-Nam, although it was published within the U.N. on December 9, was given only a limited press distribution. In fact, it was virtually ignored by the press for more than 2 weeks after its release date until some enterprising commentators got hold of the story.

I consider this report to be of such significance that I wish to propose that the Senate Subcommittee on Internal Security publish it for the information of Senators.

While it is primarily a factual report, consisting of testimony and documents, without a formal finding by the U.N. committee, I believe that any objective person would have to conclude from reading it that the accounts of massive persecution of the Buddhist religion were, at the best, vastly exaggerated, at the worst, a sordid propaganda fraud.

I wish to call attention in this connection to an interview granted to the NCWC News Agency on December 20 by Ambassador Fernando Volio Jimenez, of Costa Rica, who introduced the motion calling for the setting up of the U.N. Mission and who served as a member of it. Let me quote his words directly:

"It is my personal feeling that there was no policy of discrimination, oppression, or persecution against the Buddhist on the basis of religion. Testimony to this effect was usually hearsay, and was expressed in vague or general terms.

"When a witness tried to give some concrete proof to the Mission, the incident he cited came down to individual or personal actions. On the basis of the evidence, there was not a governmental policy against the Buddhists on religious grounds."

Having read the U.N. report myself, I was moved by these statements to call Ambassador Volio for the purpose of discussing his impressions in more detail.

Ambassador Volio told me that, based on the stories that had appeared in the world press, he had been prepared to vote for the

v

Higgins quoted Thich Tri Quang as telling her: "We cannot get an arrangement with the north until we get rid of Diem and Nhu."

Although the majority of the Buddhist demonstrators almost certainly did not realize this, this is what the Buddhist agitation was all about.

There is an issue involved in the publication of this report that ties in directly with the matter of internal security.

The American press has a proud tradition of thoroughness and of objectivity. Indeed, there is probably no country in the world where the conscientious journalist is so honored or where the competition between journalists is so keen for national awards. But there have, regrettably, been a number of situations involving vital foreign policy issues where the American people, Congress, and even the administration have been misled by inaccurate reporting in certain leading newspapers.

Important American newspapers during the war peddled the story that Mihailovich was a collaborator and Tito was a great national leader. The result was the betrayal of General Mihailovich and the installation of a Communist regime in Yugoslavia.

In the postwar period some of these newspapers told us that Chiang was a crook and the Chinese Communists were agrarian reformers; and the result was a confusion of policy that led to the installation of a Communist regime in China.

At a later date there were papers which told the American people that Castro was not a Communist but a cross between Robin Hood and Thomas Jefferson; and the result was a Communist regime in Cuba.

Now we have been the victim of still another hoax, in consequence of which the government of Ngo Dinh Diem has been destroyed and a chaotic situation has been created that will make a Communist takeover more difficult to resist.

Congress, as well as the American people, are dependent on the press for their information. Even the members of the administration, although they possess special sources of information, are greatly influenced by what they read in their newspapers. In a very real sense, therefore, the press has a policymaking role.

I believe that it might be helpful if members of the press were to ask themselves some questions about how important American newspapers could so mislead us in these situations.

Meanwhile, I hope that every Member of the Senate will find the time to read this report and give thought to its implications.

Sincerely,

Thomas J. Dodd
U. S. S.

THOMAS J. DODD.

APPENDIX 4

Three Unpublished Letters from Ngô Đình Nhu

Below are three letters that Ngô Đình Nhu wrote to his Chartist friends:

1. A letter of April 20, 1956, in which he exposes the complex political situation faced by the very young Republic of Vietnam. [Translation on pp. 141–42]
2. A letter written shortly after the Tết festival of 1963. A happy letter where he talks about Vietnam's progress in the dirty war (early 1963). [Translation on p. 153]
3. A letter of September 2, 1963, written two months before the coup d'état that would end in his death. A more somber letter. [Translation on pp. 185–86]

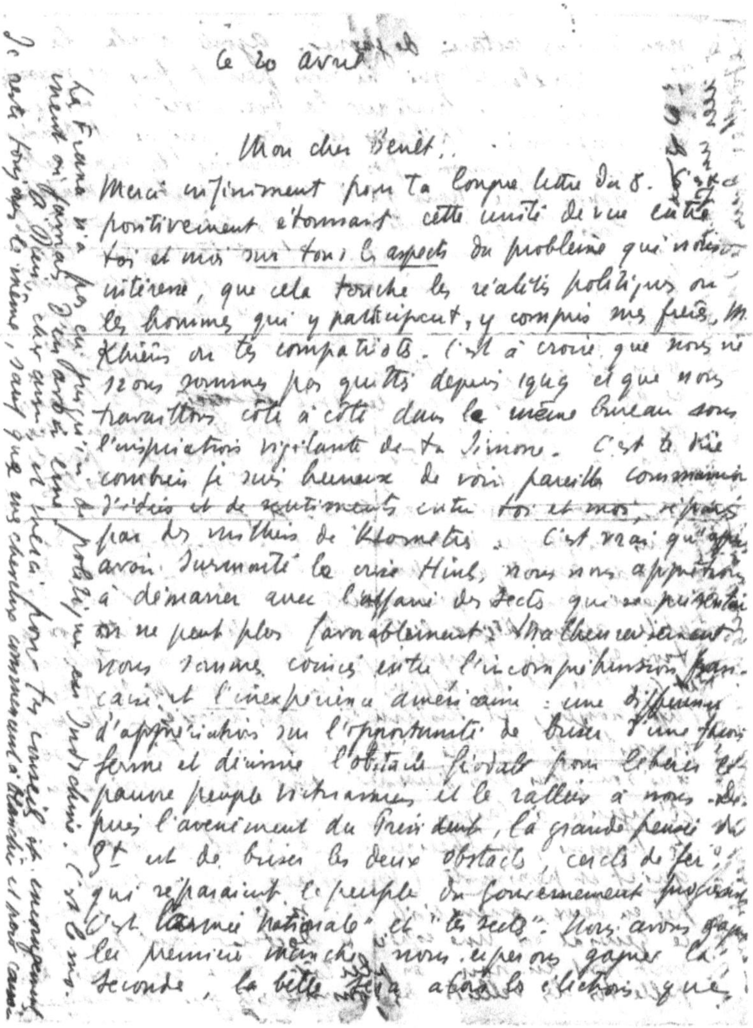
le 20 avril [illegible]

Mon cher Benét,

Merci infiniment pour ta longue lettre du 8. C'est positivement étonnant cette unité de vue entre toi et moi sur tous les aspects du problème qui nous intéresse, que cela touche les réalités politiques ou les hommes qui y participent, y compris mes frères, M. Khiêm ou tes compatriotes. C'est à croire que nous ne nous sommes pas quittés depuis 1949 et que nous travaillons côte à côte dans le même bureau sous l'inspiration vigilante de ta Simone. C'est te dire combien je suis heureux de voir pareille communion d'idées et de sentiments entre toi et moi, séparés par des milliers de kilomètres. C'est vrai qu'après avoir surmonté la crise Hinh, nous nous apprêtions à démarrer avec l'affaire des Sectes qui se présentait on ne peut plus favorablement. Malheureusement nous sommes coincés entre l'incompréhension française et l'inexpérience américaine : une différence d'appréciation sur l'opportunité de briser d'une façon ferme et décisive l'obstacle féodal pour libérer ce pauvre peuple vietnamien et le rallier à nous. Depuis l'avènement du Président, la grande pensée du Gt est de briser les deux obstacles, cercles de fer, qui séparaient le peuple du Gouvernement progressiste : c'est l'armée "nationale" et "les sectes". Nous avons gagné la première manche, nous espérons gagner la seconde, la belle [illegible] alors les élections que

La France n'a jamais pu [illegible] politique en Indochine. C'est le moment où jamais [illegible] Dieu [illegible] et [illegible] pour tes conseils et encouragements. Je resterai toujours le même, sauf que mes cheveux commencent à blanchir et sont [illegible]

nous sommes certains de gagner. Ajoutez à cela le "Temps harcelant" qui ne nous permet pas de musarder en chemin et de pratiquer la bonne vieille politique du compromis. L'heure est donc unique et décisive. Si nous ne réussissons pas à convaincre les responsables du Monde libre pour qu'ils nous aident à neutraliser les colonialistes qui soutiennent les féodaux contre le Gt national, nous irons à la Catastrophe. Car le peuple Vietnamien ~~[illegible]~~ déçu définitivement nous abandonnera. Et le Monde asiatique que nous avons travaillé ces derniers mois et qui commençait à sympathiser avec nous, se détournera de nous, isolés alors en Asie ~~[illegible]~~ et à la merci du Viet Minh. Car il ne faut plus recommencer l'expérience de 1945–1954. Soutenus seulement par le camp occidental, nous sommes sûrs d'être battus par le Communisme en Asie. Il faut avoir le concours du peuple Vietnamien et la sympathie du Monde asiatique, pour que l'aide occidentale, dominée par la personnalité du Pt Ngô, puisse être utile, ayant reçu l'étiquette asiatique. Cette conception est bien comprise par les hommes intelligents et au courant des affaires d'ici, tels que MM. Roux (Affaires étrangères) et Risterucci (États associés). Il faut travailler de manière à ce que des instructions en ce sens, qui sont, je me permets, déjà prêtes, soient envoyées d'urgence à Saigon. Le Général Ely est un homme de bonne, malheureusement il est de nature inquiet et pessimiste (voir affaire Hinh = armée coupée en deux, guerre civile etc... si le Pt touche à Hinh...). Ce général est une espèce de Docteur Tant pis, qui voit tout en noir ou plutôt tout en rouge. Rappelle-toi les velléités des Communistes qui cherchaient

[illegible]

ỆT   AM
TỔN.   ..NG PHỦ
VĂN-PHÒNG CỐ-VẤN CHÁNH-TRỊ
Số .... /CV/VP

Kính gởi ~~Ông~~ Madame Willemetz
9 rue de Verneuil
Paris
France

Chère Amie,

Je vous ai envoyé une belle carte de Noël et une de Têt aussi, à vous et aux autres camarades qui avez bien voulu penser à moi. Probablement nos services ont "trop bien mangé le Têt" et les ont égarées.

Pour la 1ère fois depuis plusieurs années, nous avons pu fêter le Têt d'une façon convenable: grâce aux progrès que nous avons pu réaliser sur les communistes dans tous les domaines.

Je suis devenu à la fois le père et la nurse des "Hameaux Stratégiques" un système que

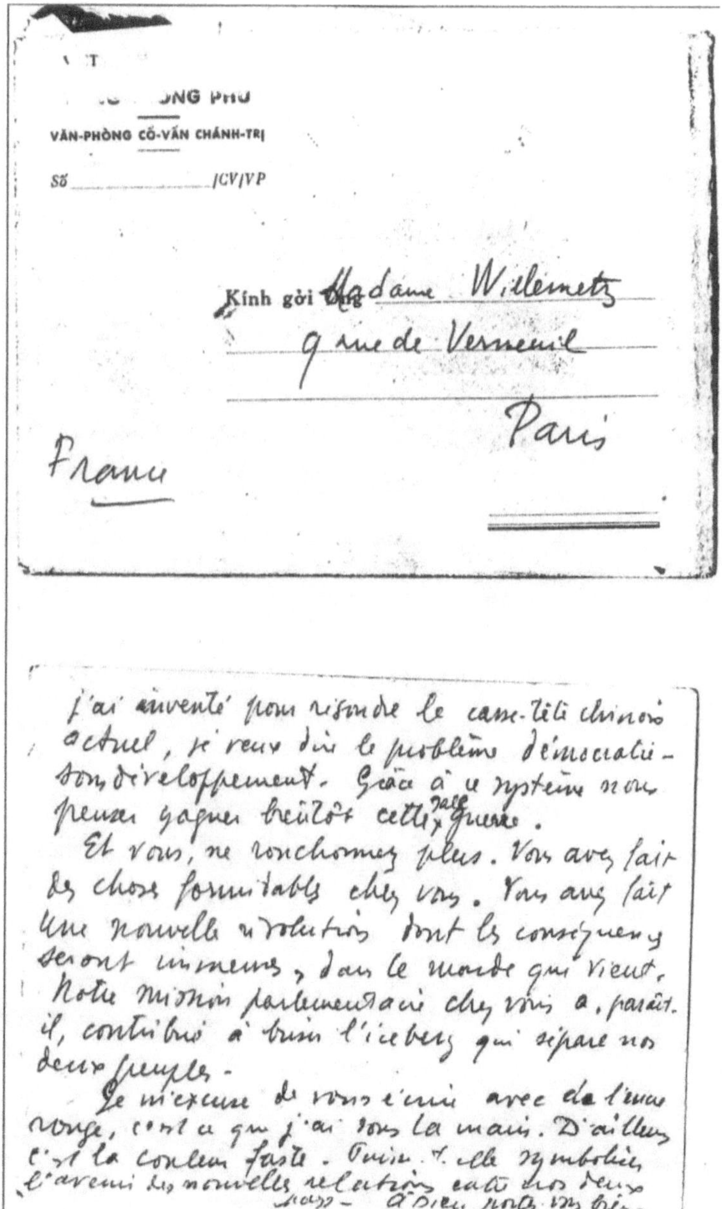

... T ...
...ONG PHU
VĂN-PHÒNG CỐ-VẤN CHÁNH-TRỊ
Số ..../CV/VP

Kính gởi ~~Ông~~ Madame Willemetz
9 rue de Verneuil
Paris

France

j'ai inventé pour résoudre le casse-tête chinois actuel, je veux dire le problème démocratisation développement. Grâce à ce système nous pensons gagner bientôt cette sale guerre.

Et vous, ne ronchonnez plus. Vous avez fait des choses formidables chez vous. Vous avez fait une nouvelle révolution dont les conséquences seront immenses, dans le monde qui vient. Notre mission parlementaire chez vous a, paraît-il, contribué à briser l'iceberg qui sépare nos deux peuples.

Je m'excuse de vous écrire avec de l'encre rouge, c'est ce que j'ai sous la main. D'ailleurs c'est la couleur faste. Puisse-t-elle symboliser l'avenir des nouvelles relations entre nos deux pays. — A Dieu, portez-vous bien —

... CỘNG-HÒA

TỔNG - THỐNG PHỦ

VĂN-PHÒNG CỐ-VẤN CHÁNH-TRỊ

Số ______ /CV/VP

Re. R SAIGON 5 №5 7 1

Par Avion.

R AVION

SAIGON 02 IX 63 8o VIỆT-NAM

VIỆT-NAM * 2 0 5 BƯU-CHÍNH Số máy 3

Kính gởi ~~Ông~~ Mme G. Willemetz

9 rue de Verneuil

7

France Paris 7ème

Cher ami, Personnel

Excusez-moi de vous avoir donné tant de soucis.
Je déteste ces journaleux avec leur amour du sensati-
onnel et leur cupidité commerciale, parce qu'ils
vous ont empêché de dormir. Au fond, il n'y a 3
fois rien autre que la conjuration américaine et com-
muniste contre le Sud Vietnam, parce que le Vietnam
veut tout simplement être lui-même et pas autre
chose, ni américanisé, ni communisé. D'où
cette affaire bouddhiste qu'ils ont montée contre nous.
Nous sommes obligés de la régler une fois pour
toute, en brisant le cercle de magie et de terreur qu'ils ont mistallé dans 5 pagodes sur plus
~~de~~ 4 000 pagodes dans tout le pays. Dans ces
pagodes ils utilisent tous les moyens, y compris
le terrorisme, pour hypnotiser quelques esprits faibles
en vue de les pousser à se jeter dans le feu, après a-

vu aussi les télévisionnistes américains, qui paient
bon prix l'organisation de ce spectacle unique au
XXe siècle – depuis l'état de siège, c'est-à-dire, depuis
le 20 août jusqu'à maintenant, il n'y a plus de suicide de bonzes. C'est la preuve que libérés de l'organisation secrète américano-soviétique (terreur, into-
xication etc…), les bonzes ont pu reprendre leur vie
normale : l'affaire est terminée. Cependant
les comploteurs, frustrés dans leur entreprise de coup
d'état pour mettre à la tête du Vietnam une nouvelle espèce de Bao-Dai, ont voulu tenter de monter
une affaire d'étudiants, comme en Corée et en Turquie :
ils en ont été pour leurs frais, car nous avons étouffé
tout cela dans l'œuf : tous ces soi-disant étudiants
ont été mis dans un camp d'entraînement mili-
taire d'où deux jours après, ils sont rentrés chez eux,
tout à fait désintoxiqués : ils ont été manipulés

par la propagande américano-soviétique, ②
et terrorisés par les bandes secrètes. Nous
savons qu'"ils" ont mis 20 millions de dollars
dans toute cette affaire : ils ne nous laisse-
ront pas tranquilles, parce qu'ils doivent jus-
tifier ces énormes frais à leurs chefs. Ils
ont dû en mettre beaucoup dans leurs poches,
et maintenant ils ont peur pour leur propre
peau.

Je vous raconte tout ceci, non pour
vous intoxiquer, ni pour vous calmer,
mais parce que je vous dois toute ma sin-
cérité, vous qui êtes une amie si fidèle et
si sensible. Si mon pauvre pays n'était

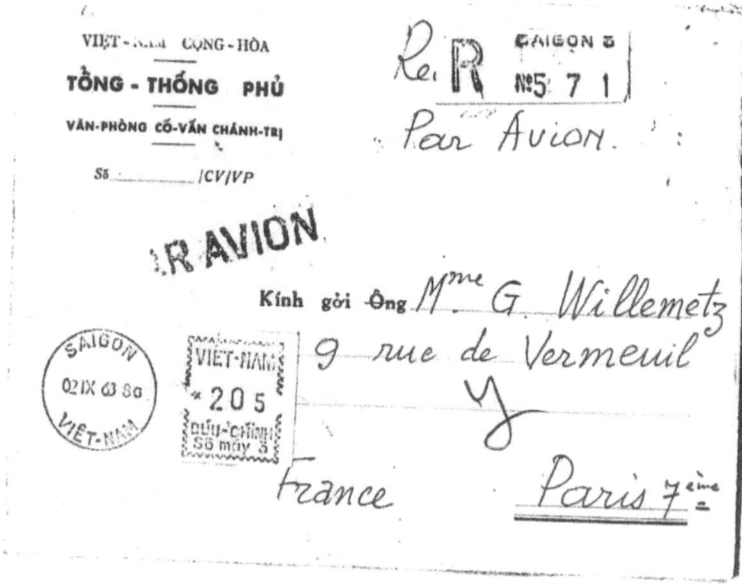
VIỆT-NAM CỘNG-HÒA
TỔNG - THỐNG PHỦ
VĂN-PHÒNG CỐ-VẤN CHÁNH-TRỊ
Số .... /CV/VP

Re. R SAIGON 5 N°5 7 1
Par Avion.

PAR AVION

Kính gởi Ông Mme G. Willemetz
9 rue de Vermeuil
7
France Paris 7ème

SAIGON 02 IX 63 VIỆT-NAM
VIỆT-NAM 205 BƯU-CHÍNH Số máy 5

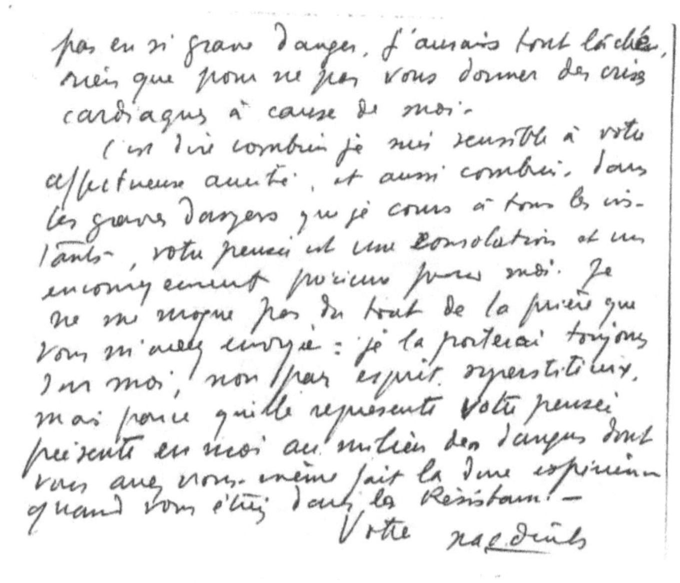
pas en si grave danger, j'aurais tout lâché, rien que pour ne pas vous donner des crises cardiaques à cause de moi.

C'est dire combien je suis sensible à votre affectueuse amitié, et aussi combien, dans les graves dangers que je cours à tous les instants, votre pensée est une consolation et un encouragement précieux pour moi. Je ne me moque pas du tout de la prière que vous m'avez envoyée : je la porterai toujours sur moi, non par esprit superstitieux, mais parce qu'elle représente votre pensée présente en moi au milieu des dangers dont vous avez vous-même fait la dure expérience quand vous étiez dans la Résistance. —

Votre [illegible]

APPENDIX 5

Excerpts from Statements (1963, 1965) and Telegrams (1963), Madame Ngô Đình Nhu

This appendix contains four documents from Madame Ngô-Đình Nhu's personal archive, including:

1. An excerpt from her typed speech with handwritten notes before leaving the US on November 14, 1963.
   a. text of speech
   b. image of speech
2. An excerpt from her handwritten draft of her statement issued in mid-1965 (manuscript IV, page 6 bis, 1–3).
   a. text of statement
   b. image of statement
3. A telegram sent from Rome to the Vietnamese Embassy in Washington, DC, on September 23, 1963, together with a part of her handwritten note about her plan for the trip to the US in October 1963.
4. A telegram sent from Rome to the Vietnamese Embassy in Washington, DC, in September 1963 (no day provided), handwritten by Ngô-Đình Lệ Thuỷ.

Excerpt from a Draft Statement by Madame Ngô-Đình Nhu Before Leaving the US (November 14, 1963)

Before leaving this country I wish above all to thank with all my heart the thousands of people who have expressed to me grief, sympathy, and indignation before the tragedy in Vietnam.

Because of them and because I am convinced that they belong to that silent majority which does not go shouting in the streets but which understands events much more than one believes, I think that in all justice, I cannot keep rancor against their country for the misdeeds of a few.

It is why I shall return here, and as long as only one version of the story in Vietnam continues to submerge the world, thanks to that too effective international communist propaganda network. I think indeed and more than ever that the sacrifices of all those Vietnamese and Americans who have died for the independence of Vietnam and the Freedom of the Free World cannot be betrayed or besmirched; therefore, each individual in his or her own sphere must dedicate himself to that duty of gratefulness.

I do not think that any government, either American or Vietnamese, would try to blockade my way, for it would be their too obvious condemnations, chiefly when my purpose has never been to interfere in the internal affairs of others, but only to make justice prevail as much as possible, even in this world of horror and chiefly for those who have accepted the greatest sacrifice for the common cause of the Free World.

I have finally decided to go and join my children in Rome instead of bringing them here, for I feel physically stronger now to undertake the trip and also because I do not want to separate them from their uncle Archbishop Ngô Đình Thục, the very cherished and respected patriarch of the family, the Ngô family, and to impose such long trip to them. I have just learned indeed that they were taken in a hurry by faithful bodyguards and hidden for days in the depth of the jungle—ironically enough trying to find a better protection among the wild beasts of the jungle—before being flown to Rome without even the nurse of the baby to accompany her should she wished to, though I learned by the Press that the State Department has announced that her nurse was with the baby.

I am grieved that this country to which the Ngô family and so many Vietnamese patriots have trusted to the end and have always been faithful and effective allies could have been the source of the Vietnamese tragedy. Indeed, all the inexplicable American official moves to corner President Ngô Đình Diệm and his brother, my husband—whose only crime was to be a loyal brother to his brother and a determined patriot to his country—and to consider them as the enemies to crush down while they were effectively cornering in Vietnam, communism, the common enemy of our two countries, will unfortunately always stay as a dark spot in the history of our two countries.

But it was reported that in death, President Ngô Đình Diệm's face was serene and that my husband had a slight smile, though his face was all streaked with blood.

I think therefore that I cannot be less serene than they and that I must consider their sacrifices and martyrdom and those of other patriots who died with them and whose number seems to have been purportedly blackouted blacked out or minimized, as the high price God wants Vietnam to pay, to awaken the conscience of the world before the communist danger which is becoming more and more traitorous under the label of peaceful coexistence which only hides a satanic program of infiltration and subversion.

Anyway, after proving so well how effectively they could intervene in Vietnamese affairs, I only hope that the US officials would never aggravate their case in Vietnam in giving another blessing even unofficial in the attempt of any new Vietnamese government to fabricate phony charges to better persecute any other member of the Ngô family, or worse to besmirched the memory of President Ngô Đình

Diệm, the father of the Republic of Vietnam and of his brother, my husband, the Author of all the new strategies and plans which have proven so successful against subversive wars and which were bringing Victory in Vietnam at such fast steps . . .

Before leaving this country I wish above all to thank with all my heart the thousands of people who have expressed to me grief, sympathy and indignation before the tragedy in Vietnam.

Because of them and because I am convinced that they belong to that silent majority which does not go shouting in the streets but which understands events much more than one believes, I think that in all justice, I cannot keep rancor against their country for the misdeeds of a few.

It is why I shall return here, and as long as one version only of the story in Vietnam continues to submerge the world, thanks to that too effective international communist propaganda network, I think indeed and more than ever that the sacrifices of all those Vietnamese and Americans who have died for the independence of Vietnam and the freedom of the free world cannot be betrayed or besmirched, therefore each individual in his or her own sphere must dedicate himself to that duty of gratitude.

I do not think that any government either American or Vietnamese would try to blockade my way, for it would be their too obvious condemnation, chiefly when my purpose has never been to interfere in the internal affairs of others, but only to make justice prevail as much as possible, even in this world of horror and chiefly for those who have accepted the greatest sacrifice for the common cause of the free world.

I have finally decided to go and join my children in Rome instead of bringing them here, for I feel physically stronger now to undertake the trip and also because I do not want to separate them from their uncle the Archbishop, Ngô Đình Thục, the very cherished and respected patriarch of their family, the Ngô family, and to impose such a long trip to them. I have just learned indeed that they were taken in a hurry by faithful body-guards and hidden for days in the depth of the jungle, - ironically enough trying to find a better protection among the wild beasts of the jungle - before being flown to Rome without even the nurse of the baby to accompany her, though she wished to, though I learned by the Press that the State Department had announced that her nurse was with the baby.

- 2 -

I am ~~sorry~~ grieved that this country to which the Ngô Family and so many Vietnamese patriots have trusted to the end and have always been faithful and effective allies could have been the source of the Vietnamese tragedy. Indeed all the American inexplicable official moves to corner President Ngô Dinh Diêm and his brother, my husband, whose only crime was to be a loyal brother to his brother and a determined patriot to his country, and to consider them as the enemies to crush down while they were effectively cornering in Vietnam, communism, the common enemy of our two countries, will unfortunately always stay as a dark spot in the history of our two countries.

But it was reported that in death, President Ngô Dinh Diêm's face was serene and that my husband had a slight smile, though his face was all streaked with blood.

I think therefore that I cannot be less serene than they and that I must consider their sacrifices and martyrdom and those of other patriots who died with them and whose number seem to have been purportedly discounted or minimized, as the high price God wants Vietnam to pay, to awaken the conscience of the world before the communist danger which is becoming more and more traiterous under the label of peaceful coexistence which only hides a satanic program of infiltration and subversion ~~and infiltration~~.

Anyway, after proving so well how effectively they could intervene in Vietnamese affairs, I only hope that the US officials would never aggravate their case in Vietnam in giving another blessing, even unofficial in the attempt of any new Vietnamese government to fabricate phony charges to persecute any other member of the Ngô Family to besmirch the memory of President Ngô Dinh Diêm, the Father of the Republic of Vietnam and of his brother, my husband, the Author of all the new strategies and plans which have proven so successful against subversive wars and which were bringing victory in Vietnam at such fast steps. About this, it would be

Excerpt from the IV Draft of Madame Nhu's Statement Released in mid-1965

For Your Information and for Release
MESSAGE OF MADAME NGÔ-ĐÌNH NHU

To the Vietnamese people, on the occasion of the Vietnamese Women's Day 1922nd anniversary of the Trưng Sisters, National Heroines (March 8, 1965), and the third anniversary of the Strategic hamlets policy as well as the second anniversary of the Chiêu Hồi campaign (return of the prodigal children) – April 17, 1965

(handwritten excerpt from the IV draft), pp. 6 bis (1–3):

> . . . Vietnam has given the name of "nhân vị" (respect for human dignity) to that democracy. That democracy nhân vị has aroused hope and enthusiasm in the Vietnamese heart, for though most simple, it has none the less proven a real sense, rarely attained, of humanity rectitude, realism, idealism. One could summarize it in these few words: man being not only matter but also spirit, man being not only individual but also member of the human community, it is therefore necessary for a solution to be worthy, that it respects all these facets of human personality, without never ignoring any, chiefly out of hypocrisy.
>
> It is therefore natural, on the plane of the spirit, that the nhân vị democracy recognizes to man not only the enjoyment of freedom – that "capacity to obey and practice virtue" as the nhân vị Constitution of Vietnam has defined it so admirably – but that it defends sincerely that freedom, by the protection of the family which it considers as the first natural bastion of man as an individual, as well as it must defend that freedom in the frame of the hamlet, which it sees as the second bastion of man as a member of his human community.

Then being also matter, the nhân vị democracy recognizes to him a material basis as material guarantees of his human dignity, a basis which would be the visible prolongation of the individual, his external roots if one may say so, which guarantee that all personal effort from him, requested by the community, cannot be exploited since his own sweat to him, an individual, trickling for that community effort, would only fall on his own roots, to water and fructify the material basis of which he is the proprietor and which is his share in the human community. Property in the nhân vị democracy can never be abusive, for it follows a margin established for all, according to the collective progress of the Vietnamese people, and where the basic property of the individual is so sacred that the state has the duty to help through agrarian reform for example – each family to be proprietor of its house and the piece of land which surrounds it and from where it draws it sustenance.

As for the military defense, each hamlet takes care by itself of its own paramilitary defense, according to its regional peculiarities and a program established for all. This reduces the role of the army to a secondary state, chiefly, and allows the population not to depend totally on an armed minority which could be catastrophic if ever so little that its elements, lacking loyalty and patriotism, become chattel of the foreign . . .

6 bis

Vietnam has given the name of "nhân vị" (Respect for human dignity) to that democracy.

That democracy nhân vị has ~~given~~ aroused hope and enthusiasm ~~to~~ in the Vietnamese ~~people~~ hearts, for ~~its its simplicity it is~~ though most simple, it has none the less proven a real sense, rarely attained, of ~~humanity~~ ~~sincerity~~ rectitude, realism, idealism. One could summarize it in these few words: man being not only matter but also spirit, man being not only individual but also member of the human community, it is therefore necessary for a solution to be ~~valuab~~ worthy, that it respects all these facets of ~~the~~ human personality, without never ignoring any, chiefly out of hypocrisy. It is therefore ~~necessary~~ natural, on the plane of the spirit, that the nhân vị democracy recognizes to man not only the enjoyment of freedom—

6 b (2)

that "capacity to obey reason and
practise virtue" as the Nhân vị constitution
of Vietnam has defined it so admirably –
but that it defends sincerely
that freedom, by the protection of the
family which it considers as the
first natural bastion of man as an
individual, as well as it must defend that
freedom in the frame of the hamlet,
which it sees as the second
natural bastion of man as a member
of his human community. Man
being also matter, the Nhân vị
democracy recognizes to him a
material basis as material guarantee
of his human dignity, a basis which
would be the visible prolongation
of the individual, his external
roots if one may say so, which
guarantee that all personal effort
from him, requested by the
community, cannot be exploited
since his own sweat to him, an individual

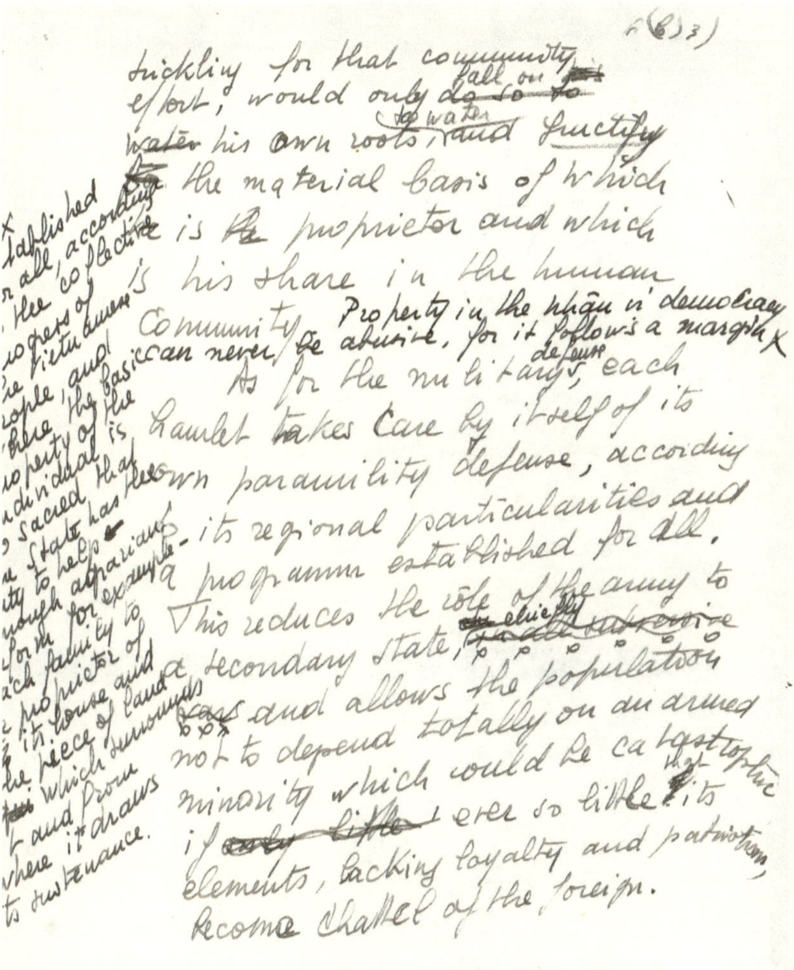
trickling for that community effort, would only fall on to water his own roots, and fructify the material basis of which is the proprietor and which is his share in the human Community. Property in the rhythm of democracy can never be abusive, for it follows a margin x

As for the military defense, each hamlet takes care by itself of its own paramility defense, according its regional particularities and a programme established for all. This reduces the role of the army to a secondary state, [illegible] and allows the population not to depend totally on an armed minority which could be catastrophic if ever so little that its elements, lacking loyalty and patriotism, become chattel of the foreign.

x established for all, according the collective progress of Vietnamese people, and there the basic property of the individual is sacred. The State has the duty to help through agrarian reform for example each family to be proprietor of its house and the piece of land which surrounds it and from where it draws its sustenance.

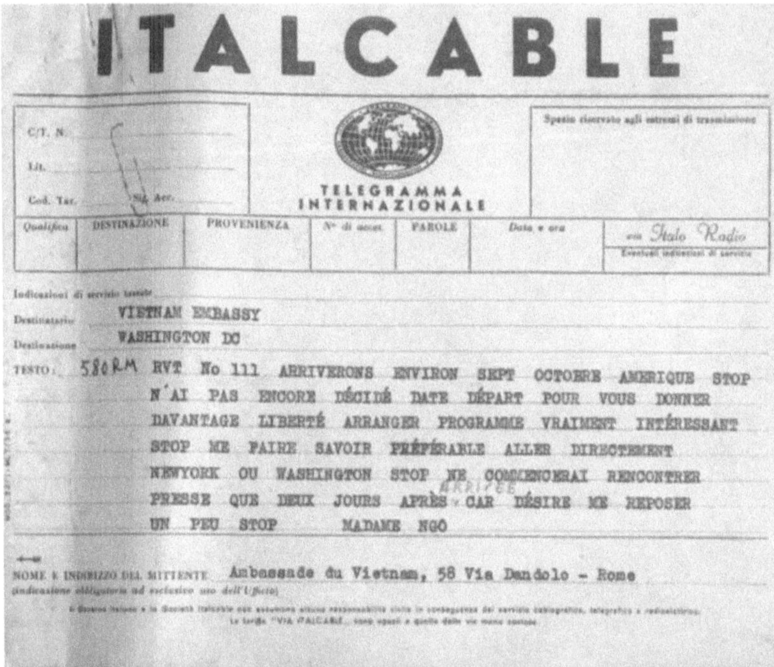
ITALCABLE

TELEGRAMMA INTERNAZIONALE

via Italo Radio

Destinatario: VIETNAM EMBASSY

Destinazione: WASHINGTON DC

TESTO: 580RM RVT No 111 ARRIVERONS ENVIRON SEPT OCTOBRE AMERIQUE STOP N'AI PAS ENCORE DÉCIDÉ DATE DÉPART POUR VOUS DONNER DAVANTAGE LIBERTÉ ARRANGER PROGRAMME VRAIMENT INTÉRESSANT STOP ME FAIRE SAVOIR PRÉFÉRABLE ALLER DIRECTEMENT NEWYORK OU WASHINGTON STOP NE COMMENCERAI RENCONTRER PRESSE QUE DEUX JOURS APRÈS CAR DÉSIRE ME REPOSER UN PEU STOP MADAME NGÔ

NOME E INDIRIZZO DEL MITTENTE: Ambassade du Vietnam, 58 Via Dandolo - Rome

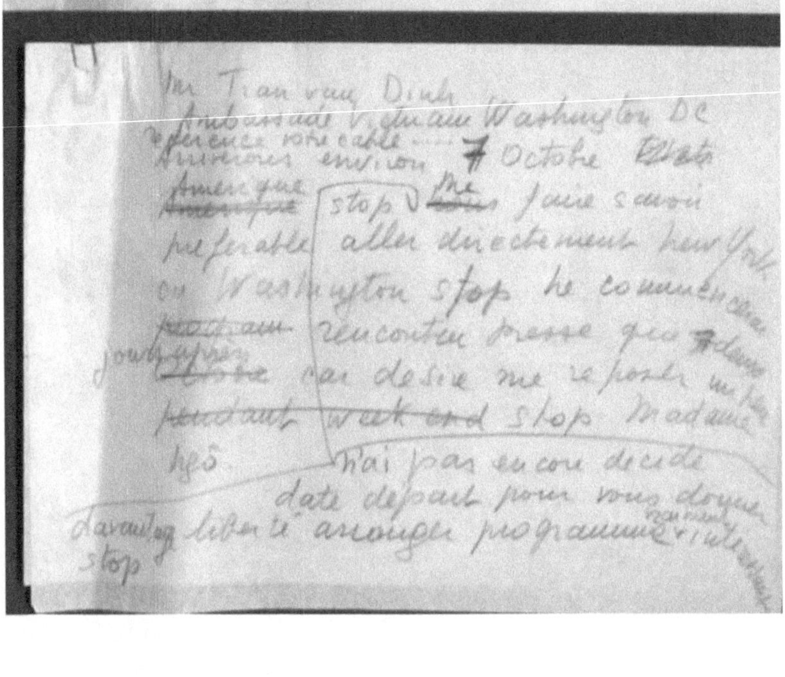
Mr Tran van Dinh
Ambassade Vietnam Washington DC
référence votre cable
Arriverons environ 7 Octobre
stop Me faire savoir
préférable aller directement New York
ou Washington stop ne commencerai
rencontrer presse que deux
jours après car désire me reposer un peu
stop Madame
Ngô n'ai pas encore décidé
date départ pour vous donner
davantage liberté arranger programme vraiment intéressant
stop

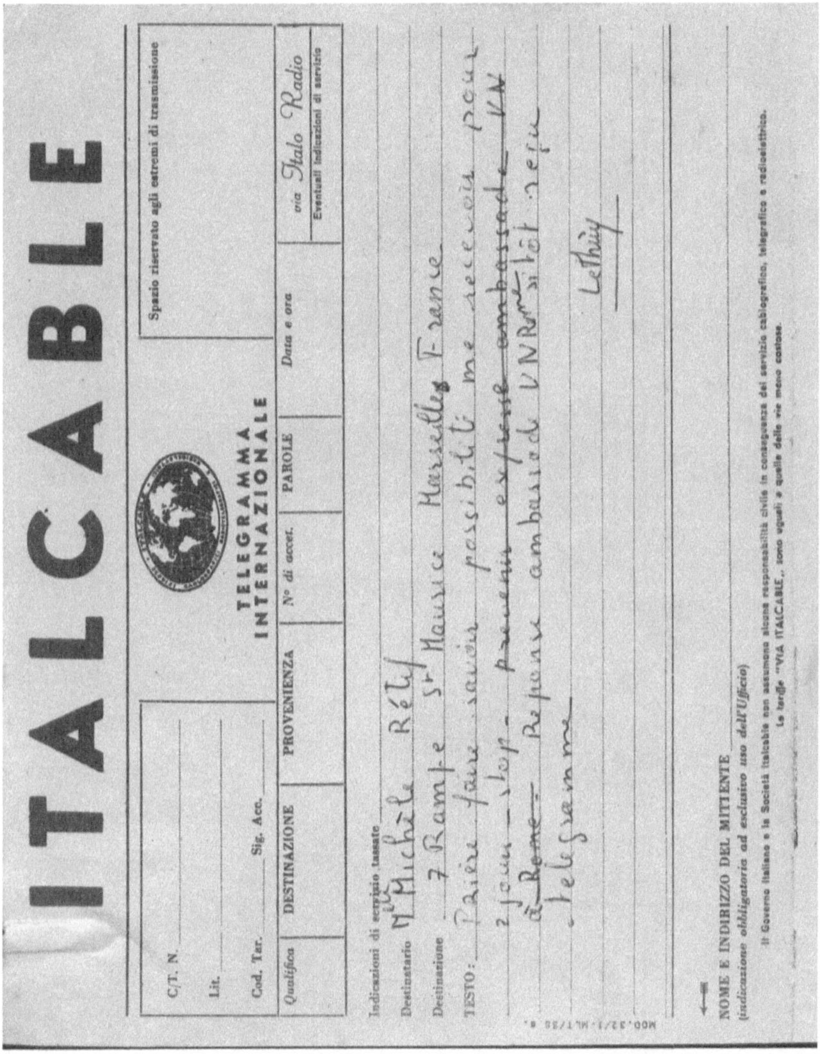
ITALCABLE
TELEGRAMMA INTERNAZIONALE
Spazio riservato agli estremi di trasmissione
C/T. N
Lit.
Cod. Ter.
Sig. Acc.
Qualifica
DESTINAZIONE
PROVENIENZA
Nº di accet.
PAROLE
Data e ora
via Italo Radio
Eventuali indicazioni di servizio
Indicazioni di servizio tassate
Destinatario
Destinazione
TESTO:
NOME E INDIRIZZO DEL MITTENTE
(indicazione obbligatoria ad esclusivo uso dell'Ufficio)

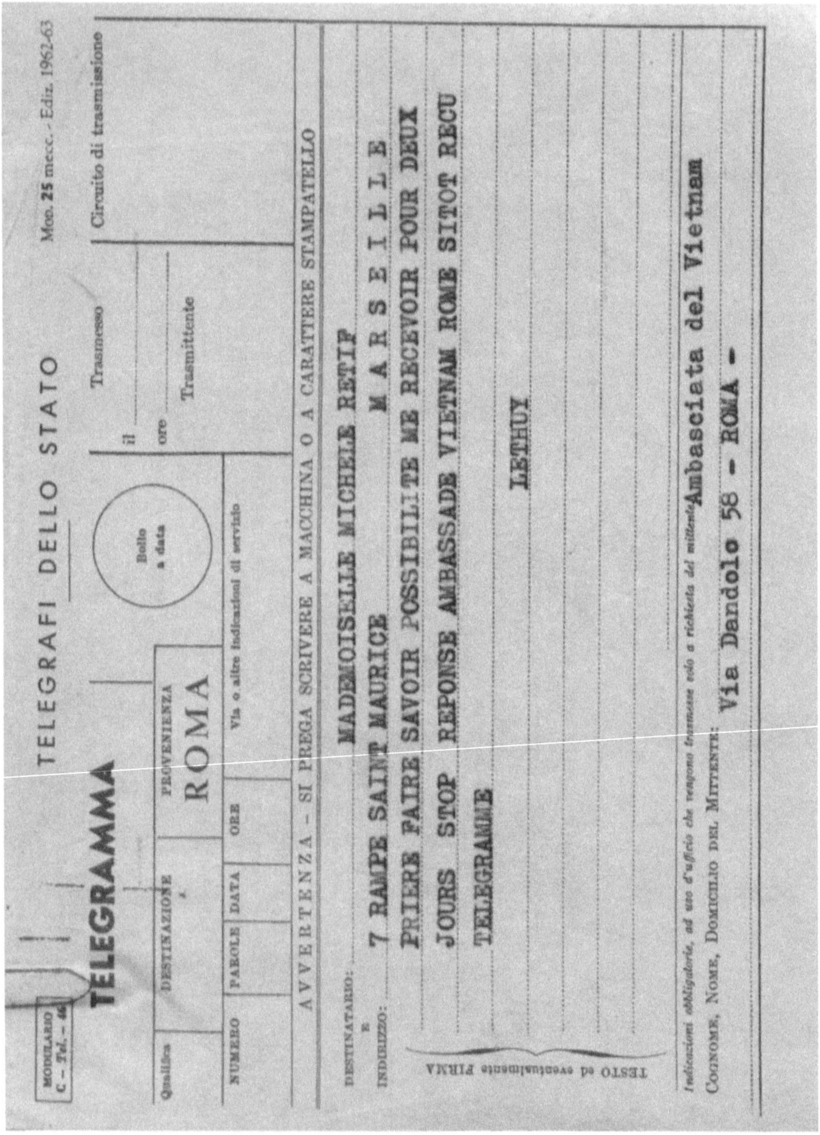

MODULARIO C. - Tel. - 46

TELEGRAMMA

TELEGRAFI DELLO STATO

Mod. 25 mecc. - Ediz. 1962-63

Qualifica

DESTINAZIONE

PROVENIENZA ROMA

Bollo a data

Trasmesso il ore

Trasmittente

Circuito di trasmissione

NUMERO | PAROLE | DATA | ORE | Via o altre indicazioni di servizio

AVVERTENZA - SI PREGA SCRIVERE A MACCHINA O A CARATTERE STAMPATELLO

DESTINATARIO E INDIRIZZO: MADEMOISELLE MICHELE RETIF
7 RAMPE SAINT MAURICE M A R S E I L L E

TESTO ed eventualmente FIRMA

PRIERE FAIRE SAVOIR POSSIBILITE ME RECEVOIR POUR DEUX
JOURS STOP REPONSE AMBASSADE VIETNAM ROME SITOT RECU
TELEGRAMME

LETHUY

Indicazioni obbligatorie, ad uso d'ufficio che vengono trasmesse solo a richiesta del mittente

COGNOME, NOME, DOMICILIO DEL MITTENTE: Ambasciata del Vietnam
Via Dandolo 58 - ROMA -

Notes

(Au.) = author; (Ed.) = Editor

Epigraphs

1. English translation from *The Holy Bible*, New International Version (Grand Rapids, MI: Zondevan Bible Publishers & International Bible Society, 1984), 911. Italics by the author. (Ed.)
2. English translation from *The Holy Bible*, New International Version, 772. (Ed.)

Foreword

1. The explanation for writing Ngô-Đình as a combined and hyphenated word will be provided by Ngô-Đình Lệ Quyên in a later passage. (Ed.)
2. André Nguyễn Văn Châu, *Ngo Dinh Thi Hiep or a Lifetime in the Eye of the Storm* (Salt Lake City: American Book Classics, 2000), 108. Another source apparently based on the Thân Trọng's family annals claims that her given name was Sắc, not Phiên. See Thái Lộc "Mỹ nhân xứ Huế - kỳ 2 [The Beauties of Hue–part 2]," *Tuổi Trẻ* [Youth], May 10, 2021, https://tuoitre.vn/my-nhan-xu-hue-ky-2-vo-vua-tai-gia-20210510095738152.htm. Her birth and death years are not known. (Ed.)
3. The three emperors were adopted by Emperor Tự Đức (1829–1883), who was their uncle and who did not have children. See Hội đồng Trị sự Nguyễn Phúc tộc, *Nguyễn Phúc tộc Thế phả* [Nguyễn Phúc Family Annals] (Huế: Thuận Hoá, 1995), 358–59. This means Lệ Xuân was a grandniece of Emperor Đồng Khánh, not his granddaughter as Monique Demery incorrectly identified in her *Finding the Dragon*

Lady: The Mystery of Vietnam's Madame Nhu (New York: Public Affairs, 2014), 20. (Ed.)

4. Chương Thâu, "Thân Trọng Huề, một nhân vật lịch sử có tư tưởng canh tân, một nhà văn hoá Việt nam đầu thế kỷ XX" [Thân Trọng Huề, a historical figure with reformist thinking and a cultural activist at the turn of the century], September 2004, https://www.hothan.org/danh-nhan/than-trong-hue-mot-nhan-vat-lich-su-co-tu-tuong-canh-tan-mot-nha-van-hoa-viet-nam-dau-the-ky-xx. See also his obituary: Louis Finot, "Thân-trọng-Huề (1869–1925)," in *Bulletin de l'École Française d'Extrême-Orient*, Tome 25, 1925, 597–99; doi: https://doi.org/10.3406/befeo.1925.3083. Available at: https://www.persee.fr/doc/befeo_0336-1519_1925_num_25_1_3083. (Ed.)
5. Monique Demery incorrectly identified her as Trần Thị Nam Trân in *Finding the Dragon Lady*, 9. (Ed.)
6. Informative books (life stories recounted by other members of the Ngô Đình family) include André Nguyễn Văn Châu, *Ngo Dinh Thi Hiep*, and André Nguyễn Văn Châu, *The Miracle of Hope: Francis Xavier Nguyen Van Thuan, Political Prisoner, Prophet of Peace* (Boston: Pauline Books and Media, 2003). (Ed.)

Chapter 1 (Part 1)

1. English translation is from *The Holy Bible*, New International Version, 753. (Ed.)
2. "Very little one," as Madame Nhu explains a few lines later, means one (adult or child) who chooses to remain "little," or humble, towards his Creator, his Lord Almighty, and so may receive his inspiration to lead him in life. (Ed.)
3. Her name was Thân Thị Nam Trân. (Ed.)
4. Her name was Bùi Thị Lan. (Ed.)
5. This refers to Thân Trọng Huề. (Ed.)
6. Trần Lệ Xuân here referred to her maternal grandparents, Nguyễn Phúc Như Phiên and Thân Trọng Huề. (Ed.)
7. Here Trần Lệ Xuân referred to Trần Văn Thông. (Ed.)

8. It is unclear what the author meant by "first," but perhaps her father was the first Vietnamese lawyer trained in France to open a private office to practice law in Vietnam at the time. (Ed.)
9. Here Trần Lệ Xuân referred to her elder sister, Trần Lệ Chi, and younger brother Trần Văn Khiêm. (Ed.)
10. In original, "sticking to their particular self." (Ed.)
11. Later on, under the communist regime, this mansion served as an embassy for various countries before falling into disrepair. (Au.)
12. Trần Lệ Xuân converted to Catholicism when she married Ngô Đình Nhu. (Ed.)
13. In Confucian norms, a married son with children takes precedence over his unmarried and childless elders, because it is the children who will assure the continuation of the cult of ancestors. (Au.)
14. Đàn Nam Giao (Nam Giao Esplanade) was the imperial altar where Nguyễn monarchs held annual ceremonies to pray and make offerings to Heaven and Earth. (Ed.)
15. These verses and their translation are from the so-called Jerusalem version of the Bible, available at https://www.bibliacatolica.com.br/en/new-jerusalem-bible/deuteronomy/33/. (Ed.)

Chapter 2 (Part 1)

1. Her name was Lucie Nguyễn Thị Danh, from a well-off family in Chợ Lớn ("Sài Gòn's Chinatown"). See Nguyễn, *Ngo Dinh Thi Hiep*, 103–4. (Ed.)
2. The "hothead" appeared to be Nguyễn Văn Ấm, who was the husband of Ngô-Đình Thị Hiệp (1903–2005), a sister of Ngô Đình Nhu. Cardinal Nguyễn Văn Thuận (1928–2002), their son, who was also known by his baptismal name François Xavier, died in 2002 after gathering the collection of his meditations in his book *Prières d'espérance* [Prayers of Hope] (1988) and after publishing in 1993 *Les pélerins du chemin de l'espérance* [The Pilgrims on the Way of Hope]. In 2000, he was in charge of ensuring the predication of the Lent spiritual exercises of Pope John Paul II. (Au.) For the books based in part on stories told

by Ngô-Đình Thị Hiệp and Cardinal Nguyễn Văn Thuận, see Nguyễn, *Ngo Dinh Thi Hiep* and *The Miracle of Hope*. (Ed.)

3. We are not able to find any information about this interview. (Ed.)
4. See Nguyễn, *The Miracle of Hope*, 152. (Ed.)
5. The term "colonialists" refers to the French, and the terms "the Legitimate Power of Vietnam" and "the Ultimate Legitimate Power of Vietnam," which appear in many places in the memoirs, refer to the Ngô Đình Diệm government. (Ed.)
6. Ngô Đình Thục (1897–1984), the second eldest brother of Ngô Đình Nhu, was one of the first Vietnamese bishops ordained under French colonial rule. During the coup d'état of 1963, Ngô Đình Thục was in Rome where Vatican Council II was being held. After the Council, he could have rejoined his diocese in Huế as he wished. Mme. Nhu reached out to the Vietnamese clergy to have their primate recalled, but there was no response. (Au.)
7. Ngô Đình Khôi (1891–1945) was the eldest brother of Ngô Đình Nhu and was married to Nguyễn Thị Hoa, daughter of Nguyễn Hữu Bài (1863–1935), who was minister of rites (*Lại bộ Thượng thư*) at the Nguyễn court. Ngô Đình Khôi served as provincial chief of Nam Ngãi but was forced by the French to resign in 1943 for his support for Ngô Đình Diệm's political activities. Together with Phạm Quỳnh and his son Ngô Đình Huân, he was executed by the Communist authorities in late 1945. (Ed.)
8. This sister-in-law was likely Ngô Đình Thị Giao. (Ed.)
9. Mme. Nhu's mother-in-law was Phạm Thị Thân. (Ed.)
10. Ngô-Đình Cẩn (1911–1964) was a younger brother of Ngô Đình Nhu. (Ed.)
11. This appears to be a mistake, as Ngô Đình Khôi was taken away by the communists in August 1945, not 1944. (Ed.)
12. Bùi Quang Chiêu (1873–1945) was a prominent leader of the French-educated southern Vietnamese elite, a newspaper editor, and founder of the Constitutionalist Party. See R. B. Smith, "Bui Quang Chieu and the Constitutionalist Party in French Cochinchina,

1917–30," *Modern Asian Studies* 3, no. 2 (1969): 131–50. Bùi Quang Chiêu was also the father of Henriette Bui (1906–2012) who was Vietnam's first medical doctor. He and his sons were executed by the Communist authorities in late 1945 in Long An. His sister, Bùi Thị Lan, was Trần Lệ Xuân's paternal grandmother (she was married to Trần Văn Thông and gave birth to Trần Văn Chương, father of Trần Lệ Xuân). (Ed.)

13. The official title was Résident Supérieur du Tonkin, the French official who oversaw the colonial administration in Tonkin under the French governor of Indochina. The mansion was called "Le Palais du Résident Supérieur du Tonkin" or "Dinh Thống sứ Bắc kỳ," now the State Guest House located on 12 Ngô Quyền Street in Hà Nội. (Ed.)

14. On Ngô Đình Diệm's detention from September 1945 to March 1946 and his meeting with Hồ Chí Minh before his release, see also Edward Miller, *Misalliance: Ngo Dinh Diem, the United States, and the Fate of South Vietnam* (Cambridge, MA: Harvard University Press, 2013), 33. André Nguyen Văn Châu provides an extensive account of Diệm's encounter with Hồ Chí Minh, Võ Nguyên Giáp, and other Communist officials in Nguyễn, *Ngo Dinh Thi Hiep*, 135–41. According to this source, it was not Ngô Đình Nhu but Bishop Lê Hữu Từ who secured Diệm's release. Yet it was possible that Ngô Đình Nhu also played a role since he was in Hà Nội at that time, working as director of the National Library. (Ed.)

15. This must have been her twenty-first birthday (see note 11). (Ed.)

16. "Colonialists" here refers to the French, while "imperialists" indicates Americans. (Ed.)

17. According to the agreement of August 30, 1940, Japan had obtained from France permission to use Tonkin as a military base for its expansion. Japan did not limit itself to the use of the airfields and naval bases of Vietnam; it also requisitioned its rice. The Vichy administration of Admiral Jean Decoux had to open the public rice granaries to which the farmers were forced to sell their rice to the Japanese at an extremely low price, sometimes lower than the cost of production. (Au.)

18. This refers to Nguyễn Thị Hoa, the widow of Ngô Đình Khôi and mother of Ngô Đình Huân. (Ed.)
19. After declaring Vietnam independent under the new name "Empire of Viet-Nam," Emperor Bảo Đại asked Trần Trọng Kim, a scholar, to form a cabinet to lead the goverment. This government existed for about five months (March to August 1945) but had lasting impacts on subsequent periods. For a study of this government, see Vu Ngu Chieu, "The Other Side of the 1945 Vietnamese Revolution: The Empire of Viet-Nam (March–August 1945)," *The Journal of Asian Studies* 45, no. 2 (1986): 293–328. For Trần Trọng Kim's scholarly contributions to constructing a new republican identity, see Nguyen Luong Hai Khoi, "Early Republicans' Concept of the Nation: Trần Trọng Kim and *Việt Nam sử lược*," in *Building a Republican Nation in Vietnam, 1920–1963*, Nu-Anh Tran and Tuong Vu, eds., 43–60 (Honolulu: University of Hawai'i Press, 2023). (Ed.)
20. The three red stripes with the broken middle stripe in the original design represent one (Quẻ Ly) of the eight triagrams of change in ancient Chinese philosophy, which was meant to indicate a bright and radiating southern civilization (*Tin Mới* [Hà Nội], August 29, 1945). This original design was accepted then, and the design with three unbroken stripes in Mme. Nhu's preference was actually adopted in 1948 by a different republican government. (Ed.)
21. The English translation is from *The Holy Bible*, New International Version, 731. (Ed.)
22. The Indochinese Federation included Tonkin (Hà Nội), Annam (Huế), Cochinchina (Sài Gòn), Cambodia (Phnom Penh), and finally Laos (Vientiane). By its Constitution of October 27, 1946, establishing the Fourth Republic, France designated its Colonial Empire as the French Union. The Preamble of the Constitution stated that "The French Union is composed of nations and people who put together or coordinate their resources and their efforts to develop their respective civilizations, enhance their well-being, and ensure their security. Faithful to her traditional mission, France intends to lead the people

she has taken in charge to freedom, to administer themselves, and to democratically manage their own affairs; discarding all system of colonization arbitrarily founded, France guarantees to all equal access to public functions and the individual or collective exercise of the rights and liberties proclaimed or confirmed above." (Au.)

23. Trần Lệ Xuân's mother-in-law was Phạm Thị Thân (1871–1964). This sister-in-law was Ngô Đình Thị Hoàng (1904–1959), an elder sister of Ngô Đình Nhu, and her daughter's name was Nguyễn Thị Hoàng Anh. See Nguyễn, *Ngo Dinh Thi Hiep*, 143. (Ed.)
24. A kind of low bench on which one can sit to read as well as to have a meal or even sleep. (Au.)
25. Her niece here was Nguyễn Thị Hoàng Anh and her mother was Ngô Đình Thị Hoàng. (Ed.)
26. This refers to Trần Lệ Chi. (Ed.)
27. In original, "accomplished such a miraculous fishing." (Ed.)
28. In original, "in the French Administration." Nguyễn Văn Xuân was a brigadier general in the colonial army who served as president of the Republic of Cochinchina from 1947 to 1948, then prime minister of the Provisional Government of the State of Vietnam from 1948 to 1949 and its deputy prime minister and minister of defense until 1950. The State of Vietnam was part of the French Union, but it was not a French administration. (Ed.)
29. Based on the Élysée Accords between former Emperor Bảo Đại and French president Vincent Auriol, the State of Vietnam headed by Emperor Bảo Đại was founded in 1949 as a free state within the French Union. While power was to be gradually transferred to the new Vietnamese state, France intended to maintain a strong influence over Vietnam. Several prime ministers had been appointed before Ngô Đình Diệm but none was able to last for very long. Few expected Diệm to last either. (Ed.)
30. Bình Xuyên was a militia with connections to organized crime. The group began as a collection of gangs that extorted protection money from boats traveling along the rivers connecting Sài Gòn to the Mekong

Delta, hence the label "river pirates." Early in the Franco-Vietnamese war, the group was led by a Communist commander but later it switched allegiance to France and was granted police authority over Sài Gòn and its adjacent areas. (Ed.)

31. There was no St. Peter Clinique in Sài Gòn. Trần Lệ Xuân likely meant St. Paul Clinique, which was built in 1938 and which is now the Ophthalmology Hospital. See https://www.entreprises-coloniales.fr/inde-indochine/Clinique_St-Paul-Saigon.pdf. (Ed.)
32. With the publication of this weekly, Nhu was trying to promote a new Vietnamese élite, capable of taking responsibility for the rise of Vietnam, free at last. (Au.) See also Miller, *Misalliance*, 47–48. (Ed.)
33. The Norodom Palace was bombed in 1962 by two officers of the Republic of Vietnam's Air Force who wanted to assassinate President Diệm. He survived and ordered the palace to be razed and replaced with a new building, which was named Independence Palace. (Ed.)
34. The Geneva Agreements divided Vietnam by the 17th parallel, north of which belonged to the Communist government of Hồ Chí Minh and south of which was placed under the control of France and the State of Vietnam. Nearly a million Northerners, most of whom were Catholics, moved to the South to avoid Communist rule. (Ed.)
35. When Bảo Đại summoned Ngô Đình Diệm to France apparently to replace him, Ngô Đình Diệm decided to disobey the absent head of state. At the urging of various nationalist groups, he then organized a national referendum in 1955 for South Vietnamese to choose between Bảo Đại and him. The referendum handed Diệm a victory, and he went on to found the Republic of Vietnam. (Ed.)
36. Mme. Nhu apparently referred to Trần Chánh Thành, who was minister of information then. (Ed.)
37. Trần Chánh Thành, who later would serve briefly as minister of foreign affairs, committed suicide when Communist forces seized Sài Gòn on April 30, 1975. Mme. Nhu's claim that he was a double or triple agent cannot be verified. (Ed.)
38. "Nhân Vị," or human dignity, was the official ideology of the Ngô Đình

Diệm government. According to culture scholar Duy Lap Nguyen, Nhân Vị was influenced in part by French philosopher Emmanuel Mounier's "personalism," which was a Marxist- and Catholic-inspired humanist doctrine that opposed both communism and liberalism. As expressed through the Strategic Hamlets program, Nhân Vị was also based on the Ngô Đình Diệm government's desire to preserve the age-old Vietnamese tradition of village autonomy. See Duy Lap Nguyen, *The Unimagined Community: Imperialism and Culture in South Vietnam* (Manchester: Manchester University Press, 2020). (Ed.)

39. Thierry d' Argenlieu renounced his monastic life to serve when France went to war in 1939. He ended his life as a monk. (Au.)

40. General Nguyễn Khánh (1927–2013) of the ARVN later would play a minor role in the coup on November 1, 1963. He launched his own coup in January 1964 and became the Head of State and Prime Minister of the Republic of Vietnam, being forced to go into exile in the US in February 1965. (Ed.)

41. The government that Gen. Nguyễn Văn Xuân headed was actually founded in 1948, not 1954. (Ed.)

42. The best work on the deteriorating relationship between the US and the RVN in 1960 places the blame on US Ambassador Elbridge Durbrow and State Department officials who tried to impose their views on President Diêm. See Ronald Bruce Frankum, *Vietnam's Year of the Rat: Elbridge Durbrow, Ngô Đình Diệm, and the Turn in U.S. Relations, 1959–1961* (Jefferson, NC: McFarland & Company, 2014). (Ed.)

43. Johnson's counterpart, the vice president of the Republic of Vietnam at the time, was Nguyễn Ngọc Thơ. (Ed.)

44. When he made the visit to South Vietnam in May 1961, Johnson had served as vice president for Kennedy for more than a year. Perhaps by this time Johnson still hoped to become president in the future. By the time of Kennedy's death in late 1963, as Robert Caro, the author of an authoritative biography of Lyndon Johnson, writes, Johnson "had given up on all his attempts to obtain some measure of recognition, or at least dignity, as Vice President. Once, as Senate Majority Leader, he had been

a mighty figure—'the second most powerful man in the country'—but that seemed a long time ago now. [As Kennedy's vice president, Johnson had] become not just powerless but a figure of ridicule. . . . He himself was worried about whether or not he would be retained on the 1964 Democratic ticket, and was convinced that whether he was or not, his dreams of becoming President one day were over. . . . 'My future is behind me,' he told one member of his staff. 'Go,' he said to another." See Robert A. Caro, *The Passage of Power: The Years of Lyndon Johnson* (New York: Vintage Books, 2013), ix–x. (Ed.)

45. These two pilots were Nguyễn Văn Cử and Phạm Phú Quốc. (Ed.)
46. The Chinese nurse of Lệ Quyên, born in the Presidential Palace on July 26, 1959. (Au.)
47. In April 1961, Ngô Đình Diệm ran in the presidential elections along with other candidates. He consented to confront his adversaries, to put up with their criticisms and those of the public. He appeared in person in front of the electorate in campaign meetings and obtained 60 percent of the vote. See Trương Vĩnh Lễ, *Vietnam, Où est la verité?* Editions Charles Lavauzelle, 1989. (Au.)
48. This refers to the protests by Buddhist monks and their followers against perceived discrimination and repression aimed at Buddhists. The protests emerged in spring 1963 and rapidly spread, offering ammunition to the government's enemies both in South Vietnam and in the US, and contributing in various ways to the success of the military coup in early November of that year. (Ed.)
49. In original, "C'est grâce à Madame," literally meaning "It's thanks to the lady." (Ed.)
50. There was at the time a multitude of diverse faiths in Vietnam with Catholics, Confucians, adepts of the ancestral cult, Buddhists, Caodaists, followers of the Hòa Hảo sect, Highlanders, Hinduists, Taoists, Animists, and Muslims. The Buddhists represented only 30 percent of the population. (Au.)
51. In original, "Grand Minh" for Great Minh and "Gros Minh" for Big Minh. (Ed.)

52. Suzanne Labin, *Vietnam: Révélations d'un témoin* [An Eyewitness Account] (Paris: Nouvelles Editions Latines, 1964); (English version) *Vietnam: An Eye-Witness Account* (Springfield, VA: Crestwood Books, 1964). Suzanne Labin (1913–2001) was a French socialist writer and political scientist who was known for her anticommunist, antitotalitarian, and pro-democracy views. (Ed.)
53. She was the godmother of one of Robert Kennedy's children. (Au.)
54. Marguerite Higgins, *Our Vietnam Nightmare* (New York: Harper & Row, 1965). (Au.)
55. Pope Benedict XVI. (Au.)
56. As referred to again below, Tĩnh Quang Lâu was the name given to her house in Rome by Mme. Nhu. (Ed.)

Chapter 3 (Part 1)

1. The English translation is from *The Holy Bible*, New International Version, 155. (Ed.)
2. See Genesis 18:22–23. The patriarch Abraham tried to obtain from God the salvation of the sinners by invoking the number of the few Just, who could alone obtain pardon for the sinners, however much more numerous than them. Thus, the just number that can save the large number (which did not transpire in this passage in Genesis, as Sodom was destroyed). (Au.)
3. Missionaries. (Au.)
4. See Appendix 2, "The Church and Vietnam." (Au.)

Chapter 5 (Part 1)

1. See Appendix 2, "The Church and Vietnam." (Au.)
2. It was at La Vang, in a desertic spot in the province of Quảng Trị, that a very small church was built on the location where the Holy Virgin appeared in the 19th century, when she wanted to protect the Catholics who were persecuted for their religion. This "Lourdes" of Vietnam has since been the annual pilgrimage site of Vietnamese Catholics. Monsignor Ngô Đình Thục, brother of the president,

obtained from the Vatican the elevation of this church to the rank of Basilica, then extended and embellished it. At the inauguration (consecration) of the Basilica in 1960, President Ngô Đình Diệm traveled there to entrust Vietnam to it. In ruins from the effects of the war, the reconstruction of the Basilica started this year, in 2012. (Au.)

Chapter 1 (Part 2)

1. Father Odorico was born in Pordenone, Italy, around the year 1286. It can be inferred from the account of his travels that he arrived in India shortly after 1321 and that he spent about three years in Southeast Asia during the period between the beginning of the year 1323 and the end of the year 1328, at which time he went back to Italy. He died on February 14, 1331, at the Convent of the Franciscans in Udine, capital of Frioul. He would be later beatified. (Au.)
2. See Appendix 2, "The Church in Vietnam." (Au.)
3. Although Confucius was Chinese, Vietnamese people considered him as one of their own. (Ed.)
4. This massacre of many Ngô-Đình family members was led by local members of the scholar-gentry movement [Văn Thân]. This movement opposed Emperor Tự Đức's concessions to the French in the 1862 peace treaty, including the ending of the government persecution of Catholics. See Charles Keith, *Catholic Vietnam: A Church from Empire to Nation* (Berkeley: University of California Press, 2012), 49–50. (Ed.)
5. "Đình" actually means a place, such as in the compound "Triều Đình" (court). The author perhaps confused "Đình" and "Định," which can mean "rectitude." (Ed.)
6. In the French original, the date was given as 1925. (Ed.)
7. In the original, it is written somewhat inaccurately that Khôi "was joined by Huân, his only son, in an August 1944 meeting organized by the Nationalist Communists of Hồ Chí Minh. . . . The Communists had seized them and let them perish by burying them alive." (Ed.)
8. Bảo Đại was born in Huế in 1913 and succeeded his father, Emperor Khải Định. (Au.)

9. For a brief account of Ngô Đình Nhu's work in this role, see Đào Thị Diến, "Ngô Đình Nhu: Nhà lưu trữ Việt Nam thời kỳ 1938–1946," *Xưa và Nay* [Past and Present] no. 444 (February 2014). (Ed.)
10. Information in the second half of this paragraph is inaccurate. As explained in the foreword, Nguyễn Phúc Như Phiên, Trần Lệ Xuân's grandmother, was a niece of Emperor Tự Đức and a half-sister of Emperors Đồng Khánh, Kiến Phúc, and Hàm Nghi. She was married to Thân Trọng Huề, who was the Head of the Imperial Censorate. (Ed.)
11. This refers to the Trần Trọng Kim government established in March 1945 under the sponsorship of Japan. (Ed.)

Chapter 2 (Part 2)

1. The Bảo Đại government with Ngô Đình Diệm as prime minister adamantly opposed the division of Vietnam and refused to sign the Geneva Accords. (Ed.)
2. It is generally accepted that popular support for Ngô Đình Diệm was much higher than for the absent Bảo Đại, but the near 100 percentage of the votes for the former appears unrealistic and has led many to dismiss the referendum as "rigged." For an analysis by a historian, see Jessica M. Chapman, *Cauldron of Resistance: Ngo Dinh Diem, the United States, and 1950's Southern Vietnam* (Ithaca: Cornell University Press, 2013), chapter 6. See also Marjorie Weiner, "Government and Politics in South Vietnam, 1954–1956" (MA thesis, Cornell University, 1960). (Ed.)
3. First name of Mr. Benet's wife. (Au.)
4. General Nguyễn Văn Hinh, chief of staff of the South Vietnamese Army and Bảo Đại's man, rejected the authority of the new government. The president was forced to order him to leave the country. But he ignored the order and even jumped on his motorcycle to crisscross the streets of Sài Gòn and derisively wave his expulsion order. This manifest insubordination could only provoke a bloody clash between the (pro-French) army under his command and the pro-Diệm forces. Nguyễn Văn Hinh was neutralized without a fratricidal combat thanks

to the pressure of the American government in an effective intervention with the French government, which was against Diệm and favored the dissident forces. Under pressure from the Americans, Bảo Đại recalled his man to France. (Au.)

5. Jacques Roux was Officer in Charge of Asian Territories and Pacific Ocean Affairs, French Ministry of Foreign Affairs. Jean Risterucci was Political Adviser to the High Commissioner of France in Indochina. General Paul Ely was Chairman of the French Chiefs of Staff. (Ed.)
6. Letter reproduced in Appendix 4. (Ed.)
7. The Hoà Hảo sect (of about 8,000 people) held the provinces of Long Xuyên, Châu Đốc Cần Thơ, and Gia Định, and the Cao Đài Sect (around 16,000 people) was in control of the Tây Ninh Province. The numbers here apparently refer to the militias, not the followers of these sects. (Ed.)
8. The Bình Xuyên were the masters of Sài Gòn, of Cap Saint Jacques (Vũng Tàu), and of the provinces of Gia Định and Phước Tuy. They rallied to the French Army and supported its struggle against the Việt Minh. They wanted to maintain the existing anarchy and retain their privilege against the new government. Most of the French in Sài Gòn, military or civilians, engineers, plantation owners, and civil servants, being prisoners of their past, would constantly feed the movements hostile to the government. They never came around to understanding the desire for the independence of Vietnam. When forced to leave Sài Gòn, the Bình Xuyên withdrew into the mangroves. (Au.)
9. At the time, the government accused the French and the Bình Xuyên of killing General Thế. See Chapman, *Cauldron of Resistance*, 133. (Ed.)
10. Bernard Newman, *Background to Viet-Nam* (New York: New American Library, 1965), 131. (Au.)
11. Although the numbers do not appear unrealistic, we are not able to locate this source. For a list of economic accomplishments by the Ngô Đình Diệm government drawn from Vietnamese sources, see Ronald Bruce Frankum, *Vietnam's Year of the Rat: Elbridge Durbrow, Ngô Đình Diệm, and the Turn in U.S. Relations, 1959–1961* (Jefferson,

NC: McFarland & Company, 2014), 205–6. (Ed.)

12. *Nhân Vị* is commonly translated as Personalist or Personalism and assumed to be adapted from or inspired by the French Catholic philosopher Emmanuel Mounier but, as seen below, the account here views such translation and assumption to be a "reductionist and superficial caricature." For the latest analysis of Nhân Vị, see Duy Lap Nguyen, *The Unimagined Community: Imperialism and Culture in South Vietnam* (Manchester: Manchester University Press, 2020). (Ed.)
13. For example, see Robert Stone's live interview of April 30, 2006, at the New York Public Library, of Dương Thu Hương, a dissident writer from North Vietnam who was sent South during the war. According to Hương, she cried when she came to Sài Gòn at the end of the war and realized that "the victorious army" (her side) belonged to a "more barbaric regime than the one that lost." See the video interview (part 4) from minute 5:37 at https://www.youtube.com/watch?v=wtx-3aRcFA58, and the transcript at https://live-cdn-www.nypl.org/s3fs-public/events/duong043006.pdf (page 7). Huy Đức, a prominent Vietnamese journalist also from North Vietnam, recalls: "South Vietnam, from what we learned in school, was a place of privation and destitution [under the old regime]. . . . In 1983, I was under [military] training [and lived] in Sài Gòn for about a year. . . . Although deprived [kiệt quệ] after 8 years of 'liberation,' Sài Gòn to me remained a 'civilized place'. . . . My book began from April 30, 1975, the day many believed that the North had liberated the South. Many, when they reflected carefully 30 years later, were shocked to realize that it was the South that liberated the North." Huy Đức, *Bên Thắng Cuộc*, vol. 1 (California: Osin Books, 2012), xi–xiii. (Ed.)
14. Letter was addressed to Mr. G. Willemetz and is reproduced in Appendix 4. The original is kept at the École des Chartes in Paris (Au.)
15. See *The Pentagon Papers*, Gravel Edition, vol. 2 (Boston: Beacon Press, 1971). (Au.)
16. See *The Pentagon Papers*, Gravel Edition, vol. 2 (Boston: Beacon Press, 1971), 690–91. (Au.)

17. Jeffrey Race provides data in his study of Long An Province showing that the number of communist surrenders rose from 14 in 1961 to 109 in 1962 and 332 in 1963. Race credited the success to the competent provincial chief, Major Nguyễn Viết Thanh. Jeffrey Race, *War Comes to Long An: Revolutionary Conflict in a Vietnamese Province* (Berkeley: University of California Press, 1972), 133. Data on other provinces or at the national level are not available. (Ed.)
18. See Labin, *Vietnam: Révélations d'un témoin*. (Au.) The scholarly debate on South Vietnam's military situation during 1962–63 continues today. Mark Moyar argues that Sài Gòn was on its way to winning the war against the NLF just as Ngô Đình Nhu believed. Some scholars have concurred with Moyar while others disagree. It is generally accepted that Sài Gòn regained the initiative on the battlefield throughout 1962 until mid or late 1963 and the strategic hamlets did pose great challenges for Communist forces. The situation in late 1963 was less clear, as the Communists seemed to have recovered some initiative while the government in Sài Gòn was preoccupied with the Buddhist protests. See Mark Moyar, *Triumph Forsaken: The Vietnam War, 1954–1965* (New York: Cambridge University Press, 2006); and Michael Doidge and Andrew Wiest, *Triumph Revisited: Historians Battle for the Vietnam War* (New York: Routledge, 2010). (Ed.)

Chapter 3 (Part 2)

1. "Supérieurs" in original, used with colonial connotations (Ed.).
2. Telegram # 276 on August 24, 1963, from the Embassy in Vietnam to the United States. *Foreign Relations of the United States 1961–1963, v. III, Vietnam, January–August 1963*. The original text is "we do not conclude that any officers with actual military strength in Saigon (Don, Dinh, Tung) is at this point disaffected with President or with Nhu." (Ed.)
3. Telegram # 391 on August 31, 1963, from the Embassy in Vietnam to the United States. *Foreign Relations of the United States 1961–1963, v. IV, Vietnam, August–December 1963*. The original text is "there is

neither the will nor the organization among the Generals to accomplish anything." (Ed.)

4. The meeting was actually at the State Department, with the participation of top officials from the White House, the Defense Department, and the CIA. "Memorandum of a Conversation, Department of State, Washington, August 31, 1963, 11 a.m." *Foreign Relations of the United States 1961–1963, v. IV, Vietnam*, August–December 1963, 69–74. (Ed.)
5. *The Pentagon Papers*, Gravel Edition, vol. 2, 207. (Ed.)
6. *The Pentagon Papers*, Gravel Edition, vol. 2, 244. (Ed.)
7. Document No. 142, *The Pentagon Papers*, Gravel Edition, vol. 2, 751–66. (Ed.)
8. Document no. 151, *The Pentagon Papers*, Gravel Edition, vol. 2, 784–85. (Ed.)
9. Document no. 154, *The Pentagon Papers*, Gravel Edition, vol. 2, 790, 791–92. (Ed.)
10. Lucien Emile Conein was born on November 29, 1919, in Paris and spent his childhood in Kansas City after his father died. In 1939, he went back to France to join the French army. After the French defeat, he returned to the US and signed up for the army there. In August 1944, he was assigned to the secret operations in France where he was charged with assisting the Forces of Internal Resistance to prepare for the landing in Normandy. After the war, he worked with the American intelligence services of the O.S.S. (Office of Strategic Services) and the CIA (Central Intelligence Agency). (Au.)
11. Document no. 148, *The Pentagon Papers*, Gravel Edition, vol. 2, 780–82. (Ed.)
12. As soon as the coup d'état was announced, Trác went into the jungle with his brother Quỳnh and his sister Lệ Quyên. Accompanied by a few well-armed faithful loyalists, they would walk through streams to avoid any traces of scent and would finally reach a runway where a plane was to take them to Rome. They would soon be met by their mother and elder sister. (Au.)

13. The accounts of the last days of the president and his brother came from the book by Trương Vĩnh Lễ, *Vietnam, où est la verité?* [Vietnam, Where is the Truth?] The author, who was president of the National Assembly until the coup d'état, was on the spot during the events. He also reported on the details given by General Trần Văn Đôn, who was one of the four principal conspirators. He had access to other sources as well. (Au.)
14. Actually, Nguyễn Văn Nhung would be arrested and presumably executed later on the order of General Nguyễn Khánh when the latter took power in 1964 from the junta that had overthrown Diệm. (Ed.).
15. Éric Roussel, *Charles de Gaulle* (Paris: Gallimard), 756. (Au.)
16. Wilfred G. Burchett, *Vietnam: Inside Story of the Guerilla War* (New York: International Publishers, 1965), 216–17. Nguyễn Hữu Thọ's comment in response to Burchett's interview actually referred to both the coup against Ngô Đình Diệm and the subsequent coup by Nguyễn Khánh in early 1964 as "gifts from heaven." General Trần Nam Trung (aka Trần Lương), sent from North Vietnam to command all NLF forces, expressed a similar view in the same interview by Burchett. (Ed.)

Chapter 4 (Part 2)

1. For a scholarly debate on whether Thích Trí Quang was communist or anticommunist, see Mark Moyar, "Political Monks: The Militant Buddhist Movement during the Vietnam War," *Modern Asian Studies* 38, no. 4 (2004): 749–84; and James McAllister, "'Only Religions Count in Vietnam': Thich Tri Quang and the Vietnam War," *Modern Asian Studies* 42, no. 4 (2008): 751–82. In a more recent article, Edward Miller argues that "Instead of seeing Tri Quang as a power-mad Machiavellian, a pacifist, or a communist, he is more accurately understood as a zealous proponent of the ideals of the Buddhist revival." Edward Miller, "Religious Revival and the Politics of Nation Building: Reinterpreting the 1963 'Buddhist Crisis' in South Vietnam," *Modern Asian Studies* 49, no. 6 (2015): 1928–29. (Ed.)
2. The correctly spelled name of this bonze is Thích Thiện Hoa

(1918–1973), who was Administrative Head of the Mendicancy Buddhist Church [Trị sự trưởng, Giáo hội Tăng già Nam Việt] at the time. According to a news article translated by Vietnam Press, he made an appeal on Radio Saigon on August 23, 1963, to "heal over the wounds dividing Buddhists and the Government," blaming "unidentified provocaters [*sic*]" who wanted to "sow confusion, hatred, division and trouble between the Government and the Buddhists, thus creating the false impression abroad that Buddhists in Vietnam were being brutally oppressed by the Government. These maneuvers were designed to pave the way for the realisation of their goals based on the repudiation of virtue and shedding the blood of true Buddhists." See "'To seek an escape for Buddhism we must remedy the action by a group of people who led Buddhism along an uncertain adventuresome road,' declares National Sangka Association Chairman, the Venerable Thich Thien Hoa." A typed copy of the original document is in Tuong Vu's possession. (Ed.).

3. This letter, reproduced in Appendix 4, is kept in the depository of the Archives of the School of Charters in Paris. (Au.)

4. The report from the United Nations is Document A/5630, titled "Report of the United Nations Fact-Finding Mission to Vietnam, December 7, 1963," is available at https://digitallibrary.un.org/record/729703?ln=en&v=pdf. This document contained information about the mission and transcripts of interviews but made no conclusion based on the grounds that the Ngô Đình Diệm government, the subject of the investigation which invited the mission into the country, had been overthrown by the coup just a few days before the mission ended. Readers are thus left to read the transcripts and make their own judgment. According to a news report by the Northern Catholic Welfare Council (NCWC) News Service on December 20, 1963, about a UN session where the report was presented but not discussed, correspondent Alba Zizzamia wrote that "the report contains no evidence that religious discrimination was a governmental policy in South Vietnam." Available at https://thecatholicnewsarchive.

org/?a=d&d=cns19631220-01.1.24&e=-------en-20--1--txt-txIN-------- (on page 8 of the foreign news section). After the UN report was made available, a US Senate Subcommittee to Investigate the Administration of the Internal Security Act and Other Internal Security Laws (under the Committee on the Judiciary) published it together with an introduction by Subcommittee Vice Chairman, Senator Thomas Dodd of Connecticut, addressed to Subcommittee Chairman Senator James Eastland. In this introduction, Dodd stated that, "While it is primarily a factual report, consisting of testimony and documents, without a formal finding by the U.N. committee, I believe that any objective person would have to conclude from reading it that the accounts of massive persecution of the Buddhist religion were, at the best, vastly exaggerated, at the worst, a sordid propaganda fraud." Senator Dodd also mentioned an interview and a phone conversation in which Fernando Volio Jiménez, the head of the UN mission to South Vietnam, provided him with a similar observation. See "Report of United Nations Fact-Finding Mission to South Viet-Nam" published by the Subcommittee to Investigate the Administration of the Internal Security Act and Other Internal Security Laws of the Committee on the Judiciary, United States Senate, United States (Washington, DC: US Government Printing Office, 1964). Senator Dodd's statement is reproduced and included in Appendix 3 of this book. For a different interpretation of the UN report (without access to Dodd's statement) by a Vietnamese Buddhist group, see Tâm Diệu, et al., *Hồ Sơ Mật 1963 từ các nguồn tài liệu của Chính phủ Mỹ* [Secret 1963 Files from US government sources] revised edition (n.p.: Nhà xuất bản Liên Phật Hội, 2017). Available at https://thuvienhoasen.org/images/file/QulgCoOb1AgQABFN/ho-so-mat-1963-finished.pdf. (Ed.)

5. Truong Vinh Le, *Vietnam, Où est la vérité?* Trương Vĩnh Lễ was president of Vietnam's National Assembly until the coup d'état of November 1963; Labin, *Vietnam: Révélations d'un témoin*. (Au.)

6. Ross Fisher, "The Kennedy Administration and the Overthrow of Ngo Dinh Diem: What Happened, Why Did It Happen, and Was It a

Good Idea?" In Ross Fisher, John Norton Moore, and Robert Turner, eds., *To Oppose Any Foe: The Legacy of U.S. Intervention in Vietnam* (Durham: Carolina Academic Press, 2006), 23–24. (Ed.)

7. Higgins, *Our Vietnam Nightmare*. (Ed.)
8. See note 1 in this chapter regarding Thích Trí Quang. (Ed.)
9. As Mme. Nhu explained to the journalist Marguerite Higgins when asked why she used such an offensive term, she "never would have thought of the word 'barbecue' if it had not been used first by the Americans." Her daughter, Ngô-Đình Lệ Thuỷ, "was at the post exchange the other day. And she heard some American photographers talking about some new 'barbecues' that the Xa Loi monks were predicting." Higgins thought Mme. Nhu's knowledge of the English language and "occidental psychology" was limited, thus she did not comprehend the different context when the word was used: private vs. public, and by some photographers vs. by the First Lady of Vietnam. See Higgins, *Our Vietnam Nightmare*, 72–73. (Ed.)

Appendix 1

1. This essay was written by Mme. Nhu but was kept separate from her memoir. The title was created by Jacqueline Willemetz. (Ed.)
2. Cf. *Toi aussi annonce ma venue* [You too announce my coming], School of Divine Radiance, by Marie-Elisabeth. Ed. Du Parvis, 2004. CH-1648- Hauteville (Switzerland). (Au.)

Appendix 2

1. See *The Risk of the Mission: Martyrs Francs-Comtois au Viet-Nam* [Texts collected by Jean-Christophe Demard and Gabriel Socié] (Langres: Dominique Guénot, 1988). (Au.)
2. See "The preface" by Bishop F. X. Nguyễn Văn Thuận in the "Complete Works, volume 1: Autobiography," from Marcel Van to Saint-Paul (Editions Religieuses / The Friends of Van, 2005). (Au.)

References

Bảo Đại. *Le Dragon d'Annam* [The Dragon of Annam]. Paris: Plon, 1980.

Cesari, Laurent. *L'Indochine en guerres, 1945–1993* [Indochina at War 1945–1993]. Edition Belin Sup. Paris: Histoire, 1995.

Chesneaux, Jean. *Contribution à l'Histoire de la Nation Vietnamienne* [Contribution to the History of the Vietnamese Nation]. Paris: Editions Sociales, 1955.

de Folin, Jacques. *Indochine 1940–1955: La fin d'un rêve* [Indochina 1940–1955: The End of a Dream]. Paris: Editions Perrin, collection Vérités et Légendes, 1993.

Feray, Pierre-Richard. *Le Vietnam*. Paris: Editions Presses Universitaires de France, 1990.

Guilmard, Dom Jacques-Marie. *Grand Monsieur, l'évêque lépreux* [Grand Monsieur, the Bishop Leper]. Paris: Pierre Téqui, 2005.

Higgins, Marguerite. *Our Vietnam Nightmare*. New York: Harper & Row, 1965.

Labin, Suzanne. *Vietnam: Révélations d'un témoin* [Vietnam: An Eyewitness Account]. Paris: Nouvelles Éditions Latines, 1964.

Le Dossier du Pentagone [The Pentagon Dossier]. Paris: Albin Michel, 1971.

Le risque de la Mission, Martyrs Francs-Comtois au Vietnam - Textes rassemblés par Jean-Christophe Demard et Gabriel Socié [The Risk of the Mission, Martyrs of Franche-Comté in Vietnam. Texts collected by Jean-Christophe Demard and Gabriel Socié]. Langres: Dominique Guénot, 1988.

McNamara, Robert. *Avec le recul, la tragédie du Vietnam et ses leçons* [Looking back, the Tragedy of Vietnam and Its Lessons]. Paris: du Seuil, 1996.

Nixon, Richard. *Mémoires* [Memoirs]. Paris: Stanké, 1978.

Roussel, Éric. *Charles de Gaulle*. Paris: Gallimard, 2002.

Tauriac, Michel. *Vietnam, le dossier noir du communisme, de 1945 à nos jours* [The Black Dossier of Communism from 1945 to the Present]. Paris: Plon, 2001.

Trương Vĩnh Lễ. *Vietnam, où est la vérité ?* [Vietnam, Where Is the Truth?]. Paris: Editions Lavauzelle, 1989.

Văn Châu, André Nguyễn. *The Miracle of Hope: Francis Xavier Nguyen Van Thuan, Political Prisoner, Prophet of Peace.* Boston: Pauline Books and Media, 2003.

———. *Ngo Dinh Thi Hiep or a Lifetime in the Eye of the Storm.* Salt Lake City: American Book Classics, 2000.

Index

Note: Page numbers in italics refer to images.

About the Contributors

Madame Ngô Đình Nhu (given name Trần Lệ Xuân) (1924–2011) was the influential and controversial de facto First Lady of South Vietnam, known for her forceful personality and striking beauty, for her advocacy for gender equality, and for her audacity in challenging powerful men, including US and South Vietnamese leaders. As the wife of Ngô Đình Nhu, brother and adviser to President Ngô Đình Diệm, she was among the most important yet poorly understood figures in postcolonial South Vietnamese politics.

Tuong Vu is Professor of Political Science and Director of the US-Vietnam Research Center at the University of Oregon.

www.ingramcontent.com/pod-product-compliance
Lightning Source LLC
Chambersburg PA
CBHW021851230426
43671CB00006B/345